A CRITICAL WORK III

ILLUSTRATIONS

STANFORD
FRENCH AND ITALIAN
STUDIES

executive editor

JEAN-MARIE APOSTOLIDÈS

editor

MARC BERTRAND

editorial board

BRIGITTE CAZELLES
ROBERT GREER COHN
JEAN-PIERRE DUPUY
JOHN FRECCERO
RENÉ GIRARD
HANS ULRICH GUMBRECHT
ROBERT HARRISON
RALPH HESTER
ODILE HULLOT-KENTOR
PAULINE NEWMAN-GORDON
JEFFREY SCHNAPP
MICHEL SERRES
CAROLYN SPRINGER
JAMES WINCHELL

founder

ALPHONSE JUILLAND

volume LXXXI

DEPARTMENT OF FRENCH AND ITALIAN
STANFORD UNIVERSITY

A CRITICAL WORK III

ILLUSTRATIONS

ROBERT GREER COHN

1994
ANMA LIBRI

Stanford French and Italian Studies is a collection of scholarly publications devoted to the study of French and Italian literature and language, culture and civilization. Occasionally it will allow itself excursions into related Romance areas.

Stanford French and Italian Studies will publish books, monographs, and collections of articles centering around a common theme, and is open also to scholars associated with academic institutions other than Stanford.

The collection is published by the Department of French and Italian, Stanford University and ANMA Libri.

© 1994 by ANMA Libri, P.O. Box 876, Saratoga, Calif. 95071
and Department of French and Italian, Stanford University.
All rights reserved.
LC 94–70643
ISBN 0–915838–97–4
Printed in the United States of America.

Acknowledgments

Permission to reprint has been granted as follows: "Man and Woman in Gide's *The Immoralist*," *Romanic Review*, May 1989; "The True Camus," *French Review*, October 1986; "Camus's Sacred: The Growing Stone," *Stanford Literature Review*, Spring-Fall 1988; "Baudelaire's *Frisson nouveau*," *Romanic Review*, January 1993; "Global Intimacy: Baudelaire's *La Chevelure*," *French Studies*, July 1988; "Baudelaire's Beleaguered Prose Poems," *Textual Analysis* (New York, 1986); "The Mallarmé Century, *Stanford French Review*, Winter 1978; "Mallarmé and/or Barbara Johnson: A Decidable," *Nineteenth Century French Studies*, Spring-Summer 1992; "Rescuing a Sonnet of Verlaine: 'L'espoir luit'," *Romanic Review*, March 1986; "Sartre versus Proust," *Partisan Review* 28.5-6, 1961; "Desire: Direct and Imitative," *Philosophy Today*, Winter 1989; "The ABC's of Richard Wilbur," *LIT* 2.2; "Derrida at Yale," *The New Criterion*, May 1986.

"Keats and Mallarmé," *Comparative Literature Studies* 7.2 (1970) 195-204. Copyright 1970 by the Pennsylvania State University. Reproduced by permission of the Pennsylvania State University Press.

for Valentina

Preface

Illustrations rounds out the trilogy, *A Critical Work*, launched in 1975. The first volume, *Modes of Art*, was an aesthetics based on an original philosophic vision, owing much to the major Symbolists, particularly Mallarmé; the second, *Ways of Art*, which appeared in 1985, presented an extension of that vision in time, a genesis, a sketch of the becoming of artistic forms through Western history, mainly French.

The first two volumes were largely theoretical, offering a method for selecting meaningfully from the vast potential material. The present volume, as the title indicates, deals more fully and concretely with a number of representative texts, "illustrates" the general approach in the sense both of demonstrating its application and also bringing "luster" to those already splendid texts, coaxing them to be luminous for us afresh, achieving, like the shoeshine virtuosi depicted by Camus in *The Minotaur.* "a double and truly definitive shine that flashes forth from the depths."

Now, since the essays collected here were, with one exception, published separately (in well-known literary or professional periodicals), there is a lingering theoretical aspect in many of them, though not, I think, heavily so, but just enough to recapitulate the mainstream of our overall argument. At times the founding vision develops new slants, or branches, in the process. Unless one gives up, one never ceases finding better ways to put those complex, totalizing matters.

This is especially true of the first essay, "A Few Miracles." Coming very late in the game, written last, unpublished, it goes back to the roots of our Western aesthetic enterprise to outline the genesis—in a would-be unshakably compact and coherent way—of the foundational imagery, or obsessions, of our major writings, particularly poetic, and art.

So it can serve as an introduction to Volume III read by itself, with no acquaintance of the preceding theoretical books; it can also be read as an epilogue, going over the whole critical conspectus, belatedly, one

He is, like Harold Bloom, establishing a canon or attacking when he calls the 'prevailing literary doctrine' that anybody's opinion is as valid as any other.

more time, with some rearrangement, like one more attempt at getting at the Montagne Sainte-Victoire or The Girl in a Peasant Blouse. But T. S. Eliot's observation that "every poem is an epitaph" applies somewhat to the elucidatory situation: we are forever going over familiar rudiments in an attempt to get the "thing" finally right.

re refinement against modish criticism

Such a stubborn viewpoint, that there is an ideal *right* way of saying something, is what sets outlooks like mine radically apart from the prevailing critical doctrine of our time: that anybody's opinion is as valid as any other. But, of course, it does not *work* that way and never has. Only those who, however naïvely, *believe* in what they are doing, can bring off anything worth staying for. Most people knew that in former years. The current ones, culturally, are painful for the caring to live through.

This is not necessarily an elitist prejudice: in their own intuitive way, the folks out there have always had a clearer sense of "I know what I like" than the modish and time-serving academics, who, when the time comes —hark, dinna ye hear it?—will change their minds again and agree with George Steiner that "music means" and, that if it does not for you, deep down, you are not "getting it."

In *Modes of Art*, I alluded to the all-importance of tone. I still think the Derridas and Fishes are tone-deaf. But we have other fish to fry...

The remaining essays "illustrate" writers, mostly French, from the modern Golden Age, which is roughly equivalent to the period (René Wellek acknowledges it, after Edmund Wilson) of Symbolism, running from Baudelaire to Proust and Valéry. Baudelaire, Mallarmé, Verlaine are key figures represented here; Proust decidedly belongs in the picture, though a *prosateur*; but so does Gide—who revered Mallarmé—and even Camus, who, like Picasso, spoke of having a sun at his center, still reflected the innocent Golden glow, enduringly Romantic under the Symbolist subtleties. Keats accordingly is a natural forebear of Mallarmé, as we show, and Richard Wilbur a grateful scion of those Frenchmen. What a bunch!

It might be wondered that, although I spent most of my career-time on Mallarmé, he is the center of only two pieces here. The reason is that a collection of my articles on him exists in French—*Vues sur Mallarmé* —and that those interested in him are apt to be fluent in that language. Offering them again in an English-language version seemed rather pointless. On the other hand, "The Mallarmé Century," it appeared to me, ought to be readily available on American shelves; readers here have found it to be of pivotal interest. Similar considerations prompted me to retain the one on Keats and Mallarmé. The other essay, on Mallarmé and Barbara Johnson, has not figured in any collection.

The most that I felt needed to be rescued from the limbo of the periodical stacks.

Our leading poet, in a gratifying postcard, endorsed my remarks on his métier (close to Mallarmé's in his use of sounds and shapes of letters) in "The ABC's of Richard Wilbur." That, incidentally, leaves Gérard Genette, in *Mimologiques*, out on a surprisingly flimsy limb.

The final essay, "Desire: Direct and Imitative," takes respectful issue with the views of my colleague René Girard, especially insofar as they pertain to original genius like Proust's.

Many other pieces could have taken their place here, but most of them—such as the long study of Proust (in *The Writer's Way in France*) —are already lodged in books. The ones that are present are those that I felt most needed to be rescued from the limbo of the periodical stacks.

Given world enough and time, there could well be a *revenez-y*, another volume. Who knows?

Meanwhile, my affectionate gratitude goes to a few people who have believed in what I was doing all along—I gave their names in the previous volumes—including, most prominently, my wife, Valentina, to whom the book is lovingly dedicated.

Contents

A Few Miracles

Our cosmos began, no doubt, the way scientists say it did, with a Big Bang. Since time, as we normally *know* it, started there and then, its essential "irreversibility"—a beginning *ipso facto* headed toward some end —establishes the two points defining any line, and, by extension (duality is the initiation of multiplicity), the dotted life-line of all (alienated from originary wholeness) fragmentariness, multiplicity, existence itself as opposed to Being.[1] The rational cognition which arises from existence can only reflect this scattered finiteness, but holistic vision (as well as, at a lower level, impulse, instinct, intuition), which stems from the silent Being-source, remains as the condition of provisional ("fake," merely indicative or suggestive) synthesis as well as a ghostly reservoir of potentiality beyond the human condition and reach, except on its own terms, when, as it were, "it is good and ready." Proust's notion of "privileged moments" and "involuntary memory" is clearly of this order. Contrariwise, the tradition of finite humanity goes back to the Book of Genesis— the Fall—and forward to contemporary humanistic "absurdist" thought and the "indeterminacy principle" of coeval science.

Mallarmé, in "Music and Letters," sums up this situation: "no twist [of thought]... falsifies or transgresses the omnipresent Line spaced [dotted] from any point to any other in order to institute idea; except under the human face, mysterious [idea], insofar as a Harmony is pure." Here, with a natural bias, he deploys terms usually applied to music or art, but he is also referring to human ideas generally, their limitations and possible miraculous leap.

[1] Even though a line may be theoretically infinite, it lacks the absolute and immediately evident infinity of a circle. There is always doubt whether a line can keep on going. Its rectitude and directionality derive from that noncircularity and, as we imagine, from the metaphysical *cut* that divided the unitary circle (circumference of a global entity) and gave it *two* ends. Hence the etymon of "time" is "to cut," according to E. Cassirer. Circle and Line are an archetypal polar pair, like the cognate "one" and "two."

1

The Bible begins with the Creation or Birth—another version of a thunderously eruptive founding event—and the first consequence is a primordial splitting up of an initial unity into a duality, represented by heaven and earth (or light and darkness).

This bipolar scheme—which we tend to imagine as vertical compared to the horizontal duality of linear time (patently, they are cognate)—has stayed with us all the way as the basis of rationality. At some point, mystics like Saint John, with one foot in transcendence and one in existence—"the Word was with God and the Word was God"—tried to overcome the rational limitation in a way that anticipates the Mallarméan or modern. Earlier, imaginative thinkers, like the Greek Heraclitus, had become aware that the original unity as a sort of persistent ghost gave underlying ambiguity to the two poles which seemed, on luminous occasion, to be the same, reversible or interchangeable: "the way up is the way down."[2]

From a rational viewpoint, the recurrent sameness of opposites appears as absurd, paradoxical. One senses a Hellenic frustration in Zeno of Elea's discovery that motion, indeed, all reality, is both continuous and discontinuous. Saint John's absurdity could be accepted, as was its cognate expression in the mystery of the Trinity, by a tradition of faith, but the rational vexation also lingered on in Christianity through the doctrine of the "excluded middle" in Saint Thomas and, *a fortiori* in modern scientific logic and Aristotelian thought generally.

But the old (e.g., neo-Platonic) ghost was always lurking in the wainscoting, certainly in Christian thought: the idea of a reversion to the unitary Source, of rebirth via psychic death ("conversion") was solidly launched by the other Saint John, the Baptist. The old thunder, or Bang, arose volcanically, from his underground tomblike cell, in his prophetic clamor against the sins of Herod.

In Genesis, we witness the formation of another fundamental psychic structure, based also on the problematic nature of knowing. When man and woman are made "in the image of God," there is born the aporia of the quasi-divine self (individual soul) vis-à-vis the quasi-divine other (mother, father, brother, sister, wife, etc.). The question immediately arises: how can infinity (divinity, or even a spark of it), a continuity, be reconciled with discontinuity, a plurality of separated selves. In this case,

---

[2]The paradox of death-birth is a close cognate of the other ambiguous couples. The moral ambiguity of God-Satan is also closely parallel: Satan as a spinoff of divinity (Lucifer) is at odds with his utter difference. In *Exodus*, God is said to be capable of "evil," until Moses talks Him out of it. Whence the need for faith, as in the instance, and Instant, of Abraham.

the bipolar paradox has become tetrapolar, since two *dimensions* are at play: the relation of self to God is vertical; of self to others, essentially horizontal. And again, the original and subliminally subsistent unity relates the two entities—here, dimensions—ambiguously. So that the other is sometimes worshipped as a sort of substitute for God and, conversely, people on occasion get rather familiar with God and address him as if he were an"other."[3] Since humor is the natural way we deal with the absurd—life impulse flowing from the source, going on (and to heck with our brittle schemes pretending to control a reality bigger than them) —these religious inconsistencies can be funny, as we all know. The ancient Hebrews who singled themselves out for avoiding that kind of familiarity with the unnamable (JHVH) spoke of His walking in the garden of Eden "in the cool of the evening," like any bourgeois ("So hoz by you?").

The bipolar paradox ("the absurd") creates problems for rationality or sanity, of course, but the tetrapolar one is even more disturbing since it involves putting into abeyance the distinction between continuity or circularity (which we associate primarily with the vertical, or metaphoric, dimension) and linearity or discontinuity (defined by terminal points), which we initially imagine on the horizontal axis (metonymic, ta-ta-ta), e.g., in our graphings of time, which for Western logic (sanity) is, as we noted, irreversible.

The ambiguity here forces us to deal with the difficult concept of cyclic, or reversible, time. That, too, has grown in the modern era and is even discussed in contemporary science (Feynman). But it still does unsettle the mind. In any event, discourse on the relation between the two kinds of time has become commonplace: circular (as on clock dials) as opposed to linear (as on calendars) time.

From a visionary viewpoint, the logical, sane perspective is a manipulatory imposition on a fuller, prior truth, which is at first purely intuitive, notably in the overwhelming feeling of Harmony, as in moments of music or the ecstatic experience of nature, perhaps a glorious morning or sunset. Paradox is the closest rational (quasi-rational) approximation to that wholeness, a hybrid, suggesting the ultimate connectedness of things through their interchangeabilities, their underlying identity, as vibrant, impressionist art does, or Hugo's "Oh insensé qui ne crois pas que je suis

---

[3]The first two Commandments forbid us to duplicate God "sideways" (a monotheistic imperative) or vertically: no "graven image" of His creation and, by extension, of Him; cf. the concept of the hidden God, JHVH. Although the authority of the father gets a major challenge from the son on the threshold of manhood (the Oedipal, of course, is more than sexual), the sacred eventually forbids this.

toi!" Hence great art, music, and literature are rife with paradox (and puns), fluidly organic chains, or networks, of images or motifs rising one from within the other, telescopically and kaleidoscopically as in the neo-Platonic "Great Chain of Being," Goethe's "nature philosophy," Kierkegaard's "repetition," Darwin's evolutionary chain, Mallarmé, Bergson, Proust, and Valéry's *durée*, and so forth, through the cream of modern vision.[4]

The notion of a Big Bang at the origin of all this is axiomatic (and recently reaffirmed) in our current science, but it deserves another look. The thunderous aspect persists in manifestations of a fearful Jehovah (or Saint John et al.), in Vico's thunderclap (echoed by Joyce in *Finnegans Wake*) as the awakener of human consciousness, and the dramatic, eruptive moment of individual birth (and the little sexual "bang" which leads to it, or any "blowout" of renewal, sacred ritual's, or Saturday night's).

Yes, but... There is a gentle, quietly beautiful equivalent in any deeply fresh apparition, epiphany, moment of grace or Grace, the appearance of a loved one after long absence, a first spring day in northern lands, the haloed sheer presence of the Infant, or any infant, especially ours.

Explosive or silent, miracles are what really count in the story of our lives.

The Big Bang and the science that proclaims it, in short, beg a question: the mere materiality of the universe. How do you get a mother's love out of that, or the smell of a garden after a rain? Mallarmé, who wrestled valiantly with the problem of belief, said decisively: "The word 'secular' doesn't offer a precise meaning." And, to a floundering atheistic poet-friend: "You can't do without Eden."[5]

---

[4]Whence the multiple beginnings critics find in major works. In some real sense, everything is a new beginning. Mallarmé: "Un livre ne commence ni ne finit; tout au plus il fait semblant" (*Le Livre*). This is the old continuity-discontinuity dilemma. Discontinuity—beginnings and endings; limitations, framings of all sorts, classic form—and continuity are equally pedigreed half-truths. **Note:** French *sens*: both (linear) "direction" and "sense" or "meaning," either as "sanity," normal sense, or (as in Medieval writing) "total meaning."

[5]Mallarmé never abandoned the referent; even the famous "Je dis: une fleur!" ends with "la réminiscence de l'objet nommé baigne dans une neuve atmosphère." The enveloping referent of nature is constant in his writing, e.g., "Crise de Vers," "Bucolique."

Agreeing with George Steiner (as well as Blanchot, Barthes, Foucault, Sartre, whonot) that Mallarmé is the founder of the modern mindset, I disagree with his coupling him with Heidegger. Mallarmé's vision and polypolar epistemology is profounder and more fluid, more artistic—though less professional—than Heidegger's. Moreover he is not "hung up" on neo-pagan critique and maintains the ground tone of late artistic Judeo-Christianity along with pagan fecundating sensuality. He has none of Heidegger's ideological poison.

From that angle, the universe both explodes, like *poésie éclatée*, and/or flows, from a prior spiritual (along with material) reservoir, emanates, in the sense of Plotinus, as its participatory incarnation. There is indeed spiritual violence—Jesus's in the entrance of the temple—but the gentleness of its deepest moments—Franciscan rather than Johannine—speaks to another mood or mode.

To some of us, not without bias, there is something vulgar in all that stir and noise at the Beginning and, by extension, the science that proclaims it. Art has more quiet dignity. It can include the violent, to be sure: Mallarmé could admire Wagner's "souriant fracas originel," but what he sought most was "sous le visage humain en tant qu'une Harmonie est pure."

The violent act of the murderer is despicable; the suffering of the victim is holy; on that point, Nietzsche was dangerously wrong. Most great novels bear out the point: there is something vulgar about murder, and, although killing is a staple of popular literature and TV, it is generally absent or rare in the masterpieces of late Western literature or art.

Might one say that the quiet aspect of the Creation stems from the fact, acknowledged by modern cosmology, that the birth was from nothing? The vibrancy of nothing-all—the surging forth of reality *ex nihilo*, the "repetition" of that phenomenon in individual birth, when, as Hegel observes, the parents are reduced to a near-nothingness, and the new entity arises from "nowhere" *between* them, follows us through various modes of modern thought. Malraux speaks of humans as being "worth nothing and everything." Camus deals with this either-or extensively in *The Rebel*, seeing the danger of its Manichean extremism for civilized living, notably deliberative republicanism. But it is omnipresent, impressively in the *hush* preceding any portentous event.

That zero, potentially all (like the whiteness at the core of the various colors) is located at the nexus of Descartes's coordinate axes, a mathematical version of tetrapolar thought. In humanistic terms, we can speak of it as a "quintessence." Paradox colors it, we noted, in the nothing-all aspect (zero-infinite, micro-macro). It is, being so "central" (or "initial," "originary"; another version of paradox is involved), an important locus of faith.

That is the way Kierkegaard saw it, in his "Absolute Paradox" (from *Philosophical Fragments*); after observing that paradox questions itself—it is both true and not true in its own terms—he is left, or bereft, with a

Paradoxically, he both liberated the signifier and rooted it. Only Joyce is comparable, though the giants of Symbolism, e.g., Proust, are close by.

central nothing, crucified psychically, as it were, amid the four poles, and from that agonized nothing makes his leap of faith, in the "Instant."

That, precisely, is what happened in the preface of Camus's *The Rebel*: trying to derive an argument against mass murder from his earlier absurdist "logic," he ended with a compounded dilemma like Kierkegaard's and, like him (despite his earlier specific rejection of such a possibility for himself, in *The Myth of Sisyphus*), leapt to an arational cry of "revolt" against murder, really a protest of faith in human decency and individual rights, derived for us, in the Judeo-Christian tradition, from the sacred-rooted value in the decalogue: "Thou shalt not kill." From that point on, despite his own reluctance to disavow his independence from religion, the word "sacred" ("I believe in the sacred"; interview with Brisville) shows up compellingly in his writings along with the comparably anti-nihilistic idea of "limits." This is hardly surprising in a literary artist who had written of the "buried sun" at our core ("The Enigma") and had proclaimed that "God is a question of beauty." At his best, as in a poignant moment of *La Chute*, he demonstrates such grace. The simplicity and liveliness of his style (as compared, say, to Sartre's) wells from that source: miracle. Alain-Fournier, before him, had dipped his pen into that transparent wellspring; he called his early collection of sketches and stories *Miracles*.

What, peering back dimly, are the major miracles, in our ongoing story, emerging from the original mystery of spirit and its initial violent act? One might speak of a colossal mating of two principles, like the fusion of sweetness and strength in Mozart's music, blessedly producing the universe and its eventual mirror in our minds.

It is hard to say which of the pair "wears the pants"; is spirit or act the Father? If spirit is *anima*, Mother, does She precede? Where Saint John saw the Word, Goethe saw the Deed. Most of us throw up our hands—perhaps emitting a puzzled Italian "è!"—signaling and settling for a stand-off. On these open-minded grounds, Derrida's plumping for the priority of "trace" (proto-writing) is arbitrary and unconvincing, reflecting his deviation from the mainstream vision of Mallarmé and Joyce (as does his one-sided critique generally, his "disassociation of sensibility," his tone-deafness).[6] Richard Rorty's pragmatism likewise rejects

---

[6]John Ellis's *Against Deconstruction* (Princeton, 1989) makes a persuasive case in favor of a more historically-grounded and adequate view.

When you reject tonality, you are left with the dreary conformities of the modern idiom (Cage, Boulez). Like natural theology, tonality is based on a paradoxical relation of matter—eternal structures, e.g., the octave—and form—the sense of harmony our psyches derive from (are beckoned to through) those structures, like the features of a

the fecund visitation into the realms of "die Mütter" (Goethe), including the ancient epistemological scuffles, and so muffs the very idea of genius. Nothing of this will last.

Sartre pretended he did not care to last. One has difficulty believing this, particularly after reading his little autobiographical sketch, *Les Mots*, where enduring on a shelf is his "fundamental project"—also in his best book, *La Nausée*—but in a way he proved his point. Who reads his other novels now? His philosophy, too, is eclipsed by the Mallarmé line (as Steiner notes in *Real Presences*, where he exorcizes both Derrida and Sartre with "Music means"). He did create a lot of noise...

What will last?

> Le ciel est, par-dessus le toit,
>   Si bleu, si calme!
> Un arbre, par-dessus le toit
>   Berce sa palme.
>
> La cloche dans le ciel qu'on voit
>   Doucement tinte.
> Un oiseau sur l'arbre qu'on voit
>   Chante sa plainte.

beautiful face. To rebel against these realities is childish, sterile, as even Nietzsche knew (whence his respect for the classic style, his general "obedience" to the cosmos).

The whole of a culture like ours has a distinctive tonality, at a level transcending the musical. The Judeo-Christian "message" is a big part of ours, obviously. We need not take the Bible literally in order to sense the miraculous inspiration and/or grounding of that line of prophetic writers or sayers, which went far to make us what we are; it worked out (even from a narrow pragmatic viewpoint). And when you include in that culture the modifying geniuses who are rooted in Judeo-Christianity but branch from it under Greek or other impulses, you have something like a row of powerful radio telescopes sweeping the heavens for a lodestar, a "North Star" and collectively locating something like its general direction, as Mallarmé more than hinted at the end of his *Coup de Dés*. That Way lies a sort of enlightened—sensitively intuited—muddling through.

Paul Ricoeur founds his hermeneutics on that perspective, and Gadamer seems to be groping his way toward it. But the negators and debunkers have nothing like that. For (individual or collective) genius, they substitute a network of chic naysayers, "in" people who band together for power on campuses and in the media, mesmerizing the youth who naturally rebel against their families and tradition. But these dog-in-the-manger adults, who should know better, block the only fertile way, which is always eventually *back* to the mainstream as well as forward. I know of no exception to that rule in the biographies of genius. See Virgil Nemoianu, "Is Literature Always Reactionary?" *The Georgia Review* 37.2: 347-65.

> Mon Dieu, mon Dieu, la vie est là,
>> Simple et tranquille.
> Cette paisible rumeur-là
>> Vient de la ville.
>
> ...

This will last, like Pissarro's "l'Entrée du village," because it is foundational, "coule de source," and is in us permanently, like a few other "classic" works of art; it structures our culture, our inner selves, as *Romeo and Juliet* did for our adolescent psyches.

The secret is the same as for a garden: the French nuances, the complexity, never outstrip the simplicity. The source is still constantly present.

After the archetypal blessed event, as direct heirs of it, chips off the old block, as we look back humanistically, the prime miracles are light (along with fire, air, water, earth), life, mother milk, love, language, and art. To be sure, each phenomenon, as it is born into awareness, is a minor miracle and sometimes, as in our best expressions, an important one. But the above are the ones that leap spontaneously from memory, and it is in the finest art, *justement*, that one finds confirmation of their specialness.

In Mallarmé's exquisite "Don du poëme," the ideal sky, *l'azur*, and the earthly bliss of mother milk are joined intimately, far in and far out. The father-poet, disappointed at his own nocturnal creation, turns to his sleeping wife (lying next to her infant girl) at naturally victorious dawn and apostrophizes her to "press her breast," musically and/or maternally to nourish his poor little abortive poem that is "hungered" by the milky azure sky he sees through the morning window:

> Ô la berceuse, avec ta fille et l'innocence
> De vos pieds froids, accueille une horrible naissance:
> Et ta voix rappelant viole et clavecin,
> Avec le doigt fané presseras-tu le sein
> Par qui coule en blancheur sibylline la femme
> Pour les lèvres que l'air du vierge azur affame?

Mingled miracles of light, life, and love, the mother-milk motif runs throughout his oeuvre and much of the Western poetic canon at its most intense (Keats, Coleridge, Chateaubriand, Hölderin, Rimbaud). That fusion of the peak of vision, essentially sacred, and the humbly concrete, the body, represents the chief aim of Symbolism altogether, in the wake of its earlier wave, Romanticism.

In this, Symbolism is an attempt to heal the mind-body rift of nineteenth- and early twentieth-century positivism, just as Romanticism tried to overcome the rationalistic limitations of the Enlightenment. Thus, T. S. Eliot, a major heir of the movement, sighed for the integrality of poetry (non-dissociated) like John Donne's and, in an essay on Mallarmé, saw him as prolonging that lineage.

Eliot's "dissociation" referred to science and art, but, since art *incarnates*, the mind-body integration is closely cognate to the one he sought. In an essay on Baudelaire, Eliot extols the Symbolist master for redeeming the body, and its weight of sin, in the form of the modern metropolis, in *Les Fleurs du mal* and *Le Spleen de Paris*.

Art like Baudelaire's or Mallarmé's or Verlaine's or Eliot's or Rilke's is, to use Joyce's still serviceable term, "epiphanous": surrounded by, and imbued with, the original hush and stillness, the silence which Debussy favored in his orchestrations and Mallarmé wanted to dominate his *page blanche*. It is resplendent with the first light of an *Apparition* (a poem by Mallarmé set by Debussy; Joyce copied the words into his Trieste notebook); behold...

Of course, they were very aware of the antecedent miracle, the appearance of the Christ child to the Magi.

That gift of the child brought us Christianity, which deepened through humility and broadened through universalization the parent faith and advanced the free creativity—"in the image of God"—announced and decisively launched in the Old Testament.

To the blessing of mother milk—Mary's flows in many a naïve text and painting—is now commingled the sanctified blood of sacrifice (seen by Musset and many others as a male giving equivalent to milk).[7] In Chrétien de Troyes' *Perceval*, a wounded wild goose bleeding scarlet drops on snow sends the Christian hero into a religious-erotic swoon (with overtones of the blood-suffused cheeks of virginal far-away Blancheflore, an ancestress of *Hérodiade*). Rimbaud is likewise entranced: "Le sang et le lait coulèrent" in the promiscuous and primal orgy of feeling in *Après le déluge*. J. P. Jacobsen's eerily stunning *Arabesque* (set by Delius) stirs our archetypal memories comparably.

---

[7]In *Ways of Art* Stanford French and Italian Studies (Saratoga: Anma Libri, 1990), I develop the theme of male expression—blood, ink, male sexual "milk"—as return gifts to the mother or Mother (cf. Freud on the child's feces as gift) in a sort of "lutte de genérosité" or ambivalent love-battle of the sexes. Jesus, like all men, needed to shake off the feminine at a certain crucial point: "Woman, what have I to do with thee?" The glowing re-embracement is all the stronger. Baudelaire, for a magnificent one, cannot be understood without this abiding truth. But the militant feminists and their legion of spineless male supporters have no interest in that.

In Mary, too, is the quietness of an apparition—John Huston exploited it in the closing scene of his pious version of *The Dead*—for her own conception was immaculate, her birth divine. Even more than for her milk, She is worshipped just for being there: "Simplement parce que Vous êtes là" (Claudel, "La Vierge à Midi").

It is not only avowed believers like Claudel who pick up all the early miracles on through the advent of the Judeo-Christian one (or ones) we know but tend latterly to forget. Commentators on Mallarmé, particularly since the 'sixties, are not at all likely to emphasize the pivotal figure of Saint John in his last work. Nor do they much note the parallel phenomenon in late Camus (*La Chute*).

The nostalgia and the critical distance together, I think, account for the choice of John, pivotal by definition, between an Old and a New, the very stuff of vibrantly original creation, late in our history but going all the way back. His head, too, is haloed on its plate, radiant, an Apparition. In Mallarmé's version—the posthumously-published fragments of *Les Noces d'Hérodiade*—the elemental blood and milk are an intimate part of the mysterious imagery.

In writers like these, or Proust or Eliot and the others we invoked—in whom all these levels of miracle are demonstrably at work—one feels a plenitude, because they build from the Ground up and recall or suggest all the stages leading to their imperialistic modern expression. Or, to resort to a familiar metaphor of flow, they prolong a cultural mainstream.

That thriving surge went underground in the Dark Ages, re-emerged in the Medieval period (Dante, Chaucer), and gathered tributary strength from various sources as it went on in the Renaissance (Shakespeare, Cervantes), reaching a peak of psychic power in the late nineteenth and early twentieth centuries, our modern Golden Age.

After that, critics started worrying aloud about the decline of culture —Ortega still reads convincingly—and, patently, it is threatened by virulent new strains of spiritual disease and neo-barbaric vandalism. But miracles will never cease: one can only wonder at those sublimely oblivious figures who manage to ignore all the stridency, the whimperings, the ugliness around and just go on turning out authentic art. One could name quite a few, but, prominently among them: Wilbur, Updike, Bellow, Welty, Olmi.

Man and Woman in Gide's *The Immoralist*

André Gide's short novel, *The Immoralist* (1902), has held up better than his other works, even *The Counterfeiters*, in the esteem of excellent critics, notably Albert Guerard, Jr., who wrote a model study of the man and the oeuvre. If one seeks reasons why this is so, some come forth readily: it presents a tensely dramatic plot—centered on a male-female relationship—in a precise, lively, modern style. The Gidean classic sobriety is perfectly melded with a late-Romantic depth of feeling. The story carries us through varied scenery, excitements, passions, losses. It maintains a tempo of urgency and unpredictability. We get immensely involved in the fate of these two young adults.

In his preface Gide tells us that (despite the title, which seems to take sides) his book makes no clear judgment for or against his protagonist. Not that he is at all indifferent—he fervently assures us of the contrary in terms which remind us that he is still a child of the earnest nineteenth century: "he has put into this book all his passion, all his tears, all his care." But he insists that "many great minds have been greatly disinclined to ... conclude," and he obviously is among them.

Of course he is right. One reason why *The Misanthrope* keeps coming back as our all-time favorite play of Molière is that we never know whether Alceste is butt or hero, and successive actors bring out one or the other aspect, refreshingly. And then along comes a memorable performer like Paul-Emile Deiber, of the *Comédie française*, who manages to make Alceste funny and painful *at the same time*—like certain physical contortions or a strained neck—and that higher synthesis applies to Michel as well, though in a slightly different way: he is both odious and attractive through most of the book and achieves the status of a *monstre sacré* or a "monstrous child," beyond good and evil in the Nietzsche sense, in the intertextual wake of René and Pechorin.

11

And yet there remains the fact of the title, indicating some subtler tilt in Gide's mind, and a conviction in many of his readers who find him not to be all that neutral in the final images he leaves us. It is the old problem of *Geniemoral*: isn't there an ultimate ethic which binds a Céline, a Pound, as well as the rest of us?

In other words, one can have it, in a sense, both ways: a sustained balance and suspension of judgment which raises the novel to high art throughout and yet, *in extremis*, some notion that, as the British are apt to put it, "It isn't done." One doesn't do to an ostensibly loved and frail wife what he did to her, neglecting her through a difficult pregnancy, dragging her around Europe and North Africa in a harebrained scheme to strengthen her, turning against her emotionally in her weakness, and finally betraying her, until she dies... Not even if he didn't cherish her as much as he repeatedly assures us he did. And not even if that was the price of his own self-esteem and eventual achievement.

The teetering "high wire" balancing act of Gide obviously has a great deal to do with the power of his novel whether one agrees with a final tilt or not. I find a certain parallel in this regard between Michel and Proust's Charlus, who is also exquisitely ambiguous, not so much in terms of guilt or innocence but rather of the cognate homosexual doubleness, the male-female wavering. In Charlus this becomes comic-tragic at times in a way that does not apply to Michel. There is no doubt that the latter is hesitant sexually or even primarily homosexual (like Gide himself); nor is there any doubt that for Proust and Gide both—who discussed such matters in a well-known passage of Gide's *Journal*—there were raised anxious moral questions which influenced and filtered into their novels. To put it impertinently, we have in both cases a dialectical principle which not only *elevates* the art and the interest—an *Aufhebung*, as Hegel would put it—but conversely brings about a *low*-wire act, plunging us into embarrassingly intimate realms as well. (The two together, the high and the low, are standard stuff of metaphoricity, the steep dimension of art). And therein lies chiefly the compelling hold *The Immoralist* has on our psyches, after all these years and readings.

Not so much, I would claim, because of the homosexual tension itself. That is certainly a part, or layer, of our involvement, and the critics largely do justice to it. No, and this is the gravamen, the sole *raison d'être* of our piece: beneath the homosexual drama, which I see as a sort of "screen" for even more troubling regions of the *id*, lies a dangerously murky realm of male-female relations, insufficiently explored hitherto.

Thomas Mann, who was attentive to Gide—he wrote an admiring preface to Albert Guerard's book—can serve as our Virgil guiding us into this nether region.

In the crucial chapter of *The Magic Mountain* entitled "Snow," Hans Castorp undergoes an ordeal which results in a vision marking the peak of his stay up there. first, there is an idyllic Mediterranean scene, paradisial as Mignon's dream in *Wilhelm Meister*, or Baudelaire's in *L'Invitation au voyage*. Amidst it:

> A young mother, in a brown robe loose at the shoulder, sat on a rounded mossy stone and suckled her child, saluted by all who passed ... as the worshipper does when he passes the high altar... This mixture of formal homage with lively friendliness, and the slow mild mien of the mother as well, where she sat pressing her breast with her forefinger to ease the flow of milk to her babe, glancing up from it to acknowledge the reverence paid her—this sight thrilled Hans Castorp's heart with something very close to ecstasy.

But the scene turns into its opposite, horror:

> Two grey women, witchlike, with hanging breasts and dugs of finger-length, were busy there, between flaming braziers, most horribly. They were dismembering a child. In dreadful silence they tore it apart with their bare hands—Hans Castorp saw the bright hair blood-smeared...

Gide lacks the frank *Schaudern*, the blood-curdling honesty of Mann—which is why Mann is helpful for our expedition. And Gide lacks the wise, healthy, balanced, fully *human* final vision that Mann, like his protagonist, derives from the agon.

The closest Gide comes to this primal realm of *die Mütter* (Goethe, *Faust*) as life-giver and witch (Jung's Terrible Mother with whom we associate the "Pleiad" of infantile fears, such as being dropped, roasted in an oven, dismembered...) is a passage in his early *Cahiers d'André Walter* where he describes a nightmare: a monkey comes and lifts the skirts of his ideal woman—"Elle"—and underneath is... nothing. Clearly the "Elle" is Madeleine, the cousin who became Gide's wife ("Emmanuèle" in the *Cahiers*), and there is every indication that behind her, palimpsestically, is Gide's mother. Of Alissa, in *Strait Is the Gate*, who corresponds point for point with Madeleine, an intimate friend says "it is your mother that Alissa is like."

André's dream is quite horrible enough, and in a way worse than Mann's scene, at least in terms of what it meant for Gide's character. Negation, even the dreadful sort described by Mann, is in some sense more human than total annihilation. What goes down can come up. But what hope can derive from nonexistence? A sexual encounter with a figure who unquestionably echoes the forbidden mother[1] in a dream

---

[1]In Rimbaud's *Les Déserts de l'amour* a similar woman appears in a dream, and he is similarly frustrated and weeps as Gide's André did, unconsolably.

fantasy seems like healthy feedback against incest repression compared to that devastating emptiness Gide ran into. In short, it would have been better, I submit, if under "Her" skirts there had been *something*.

Freud tells us that it is best for the boy child if his desire for his mother is "shattered" in the Oedipal crisis. But, patently, Freud also believed in bringing these underground desires to light in order to overcome excessive distortion of the libido, and one can be confident of his opinion in this case, seeing what became of Gide's marriage, despite the sympathy Freud showed for the artistic personality in his "Leonardo."

All the evidence points to the fact that with Gide love and sexual desire for a man or woman were very separate. This split is commonplace throughout Western cultural history, starting at least with the Greeks and Romans (Venus cloacina and purificatrix), and we are well aware of it in literary figures from Shakespeare, Swift, Goldsmith, through Baudelaire and Proust. D. H. Lawrence, in his *The Psychology of Sex*, sees it as an essence of male emotionality as opposed to female: women have far less difficulty accepting one as part of the other, usually; they are more centrally integrated and temperate, "flowing" in that sense. This polarization in men generally is closely linked to their bent toward extreme psychic patterns and actions (theology-porn, ambition-suicide...). But with Gide we have to say that the pattern is aggravated into a "fruitfly" magnification.

The *dimensional* dialectic between the sexes accounts for well-known phenomena, such as the projection of male excessiveness onto women: a Jimmy Swaggart sees exciting hellfire in a prostitute who, when interviewed, turns out to be just a gal "turning a trick," trying to get on in life and raise a child. The intense executive in Fassbinder's *Lola* believes he is plunging into siren depths, but Lola is planning to open a bar with the proceeds. Swann falls headlong into love with a woman, Odette, who is almost a *femme fatale* in his jealous mind, but she keeps her cool indifference when it counts, and life just goes on after a while, through their progeny, Gilberte.

Gide and his Michel lack the saving flexibility of Swann, who makes the turn, pivots, and becomes a model bourgeois father.

Mind you, we are not engaged in a Philistine accusation against Gide's writings, or even his life, here; merely, we are trying to understand what lies behind both in the name of a general comprehension which belongs to the literary critic as much as to anyone. For this, provided we are wary of psychologizing or reductionism, we are entitled to draw on clues taken from the biographies or anywhere else. What counts alone is what we *make* of them.

The principal clues in the case of Gide are widely known. Most readers of Gide are aware that early in life he married his shy cousin Madeleine whom he worshipped, "put on a pedestal." That the marriage was never consummated. That he betrayed her frequently with men; even on his honeymoon, as revealed in *Et Nunc Manet in Te*, he made passes at a youth in the train. That Gide wrote hundreds of letters to her and that she burned them all in womanly revenge. That Gide also betrayed her with the opposite sex, notably with the woman from whom his daughter, Catherine, was born.

The Immoralist reflects the main lines of this relationship rather closely, including the part which came after the publication date, by anticipation. At that time (1902) Gide had been married to his cousin for seven years; he had known her since childhood. We will return to the biography later. For the moment, the initial events of the novel which interest us most are the following:[2]

Michel, a promising young scholar of cultural history, marries, in order to please his dying father, a woman whom he does not love, and we learn that he has loved no other; she was twenty, he twenty-four. His mother had died when he was fifteen: "her stern Huguenot teachings had slowly faded, with her lovely image, from my heart..." (9). His health was fragile; he was a loner, with few friends; he "prized friendship rather than friends" (10).

The "Huguenot mother" is true to the life, but her early death isn't; it was Gide's father who died when he was young (age twelve). The lack of interest in women is also a well-documented fact. His remark about friendship is part of a consistent theme which runs through the novel and points to the heart of Gide's and Michel's character-structure: the vertical of narcissism, high-mindedness, ego-ideal is a fixation, a "hang-up" which is all-determining here. His inability to pivot to the other—wife, friends, normal folks altogether—stands in stark contrast to Mann who over and over, in *The Magic Mountain* and all his writings, indicates a need to *cross* his ego-ideal with the horizontal of existence, "the need to catch the eight o'clock bus" ("The Artist and Society"), in a higher balance, a mandalic plenitude.

We learn further, reading on, that Michel's health was "extremely delicate": whereas Micheline was "quite strong; that she was stronger than I we were soon to learn" (10-11).

Gide had more than a touch of the tuberculosis from which his father had died and had been twice invalided out of military service. Madeleine herself was not very robust. But Marceline is made to be so here, at least

[2]Page references are to the Vintage paperback edition, 1970.

initially, in a pattern which no doubt reflects his earliest sense of weakness vis-à-vis his mother who was, as Harold March[3] informs us, "deeply religious, self-effacing, and possessed of a strong sense of duty." "On her only son... she lavished her high-principled attentions to the point of endangering his affection for her" (22-23).

With all that French Protestant and female energy focused on him, André Gide was evidently a scared-running little boy. In his autobiography he is described as "stupid, silly, sly," living in a state of "half-sleep and imbecility." The loss of the father, whom he had admired, further focused that energy on him, an only child, alone with two formidable women: his mother and her former governess and later companion, Anna Shackleton.

Awesome feminine power, the male need to prove and justify oneself in the face of it, is a main wellspring of masculine motivation and achievement.

Michel says: "I have kept, I think, from my puritanical childhood this hatred of any surrender to weakness" (17). What we read between the lines is a specifically male need to be macho. That transpires unmistakably from the bravado of "what need had I now of her constant care and of my selfishness? Was I not stronger than she at this moment?" (64). Later in the book this theme expends into a full Nietzschean refusal to pity the weak, meaning his ailing wife.

Gide, we know, had read his Nietzsche by this time, but he did not really require him for this rigidly upright ego-ideal; he derived it from his own total fear, not unrelated to the psychic mechanism that made Jesus say to his mother, "Woman I know thee not"; that made Saint Paul transcendentally celibate and the Catholic priesthood in his lineage; that made Percival (who also lost his father early) leave his mother fainting, and eventually dying, behind at the bridge as he set out for his initiation into manhood through knightly and spiritual prowess, leading directly to the modern cultural hero who wields a pen, not a sword, e.g., Baudelaire replacing General Aupick.

Anthropology offers us endless examples of the ritual ordeals young men of the tribe undergo to purge themselves of all mother influence as they constitute themselves as adult hunters and fighters, men among men. This becomes much more problematic in modern Western individualistic society, where the role model of the individual father is so important, if the father is missing or inadequate.

In an essay "Plumes and Prisons" I have taken note of the many leading French (and other) writers who have lost their fathers early in life,

[3] *Gide and the Hound of Heaven*, University of Pennsylvania Press, 1952.

hence lacked that model and had more to prove. I cited there the Spanish psychiatrist Enrique Guarner, who had exclusively matadors as his patients: without exception they were fatherless! I noted Michel Leiris's *Literature as a Bullfight*. A close friend of Camus—who was orphaned of a father and whose mother was of Spanish ancestry— thought of him as a bullfighter.[4]

Thomas Mann, in his *Doctor Faustus*, observes the urge to put the feminine behind them in special men, most prominently Christ. Apparently, few have had his honesty in delving into the male psyche, including homosexual temptations that go with that specialness.

We know about womb envy from Karen Horney and Lillian Rubin and from unsurpassable writers like Proust, whose little Marcel cackled like a hen when he had brought off his first successful prose; or like Mallarmé who, in *Don du poème*, begs his wife to give life, creation, to his abortive poem.

Camus, who owed much to Gide, is very helpful here: in his youthful lyrical essays, *L'Envers et l'endroit*, he describes a mother cat that has devoured some of her kittens. The young Camus sat there utterly transfixed, hypnotized, staring at her for *hours*. He was utterly pious to his mother, as we know from all accounts, and in the preface he later wrote for that reprinted work he mentioned his attachment to her as one of the absolutely central themes of his authentic work to come; the other main theme was, precisely, the need to be a man...

This is the inner bullfight, the structuring crisis, in which Gide went one way, Mann and Camus another.

Camus stayed with the male-female dilemma all the way, struggling through setbacks such as the betrayal by his first wife, and came out with *both* his commitment to woman and his male identity intact, as Mann had done (balancing, at one excruciating point, between Claudia Chauchat and Peeperkorn). The episode in which Camus lies on the bed next to his frightened silent mother after she had been threatened by a strange intruder, breathing in her sweat and anguish, *staying* with her, is most telling (that vinegar smell remained in his system and shows up in his portrait of Prague). He spoke, in that same piece of *L'Envers et l'endroit*, of the "indifference of that strange mother" (she was a deaf-mute) and shows the highest respect for it: it is a source of his own silent authenticity, reflected in the indifference of an absurd cosmos.

This is the nothing-axis of the Terrible Mother: every child knows that her cold-treatment is worse than the father's physical punishments.

[4] In Patrick McCarthy, *Camus* (New York: Random House, 1982) 22.

In the war, when it got unbearably freezing we soldiers used to exclaim "It's colder than a witch's tit!"

At times Camus purged the horror of the devouring cat and the indifference of world and mother in homeopathic expressions such as *The Misunderstanding*, where a mother kills her incognito son and commits suicide. At other times the tilt which emerges from the courageous struggle results in his putting woman at the core of his cosmos as in *The Plague*. This is ultimate faith: in life, in his mother's central role in it, and his own meaning. The victory at the core where women and men become co-human also allows the flexibility, the capacity to move into the feminine dimension and fully sympathize with woman as mate and comrade, as in the portrait of Janine in *The Adulterous Woman* or of Jeanne in his youthful sketch under that name (reflected in *The Plague*'s Jeanne).

Sartre, curiously, is closer to Gide. He was not homosexual, but he did not succeed in accepting and developing the feminine side of himself ultimately (his anima) with the power of a Goethe, a Proust, a Joyce. He began fatherless and vulnerable. In *The Words* he presents an episode where, as a little boy, he accompanied his mother on a walk by the Seine. When a stranger accosted her, he felt accosted too, a member of the feminine. Homosexual dread haunts most of his work. In *Nausea*, having read of a little girl named Lucienne who is raped from behind, Roquentin is obsessed with the image. Sartre is altogether obsessed with Genet, with Daniel in *The Roads to Freedom*, with the fascist homosexual in *Childhood of a Chief*... Thus, we can understand the wild exultation of Orestes in *The Flies*, when he has killed his mother, Clytemnestra, and screams he is free at last, a man among men![5]

There is nothing like that matricide in Camus or Mann. Sartre's obsessions take us, rather, to Gide's way; altogether women come off badly in Sartre's fictional world. In Gide's first play, *Saül*, the Biblical king kills his hated queen, and the homosexual undertones are very plain.

Here we are on delicate ground: one cannot prove that Gide (and Sartre) went one way and could only have gone that way. There are books of his—*Isabelle, Geneviève, The Counterfeiters*—which portray

---

[5] I doubt that this is primarily because his mother remarried, like Clytemnestra (cf. Hamlet, Baudelaire). The raw mother figure is problem enough. In a way, the remarriage helps the psyche, by a divide and rule device: there is a man to hate along with the mother, and that is tempering. Gide did not have this advantage. Sartre managed better. He had many affairs with women, and no homosexual experience.

women with true sympathy and understanding, even a sort of feminism.[6] In lining up a number of writers like this, we can hope, at best, to glimpse a common crisis of being and growth which can lead in various directions, and not necessarily permanently. Camus changed his view of women over time, it has been persuasively demonstrated, by Donald Lazare and Herbert Lottman, for example. Even Sartre has his warmly *sympathique* Sarah, in *The Roads to Freedom* (it helped her to be Jewish). Nonetheless, all these writers do point to the terrible subterranean problem and make us feel its tragic power, its skin-of-the-teeth dangers, and help us to see how a decorous citizen like Michel, Gide himself, could come to do the quite unspeakably cruel things he did *compulsively*, with the relentless insistence that is the pulse-beat of *The Immoralist*.

Shall we make a plunge on our own?

What, after all, is the awesome quality of women that men lack? Obviously, the power to give birth. With that there is the ovum centrality, the closeness to Being that is implied therein (the heart of things, the hearth, the home to return to). Woman is central and also prior. She is closer to the original unisex creature: for the first weeks a fetus is visibly female regardless of gender. As such, she is more natural; whence her grace, gracefulness, graciousness. She flows through time more like a river, undulating more gently than men, who have hang-ups, are dammed up, Icarian, fly high and fall low: she is Anna Livia Plurabelle; Goethe's *Ewigweibliche* which pulls us onward (*hinan*). So earth surface, time, memory, the horizontal (flow) are her particular dimension. She lives longer and is more temperate: men commit almost all the violent crimes, outnumber her on death row 1200 to 8 or so, kill themselves three times more often, do all the fighting and governing practically, and so on. She faints, weeps, laughs, eludes like Ondine, moves on (*è mobile*). Supple as a cat, with claws hidden. Not a channeled violence, but an enveloping power. Electric.

The boy child at first is of his mother, *is* her. Then he has to be weaned, ousted, pushed out into male doing and separateness very differently from his sister. He is for a while distinctly nothing at all. That is what he must work with: so he learns to abstract, fly, create in *his* way. Make something of himself. Be a man.

If there is no father to imitate and if he is sensitive and thoroughly mama-dominated, he is apt to dream, at least, of making nothing of Her, killing her in revenge. It is the equivalent of the Promethean impulse

---

[6]Still, there is something forced in his siding with Geneviève versus men, the sort of shallow shift that we find in his *déculture*, his politics during the war, his cult of Simenon, etc.

which gets back at God for being all and our being nothing. At least, blaspheme against her as happens in Proust's *Contre Sainte-Beuve* (reflected in Mlle Vinteuil in *Swann's Way*). Baudelaire's misogyny and fantasied violence against women is in proportion to his lifelong adoration of Caroline.

Modern men go off and live in homosexual colonies in big cities in a breakaway attempt. Yet once there, they live permanently under Her aegis: dressing, walking, talking like her. Often they seek a Queen Bee, a woman they group around, or a cult figure like Barbra Streisand or Jane Olivar. All that is the narcissistic male love of woman Gide offers Madeleine—not humanly livable in the sense of fruitful structuring in a family way. Other, normal men may childishly worship their wives too, but they know how to swivel into the other direction intermittently: they win that capacity in their core as Leonardo won his flexible genius, his power to change directions when it counted, as Valéry noted in his later essay on him.

If a homosexual rejects her as a sexual partner it isn't because he doesn't love her enough, *au contraire*: he can't *handle* her power. She is too integral, like life itself. A penis is more limited. Sex can be manipulated; love can't. So they have a thousand partners, not the One that counts. Neither can they pivot into her life-flow, toward progeny, for that, too, is all-powerful and leads to death, away from the ego-ideal of the narcissistic self. Ego-ideal and libido are at odds, Freud observes. With the other being a male, the flow-risk is avoided: such is the role of Ménalque, based on Oscar Wilde, in *The Immoralist*. If he risks, or Michel, and they do, it is in their own male way, in the name of their own male production.

Thus Ménalque preaches the now. Time before and after, in memory or bourgeois calculation insuring a future, is ruled out as sentimentality. Throughout the novel, every move *sideways* is checked by Michel and his Nietzschean mentor.

Summing up provisionally: Michel lets his adored wife die for the same almost-inscrutable reasons that Sartre's Orestes murders Clytemnestra, or a character in Baudelaire's *Portrait of Mistresses* kills an unbearably angelic wife... No doubt, for the same deep reasons of rejection—for to be a male at all is to be in some real sense rejected by woman, as an organ transplant is rejected, as the sperm is repelled by deadly acids as it swims toward the ovum—that sends men every day to attack women in one compulsive form or another. Often enough, as in the case of a Ted Bundy, it is clear that it is out of a profound sense of weakness, of rejection (he never got over a spurning, apparently), in a totally mistaken attempt to prove one is strong, to get one's own back. Lord help us...

Returning to *The Immoralist*: in its subsequent pages it confirms this perspective at every turn:

Michel begins to fall in love with his bride on the boat ferrying them to Africa (Gide, contrariwise, had loved Madeleine since child-hood). Since he had not taken women seriously before, he is surprised at her depth and stirred to his own depths. But it is soon plain that his emotion is, as consistently later, purely vertical: what turns into adora-tion, upward, begins as pity, downward: "I kissed her on the eyelids and suddenly felt, in the wake of my kiss, a new kind of pity; it filled me so fiercely I could not restrain my tears" (13). That fierceness and con-descension contrast sharply with the quality of her awakening feeling for him: "She stared back in her turn; then, very tenderly, smiled at me" (13). The smile and tenderness are essentially calm, sweetly peaceful and gently flowing—yes, feminine. Men's and women's emotions are very apt to *cross* in this way. Need one add that men are not "just" men, women not "just" women, and that they often change positions in a sort of *chassé-croisé*, or morris dance? But there are still prevailing patterns linked to sexual identity, and this pair is exemplary in that respect, and will remain so throughout the story. When he falls violently ill, spits blood, is pronounced probably incurable, Marceline cares for him with maternal generosity: "Marceline, my wife, my life, I know that her devoted care, that her love and nothing else saved me" (21). Wife, indeed, ideally means life as on-going, a river of tendresse, an inner melody. But we have some idea now why he couldn't stay with this life-force which threatened him with his own insufficiency. He becomes utterly self-concerned, proud that "death had brushed me... with its wing" (21) and that he had survived the challenge, as he convinced himself gradually, on his own, and risen anew so that "the daylight acquired an unhoped-for radiancy" (21). It is soon evident that he is seeking self-reliance. Of his cure he says succinctly, "It is a matter of will" (26). Hence, he cannot accept Marceline's praying for his recovery. Although he claims not to be interested in God (Gide often was), or her religion, we are aware that it is *her* intercession that bothers him: "I don't like to be indebted..." (29). Which forcefully recalls the young Nietz-schean James Joyce who refused to bow down to his mother's religion even at the bedside of her final illness, and the corresponding episode in *Ulysses*: "No mother, let me live and let me be." He fled that provincial mother-place ("doublin his mumper," or Dublin his mother, in *Finne-gans Wake*) and its parochial belief, for his creative life abroad.

Henri Peyre taught us, at Yale, that Frenchmen tended to be anti-clerical because their wives, "the memory of the race" (Thierry-Maul-nier), carried on the church tradition in cahoots with the priests. Gide, too, revolted against traditional faith and came up with one closer to his own needs, in which the figure of Christ stands out versus Pauline ecclesia.

At the end of the novel, this motif recurs poignantly: Michel puts a rosary into the hands of his dying wife, and she deliberately lets it drop, as if to say: "You rejected my faith and my life-rhythm; I cannot accept its symbol from your selfish hands."

Meanwhile, as Michel slowly recuperates, we see him turning against that rhythm subtly. He takes an interest in Arab children with more than a suspicion of budding homoeroticism. "I was upset by her presence. If I had stood up she would have followed me; if I had taken off my shawl, she would have offered to carry it... I saw she had her protégés; in spite of myself, but stubbornly, I took an interest in the others" (33). Later, he notes that she seems to prefer the sickly children and, like Nietzsche, he sees that as a namby-pamby sentimentality: feminine, in a word. He pays homage to her maternal kindness momentarily (36), but the Juggernaut of his too-male project sweeps on: "I lost my temper with her and with them, and finally drove them away. To tell the truth they frightened me" (43).

Rimbaud (in "Childhood") and Sartre (in *Nausea*) betray a comparable fear of the biological forces which lead to decay and death, hence their clinging to a male image of safe hardness, a "ball of saphir," a "steely" jazz tune.

Michel favors particularly a boy named Moktir who steals a pair of scissors from him while he watches fascinatedly in a mirror (43-44). The fatherless Rimbaud admired the "forçat intraitable" as Sartre admired jailbird Genet. The mirror of *The Immoralist* adds to the safe structuring of this perverse fall-rise. This dialectical movement will carry him into a flirtation with all sorts of muck, incest, dirty beggars, poachers. A *nostalgie de la boue* is universal but not so consistently. Baudelaire, in his *Journaux intimes*, speaks of the unique pleasure of sex being the consciousness of doing evil. That, too, is excessive, Manichean (*fleurs-mal*); fortunately, there is another Baudelaire.[7] Homosexuality is easily involved here: we see it in the lesbian scene of *Swann's Way* where evil itself seems to be the main motif emerging from a person who, like Gide, was raised in puritan ideals. Proust makes it clear that Mlle Vinteuil is "an artist in evil," i.e., a sort of disturbed genius reflecting his own complex makeup and, indirectly, Gide's.

---

[7]Notably in masterpieces of male-female love like *La Chevelure* and scattered homage to women throughout the oeuvre.

Michel is terrified of dying and tries to seize his life before it is too late: "I read these words of Christ to Peter: when thou shalt be old, thou shalt stretch forth thy hands" (47-48). So Gide, Michel, do take the Bible seriously—on their own terms.

As he discovers this new independent self, Michel feels the necessity to hide it from Marceline, to lie to her. He professes "an ever greater love" (60), but he is going off in a radically different way. At one point, nevertheless, the pair make love, but it is a sort of fluke, brought about by a violent adventure (this never happened between Gide and Madeleine). The result is that, instead of growing closer to her in the sense of being able intermittently to enter into her feminine life-flow, he becomes more entrenched in his own pattern. It is then, precisely, that he utters the telltale phrase: "Was I not stronger than she at this moment?" (64). Just before that we read: "It seemed to me, now that I was stronger, that she had become even more delicate" (63). And just afterward: "overcome with pity, with tenderness, I gently rested my lips between her closed eyes in the tenderest, the most loving, and the most reverent of kisses" (64).

Clearly, this "tenderness" is of a radically different order than hers. It goes with "pity" and "reverence," down and up, and is characteristically excessive, self-important.

They plan to go home, and Marceline, like most women, is overjoyed at the prospect of staying put in a *chez soi* (65). But Michel is busy with a drastic change in his professional direction: he is, in a Nietzschean way, "breaking the tables," revolting against traditional scholarship in his field, embarked on the well-identified historical path of *déculture* involving—as in *Les Nourritures terrestres*—a neo-barbarism, a "trashing" of the past not unlike the one we have seen since, roughly, 1968. Hence, he is intrigued by the Goths who invaded Rome and helped to precipitate its decline and fall: "the figure of the young king Athalric was what attracted me most to the subject. I imagined this fifteen-year-old... rebelling against his mother Amalaswintha, balking at his Latin education, rejecting culture... dying at eighteen, utterly corrupted, glutted with debauchery" (66).

Gide is known for favoring the literary device called *en abyme*—a sort of play within a play (he speaks of it in *The Counterfeiters*)—and this microcosmic revolt against a mother in the name of a male fling cameoed in mid-novel is true to the macrocosmic whole.

Marceline's pregnancy becomes visible back at the home farm in Normandy, and Michel, momentarily, dreams of an ideal balanced life (71-72). He is happy and serene. But that lasts no more than the never-repeated sexual encounter. On the contrary, he plunges into an intricate series of adventures with <u>low-lifes</u> working on the farm. He gets to the point of endangering his patrimony through encouraging poaching and odd double-dealings with various characters. He is engrossed by what he hears from one of them about the lurid, incestuous carryings-on of a local family called Heurtevent. His distorted love for Marceline remains characteristic in this phrase: "I bent over her as over a deep, clear pool which revealed, as far as one could see, nothing but love" (86). A pool down into which one gazes, like his Narcissus, is not a flowing river of feminine life. Something is wrong, he intuits: "I sensed, close to our happiness, something besides happiness, which certainly stained my love..." (86). This new Adam (he spoke earlier of the old Adam he was leaving behind) is listening to an inner snake—"You will be as Gods" has become "You" singular—which will soon take on human form.

They go to live in Paris, and Michel cannot abide ordinary bourgeois existence, the banality of salon conversation, "others." Such is the familiar style of genius: Montaigne, Rousseau, Camus... Ménalque shows up —he is modeled on Oscar Wilde who played a similar role in Gide's development—as a human version of the whispering snake, telling Michel to break free from his middle-class limitations, the world, in a word, of his wife and child-to-be. Ménalque, we noted, lives only for the moment. No calculation for the future, no memory. He reinforces what has been building in Michel since his steep fall and rise from tuberculosis. Marceline instinctively dislikes him, exactly as Settembrini dislikes Naphta or Chauchat: he is at cross purposes with them.

The baby is abortive, and Marceline falls deathly ill. Michel, stiffened by Ménalque's injunctions, is heartless when she seems to want a rosary for comfort: "I did manage to get well by myself " (116). Normal people would think this fleetingly, no doubt, but, out of fellow-feeling, *sympathy* (not the *pity* he specialized in) would have put it out of their minds. But Michel develops it into a major motif. "Did the two black holes of her nostrils always look like that?" (143). Again: "I knew all too well that my eyes, instead of trying to meet hers, would slide down to the black holes of her nostrils" (165). That is all-too-honest.

Those black nostrils are "deux trous noirs!" in the French. In the episode of the lifted skirts in *Les Cahiers d'André Walter*, the awful nothingness we alluded to is followed by "c'était noir, noir comme un trou: je sanglotais de désespoir" (179). Nothing can be proved, of course, but this sounds familiar, striking: something like the fearful essence of feminine sexuality for a man, an underlying threat of nothing, a black pit in which one can drown, obverse of the pool of love into which he gazed, almost a cosmic Black Hole.

It is also a horrid fact that men are known to secretly hate their wives for being sick. Should she not buoy us up? There is a basic selfishness underlying both sexes in that sense, no doubt, but perhaps a revenge motif creeps in particularly with the vitally outdone, *de trop* male. Anyway, it is a recognized surprising fact. As is the fact that men resent their mothers' getting old—critics have alluded to this in reference to the Stranger's indifference toward his aged mother. Again, normal human sympathy should balance that out; but that is what Michel, like Nietzsche, lacked most. And so he says to himself: "only the strong deserve sympathy" (143). He even brags: "It seemed to me I coughed better than that" (143). On the next page: "I was strong now" (144). And he goes, not out to her need but down: "so weary was I of the heights" (147). "Our descent into Italy gave me all the vertigo of falling" (148). He has dragged Marceline into a hectic traveling despite her weakened condition, just as Gide had done with Madeleine. The thought seemed to be, in both cases, that he had recovered in North Africa, why not she? A *pavé de l'ours* if ever there was one. People do tend to be that way: imposing their pattern on others in a clumsy well-meaning manner. But to that lethal extent? And on the way he *falls* again and again into the muck of homoerotic encounters, groveling with lice-infested beggars, and the like. He swears, "I loved her passionately" (150). "But how can I express this —that insofar as I respected myself less I revered her more" (151). He is on a sort of wild psychic elevator that can only ascend or descend.

Marceline chides him at one point because of this fixation of perversity, and he muses, "I had to admit that to me each man's worst instinct seemed the most sincere. Then, what was it I called sincerity?" (157). This is the crossroads tension between these two: she sees her normative truth as sincere, he sees his Manichean one, and both are right. Gide wrestled with this problem of sincerity in work after work and lost. Wisdom should have told him that there is a higher balance of the two dimensions in a healthy life of the sort that neither his masterpiece nor his own marriage reflects at all.

Marceline approaches death, and Michel goes off to sleep with an Arab prostitute (admitting later that it is her little brother who interests him more, perhaps). He returns to find his wife far gone and clumsily offers her the rosary which, we noted, she deliberately drops.

Perhaps we can read that as a terminal independence of her own, i.e., from his and from her belief both. That would be a sort of final getting-even with Michel for his cruelty and neglect, showing herself to be strong enough to do without God or that kind of man. A woman's self-assertion, in short. It would be only fair. Fair? Who does not prefer her as a person? I think of his mentor Mallarmé's remark about Gauguin: "One doesn't have the right to abandon one's children even to found a religion." He would have applied that surely, as well, to his good wife.

Michel falls into a strange numbness. He cannot decide on his own guilt or innocence: "I must prove to myself that I have not exceeded my rights," he says to his friends who have come to help him. Clearly, he is suffering and asserts that "Something in my will has been broken. Sometimes I am afraid that what I have suppressed will take its revenge. I want to make a fresh start" (170).

The friends are deeply disturbed by what he has done: together with the title and his final self-indulgent acts, we are left with the "tilt" of ultimate judgment, despite the moral suspension posed in the preface.

Still, many readers over the years have come down on the side of that suspension and refuse to blame Michel. No doubt, that is partly a reflection of our own indecisive era.

Camus puzzled about these matters in an exemplary way and came up with a notion of "reasonable innocence" (*The Rebel*). He knew that moral relativism in the time of Nazi nihilism could be very dangerous to civilized society. In *The Fall*, for similar reasons of *value*, he implies that we should not be too quick to give up an *eventual* Edenic goal of true innocence, like a far-out North Star that guides us even as we muddle our way through messy existence. On either of these grounds, the reasonable or the absolute, Michel is found seriously wanting and Gide, alas, along with him. But what can one do about it? *The Immoralist* remains a wonderful book.

The True Camus

Let us start modestly, as Albert Camus did. By the time he was stopped, when he died brutally in his forty-seventh year, he was widely regarded as the most important literary figure in the Western world.

He could hardly have come from humbler circumstances. His French father, who died in World War I almost as soon as Albert was born, was an agricultural worker in Algeria. His Spanish mother could not read, seldom spoke, and was partially deaf. Her mother was a straight-laced old lady who raised Albert and his older brother with strictness and, at times, the whip. Camus grew up in Belcourt, a working-class neighborhood of Algiers. As he looked back on it later, his childhood seemed happy despite the hardships. He loved the life of the streets and the beaches in the sun. A dedicated teacher took an interest in him and encouraged him in his studies. Camus worked with fierce concentration and went on with scholarships to the University of Algiers, where he specialized in philosophy. But at age seventeen he contracted the tuberculosis which never really left him, though it came and went. He dropped out of school and took a series of odd jobs. At age twenty he married but divorced a year later: his first wife, Simone Hié, was a beautiful drug addict who betrayed him and wounded his psyche deeply. Camus's affair with the Communist Party shortly after this was rather similar: youthful hopes and swift disenchantment. Simultaneously, he founded a politically inspired theater group which attracted some local attention. He did some writing as well as acting and directing for it, loved it all passionately. He had, meanwhile, recovered enough to go back and get a diploma in philosophy. In 1937 he published his first little book, *L'Envers et l'endroit.*

This brings us to the literary Camus who most concerns us, for it is a marvelously honest and tender piece of writing about his early years, and when it was republished shortly before his death, he said that unless he returned to the unspoiled simplicity and piety of that book he would never do anything worthwhile. So let us have a look at it, remarking only that what happened to Camus after that is quite well known: how he fought for justice to the Arabs in the local press, went on to help edit and write for the Resistance paper *Combat* during the war; how he remarried and had twins, how he became famous with *L'Etranger*, *Le Mythe de Sisyphe*, *La Peste*, *L'Homme révolté*, and so on; the quarrel with Sartre; the Nobel prize; his dismay at his fame; and at the Algerian conflict in which he refused to take sides, out of loyalty to his mother; his stupefying death in a car accident in 1960. We will return to some of these items later.

The title *L'Envers et l'endroit* refers to the deep, honest ambivalence that runs throughout Camus; typically for him, particularly in his first manner, love and hate, beauty and ugliness, life and death go hand in hand. Eventually, this total cancellation will be identified with the absurd, referring especially to the tension between the mind's quest for unity or meaning and the world's chaotic refusal of it. One would speak too of heaven and hell, if it were not for the fact that Camus, like his parents, had little use for organized religion though he was baptized a Catholic. But he was a profoundly religious man in his own way and said "God is a question of beauty" to an intimate friend. Later, he will reintroduce into a world threatened by valuelessness the moderate religious concept of "the sacred." Altogether, a pantheism not unlike that of the other great artists of modern France or Europe, or Emily Dickinson here, is close to his untrumpeted belief. But the God of beauty, or of the wistful sacred, is remote indeed from often-grim human affairs, and in these pieces we see an old woman whom no one is interested in staying with any more. The young folks go off heedlessly to the movies and leave her alone with her cold crucifix. Young Camus goes off too, but with a stab of concern in his heart, and we see him, in a sense, betraying those other young'uns, becoming himself with his deeper awareness. There is another sketch about an old man, similarly avoided in a café, going home alone in the dusk toward his eventual death.

There is a scene where Camus is sitting in an Arab café overlooking the twinkling port alone, listening to the foghorns in the night and wondering about his future itinerary through life. The key notes are sounded in the darkness of his love for his strange "indifferent" mother —she never caressed him but they were utterly in league and he knew it—and his need to be a man.

This is a telling point. He was fatherless like his Stranger, of whom it is said, tersely, "He had never known his father." In *La Chute*, equally tersely, Clamence laments, "Il n'y a plus de père, plus de règles!" It is suggestive to note that any number of France's greatest writers, from Du Bellay and Racine through Baudelaire, Rimbaud, and Sartre were orphaned or otherwise deprived of their fathers. The impact is fairly obvious. The normal father provides a role model which mediates the boy's struggles to manhood. Failing that, the process of dissociating one-self from the mother becomes quite problematic, and an excessive pattern is apt to develop of "proving oneself as a man." This is confirmed by Enrique Guarner (revealed to me by Charles McCabe), a Spanish psychiatrist whose clientele was exclusively matadors. Without exception, they were fatherless. Before I had learned that, I had spoken in print[1] of Camus's bullfighter psychology, mindful of his Spanish inheritance as well as Michel Leiris' essay, "De la littérature considérée comme une tauromachie."[2] I was naturally pleased when Herbert Lottman's biography disclosed the fact that one of his closest friends thought of Camus in just that way. The fact that Patrick McCarthy in his recent book[3] dismisses this notion loftily causes me no particular pain. McCarthy's book is often hasty and insensitive, though it has its uses and is cleverly packaged.

In another scene, Camus stares for hours at a mother cat that has just devoured some of her kittens. This is the other side of his special courage and one which I particularly admire. He describes in an unbearably powerful understatement of tenderness a night he spent lying next to his mother after she had been frightened by an unknown assailant, breathing in her perspiration and her silent anguish. In this daring to *stay* with the unmediated mother, he resembles Proust whom he, unlike Sartre, worshipped. We know about Proust's stubborn relation to his mother; few normal people are honest about their deepest affections and anxieties as this pair of artists were.

Further, as in the case of Proust whose mother could become an object of fierce hatred out of jealousy, in *Jean Santeuil*, to the point of wishing her death, so too Camus sees in the mother cat the hideous "wrong side" of his total attachment, what Jung refers to as the "terrible mother." The Stranger tells the examining magistrate that his indifference before the death of his mother can be partly explained by the fact that everyone desires the death of loved ones at times. This is repeated elsewhere in Camus, and it is an important theme of *La Chute*. Camus's play *Le Malentendu* is about a mother who, with the help of her daughter, strangles the incognito traveler who turns out to be her son.

---

[1]*Diacritics* 4.2 (1974).
[2]In *L'Age d'homme* (Paris: Gallimard, 1939).
[3]*Camus* (New York: Random House, 1982).

No doubt the betrayal by Simone Hié has something to do with all this and with the well-known donjuanism of Camus, but, of course, beneath all that, there are universal facts of life, which some people are more candid about than others. Not that one should wallow in them; Camus thought of his *Misunderstanding* as a modern tragedy, and that, one feels, is the proper way to handle these matters, just as Sophocles did with his *Oedipus*. But let there be no misunderstanding here: woman is at the core of Camus's earthly world, where the mother securely is in *La Peste*.

In *L'Etranger*, which came out in 1942 and made his reputation, Camus's protagonist seems dazed at first. He has been inwardly stabbed by a new awareness, as we gradually learn with him; he is "on to something," the absurd. The consolations of religion had departed from lots of lives in his time, but it is another thing to feel in depth that the world is made of a profound cleavage between mind and reality. The fact of mortality alone when it hits you truly can make mockery of the quest of meaning; or the simple confrontation of self too close-up in a mirror when you see a sort of alien moon-landscape. Where is our identity, or anything fixed in this fleeting, ephemeral existence? But all that *Angst* is familiar by now, and I would like rather to emphasize that this is one of those dazzling, infinite half-truths of which reality is obviously made, such as freedom and determinism, continuity and discontinuity, heredity and environment. Since each is infinite, one can get hooked on it as on an infinity-opening drug, and Camus did for a youthful while, as did a lot of young people in his time, partly through reading him. As a result of the impact of World War II which, as he said, "made me modest," he discovered or rediscovered the other half-truth, that life is *not* absurd. From then on, those two half-truths *together* interested him more in what he described as a "higher balance," in connection with his doctrine of limits and moderation. One infinite balances off and limits the other in his more mature perspective.

But, for the moment, his hero is stuck in his half-truth of the absurd which Camus will further explore in *Le Mythe de Sisyphe*. The vertical posture of the young matador can usefully characterize this steep, excessive, and one-sided honesty which leads or allows him to commit murder. Everyone remembers the scene where he yields to a sort of universal indifference under a dazzling sun on the beach and numbly shoots the Arab who is harassing his friend, Raymond. The fact that he shoots one shot and then four more has been often explained: his honesty dictates that he, as it were, *endorse* his dazed act, take full responsibility in a sort of Nietzschean mood of superman suspension of ordinary morality. The

Stranger becomes, it is widely agreed, the full conscious absurdist at this fateful juncture. But the usual comments are less sure of the puzzling accompanying thought which runs through Meursault's head, that he was aware that he had "unbalanced the day." Though nothing can be proven here, I submit that this is the germ of the movement to maturity in the "higher balance" I alluded to earlier. The Stranger's steep, vertical, infinite honesty is tentatively crossed by a ghostly dimension of other-relatedness, equally infinite as he will discover later, in *La Peste* and *L'Homme révolté* and which moderates our individual juvenile-omnipotent drives.

This dimension had already existed in his play *Caligula*, written a few years earlier, in the mouth of his spokesman for decency and sanity, Cherea. But Camus had gone on to get smitten by the new kind of awareness which, as he said in the preface to *Le Mythe de Sisyphe*, he had found on the "street corners of his time."

In that essay, published in 1943, Camus accepts practically as axiomatic—though he hedges a little in the preface about its being merely a tentative proposition—the manifold contradictions he finds throughout Western culture from Zeno and Aristotle on to the existential exponents, such as Kierkegaard, Jaspers, Heidegger, and Chestov, of "humiliated thought." So taken is he by this view that he seriously considers whether suicide might not be the proper response to the universal absurdity of our lives, and that is the subject of his essay. To explore, as he puts it, a logic to its extreme consequences even if it dictates our death. A Spanish stubbornness, which Camus was known for, is at work here, very clearly, and I think a succinct comment might be: *Olé*. Fortunately, he finds for life. Suicide, it turns out, would be a sort of evasion, a copout or "leap." This is a term he applies to a number of thinkers such as Kierkegaard, Chestov, Jaspers, and Husserl, who accept the absurd to a point and then find a way out through religious salvation or some equivalent resolution. In this sense, they abort the unending tension which is the essence of absurd contradiction. Suicide would obviously do the same thing. But for this Camus the absurd is our only reality, our only good, and must be lived with all the bitter-sweet way, with passion, lucidity, revolt—by this last term he means never giving in, as in suicide or consoling religion. It is equivalent to consciousness or high consciousness. In other words, suicide would take away all we have, bitter as it is at times, and even in essence. A long, lucid, and intensely indifferent life is the defiant *révolté* answer to such a fate, and he imagines Sisyphus, rolling his eternal rock up the hill only to have it roll back down again, as being happy, as he says at one decisive point.

All this can bear another look. What is really going on underneath is this: at the point where Camus considers suicide as a solution to the absurd, he is confronted with another kind of absurdity, namely, that it makes no sense to end a life to solve a life's dilemma because, at the moment you die, the very problem disappears; at death, you have solved nothing since there is no more problem. Or if one imagines a tiny instant *between* life and death and the *wavering* that would occur between a problem to be solved and a no-problem (in death), then you have what can be seen as the absurd formula folded back or turning on itself. The absurd, which is a contradiction, can—as a total proposition of truth—be seen itself as contradictory. The absurd is both true and not true or, as I said earlier, it is a *half*-truth.

In the case of Meursault, a *tilt* from the vertical bullfighter dimension to the horizontal dimension of other-relatedness occurred at least in his mind: it would have provided a balance, the "balance of the day," which he sensed he had broken. Here too, an excessive drive to honesty, a kind of mortal logic which could dictate his death is providentially moderated by a tilt or pivoting: the logic of the absurd, and the suicide which might result from it, give way to an illogical, merely human impulse. Incidentally, even in his early lyrical essays, we find that promising, humane giving-in in terms of tenderness and, at times, a flow of tears. If suicide turns out to be the problematic, wavering solution we just saw it to be, then there is no point committing suicide. Rather, one does nothing drastic in that self-canceling direction but just keeps on living impulsively, which is what we all do all the time. Camus's "logic" has encountered a limit in the breakdown of the absurd, contradicted by its own self, fortunately. It is precisely such a tilt that characterizes the "happiness" of Sisyphus, which is not at all warranted within the absurd. In fact, it looks suspiciously like what he accused others of: a leap into another dimension of existence, away from the too-perfect logic of the "absurd." This is also true of the statement the good-hearted Camus makes at one point in his essay. Although theoretically his absurdist heroes accept no conventional morality, at this point Camus, obviously frightened of some of the implications, says that there is no reason to commit a crime any more than there is not to commit it, adding that to perform evil would be "childish." If that is not an arbitrary "leap" in his terms, what is it?

Still, the whole doctrine had an immense appeal, as we know, and set the tone of Camus's reputation at that time. Even recently, one heard William Styron speaking of Camus as his guide to whatever replaced religion for him.

But for those who followed Camus into his later phase, during and after and occasioned by the war, we find something quite altered. The tilt to the horizontal of other-relatedness is fully described and accepted in the preface to *L'Homme révolté* in 1951.

Partly because his reputation was so bound up with it, Camus at this point is at some pains to square his new view with his previous absurdist "logic." But now he clearly states what I have stated a few moments ago: the "profound ambiguity of the absurdist position," or what we have seen as the absurdity or arbitrariness of the absurd. Camus is left quivering at a crossroads: between the two horns of the original absurd contradiction in one direction, the vertical, and between its acceptance and rejection in another direction, the horizontal. At this crucifying juncture, he throws up his hands and sees himself bereft of all but a blind "impulse," life itself just going on at this crossing of dilemma and protesting against the mess. Moreover, the protest is against a world which has seen murder on such a staggering scale in World War II. Indeed, the book *L'Homme révolté*, which he is prefacing, is an attempt to answer the problem of mass murder in his time, just as *Le Mythe* was supposed to deal with individual suicide. So he is left only with the protest, this "impulse" which he now calls "revolt." Earlier, you will recall, revolt was the expression of a defiant response to life's absurdities and it just kept you living *in* the absurd, not copping out. That revolt led to no solution to anything. But now it is his answer to murder, as follows: a "révolté," or rebel, is a person who says *no* to an unacceptable situation, for example, an exploitative master. But he says "no" in terms of a right, a right to be free of exploitation or injustice. This right is a "yes" which goes with the "no." In other words, a true rebel revolts in the name of a principle which is universal, a right. Since a principle is by definition not just for one individual but a general law, the tilt to the horizontal occurs here, of which I spoke earlier. Since that right encompasses all men, one has no justification for murdering anyone in the name of rebellion, Camus claims. One may well sympathize, as I do, and still see that this pivoting or tilt is just another impulse with no real foundation in logic, absurd or otherwise. It is just the feeling one can have that I and you are all bound up and one slides into the other easily, as in life. There is, indeed, a great mystery of reality here—the problem of identity and intersubjectivity—but it is obvious that people who do not feel it just go ahead and murder anyway, and by the millions, in wars. Camus *is* sensitive and does feel the connection and compassion, just as he did for the old woman in the early essay we spoke of. He wants us all to feel it and stop killing each other. He is singularly good-hearted. Alas, his notion that we must in true revolt always balance the "no" and the "yes" as well as the I and the we—the striking and the caring or scrupulosity—is not easily observed in the heat of *action* which is *not* simultaneous, balanced, but serial or successive. Typically, one will strike and then regret it, or mourn a dead enemy if it comes to that; but not both together.

In a section of *L'Homme révolté* Camus alludes to Ivan Kaliaev, a Russian poet who insisted on giving his own life to pay for the life of the tyrant which he took. Camus called him "an innocent assassin" and wrote an admiring play about him called *Les Justes*. Well, not too many will emulate him, and it is clear that there is no surefire formula here. Yet, I think Camus is doing as well with all this as one can. By adding the horizontal dimension to his earlier perspective and maturing into his doctrine of limits and "higher balance," he has powerfully and convincingly shown at least what is desirable. He knows that this impulse toward The Other, including an enemy, is just that, an impulse. It is a *tilt* to the side and The Other and on-going life, even as you radically revolt in depth and cut through (vertically) a status quo. But, *knowing* that, he *nudges* us in the humane direction, and that is a good thing. In this way, he gives comfort to all those who would temper the ruthless revolts of Marxism by a limit, a cross-cutting dimension of humanity, as in the views of Silone and Gramsci in Italy and the modern Socialists in Western Europe generally, including France under Mitterrand.

If you look at this another way, viewing history along a time-line—seeing a ruthlessly goal-directed drive in the modern totalitarians, a deification of history as leading to a final justice for all, then Camus's good heart and sense of balance tell him, in *L'Homme révolté*, that we must limit the drive of that "horizontal religion" by a perspective of the sacred, which cuts across it in the name of individual (vertical) human rights, a *value* outside of history. In this sense, he contests the Sartrean doctrine of existence always preceding essence, and a constantly open relativistic "situation." Rather, he rediscovers that man has a nature after all, a sort of moderated essence which can serve as a value; this or that man is infinitely precious in himself, stemming from the sacred, and history has no right to treat him as a mere pawn toward some utopian end in a remote future.

In this way and others, I believe Camus got the better of Sartre in their famous quarrel. I totally disagree with Patrick McCarthy as to the value of *L'Homme révolté* and Camus's thought in general. *L'Homme révolté* is a heart-warming attempt to figure out what went wrong in our Western culture to the extent of the massive atrocities of the twentieth century. He traces our sins of imbalance and hubris from the roots in Judeo-Christianity, which is too obsessively judgmental and goal-oriented as compared to the temperate and relatively now-oriented Greek view of life. His investigation and analysis take him through numerous figures of our tradition, up through the Hegels, Marxes, and Nietzsches. He does not always do them full justice—though he is usually generous in admitting this too—but he tries to, and mightily, and for me this is the key book of modern historico-political theory. Camus is not a philosopher and says so, but he is a nonspecialized thinker, a poetically visionary, intuitive one, rather like Heidegger's *Denker*. The wrestling with the absurd dimensions which I noted is right in line with the most sophisticated patterns of thought such as we find in Lacan, Foucault, and Jakobson. If he gets no final answers, it is because there are none, for these others as well.

The new social concern and the mature higher balance were already evident in *La Peste* of 1947. There is now a definite tilt away from the perfect tension or ambivalence of the absurd in the new formula: "There is more to admire in man than to despise"; such a tilt is, also, sideways, into a flow of time and humane emotion. The hero, Dr. Bernard Rieux, is described as being square-jawed, aged thirty-five, and stocky. It would be hard to be more four-square balanced than that... Because of the new emphasis, Rieux is a doctor, and the people who are too individualistically concerned about (vertical) salvation, such as the Jesuit Paneloux and even the philosophical Tarrou, are somehow doomed and succumb to the plague, whereas an ordinary guy, the journalist Rambert who just wants to be happy with his girl, makes it. For similar reasons, the artist-figure Joseph Grand is cut radically down to humanity in that his art is risible though his decency is great; he too survives, partly because in the midst of the crisis he burns his manuscripts, which is a surefire way to lower your hubris. The later Camus was much concerned about his reputation, pride, and ego getting in the way of breathable life and creativity. Everything in *La Peste* moves in this direction in emphasis, though the vertical is preserved too in proper proportion through Rieux's meditative depth and even Grand's renewed art, in the end. The very tone of the novel is moderated, cool, a chronicle, with a new objectivity and workaday calm befitting the doctor narrator. The emphasis is collective, and the events of the chronicle are seen from several viewpoints. Fraternity, unpretentious struggle against a still-absurd fate which brings plagues that come and go when they want, courage with refusal of heroics, just life wanting to go on and be normally happy, all this had a considerable appeal to young people who were looking for guidance in a world without much belief after the second World War.

One of his last books, and some think his best, was *La Chute*, of 1957. It is a bitterly funny portrait of a former Parisian lawyer living in Amsterdam. He had a golden youth and thought very highly of himself as a lover of his fellow man until one day he failed to respond to a dangerous call for help from a drowning woman in the Seine, and then his whole ego-structure collapsed. "The lights went out" on the party, as it did for Salinger's girls in *Uncle Wiggly in Connecticut* or, really, all of us privileged people. No longer being able to keep up an image of his goodness and innocence, he resorts to a stratagem of spreading universal sense of guilt; "misery loves company." This was his fall from a sort of grace, and his name and much of the symbolism allude to Saint John the Baptist and the theme of baptism which the plunge into the nocturnal river would have been, a sacrificial descent leading to salvation, rebirth. So he calls himself a "false prophet," living in duplicity like all the rest of existence, and this is the constant, searingly amusing theme: all our little self-deceptions and hypocrisies are paraded before us. And there is the higher duplicity of the Hegelian notion that evil is just a part of the ongoing synthesis of good and evil, which Kierkegaard trenchantly revolted against with his either-or. Camus is solidly, underneath, on the side of Kierkegaard here, though he is never mentioned. The muddy, verbose dialectics of his own time, Sartre's included, are being subtly invoked. But the pure light of the Greek islands stands for that clear innocence we can never find again in our northern mists amid the hustling, hassling, self-seeking, lobbying, conniving, half-lying millions in our semipolluted cities like Amsterdam, the site of one of the greatest crimes in history, as Camus puts it, the genocide of the Dutch Jews. But the protagonist, Jean-Baptiste Clamence, goes rattling on about this and that, always worrying about his own self-justification. He even tries to pull Jesus down to his all-too-human size, seeing him as guilty because of his awareness of the children of Rachel, the slaughter of the Innocents killed for his sake, and he hears the cries of Rachel refusing to be consoled. Here, Camus and Clamence want us to break through at least for an imagined instant, a flash. There is not the slightest question of Clamence speaking for Camus, as some (like Simone de Beauvoir) thought; Camus denied this roundly in an interview, and poured scorn on Clamence. No, but in those breakthrough moments, we see the original Camus whom Patrick McCarthy and others rightly deem a deeply religious man without a church—a man who could reject organized religion and the afterlife again and again and, yet, say to an interviewer, "The anti-religious view is vulgar," or "God is beauty", and speak of the sacred as a resource —a Value—against the ruthless nihilistic plunge into merely secular

' sublime muddler-through '

history. A beggar who comes up to Clamence in the street whispers humbly, "We have lost the light." Those few words are quite sufficient for those who have eyes to glimpse with.

Camus, in an interview, put truth above all other values, but, as we noted, he was a good-hearted decent man and, on the whole, he was a sort of higher centrist. He stayed in the middle of controversies such as the Algerian war for independence, and at the end of *L'Homme révolté* he came out for a whole series of mid-positions: moderation in revolt, the mild, reasonable Mediterranean, and an idea of Europe as being humanly in-between excesses in Russia and technology-driven America (as he saw it then); the village as opposed to big cities—he detested aspects of New York and did not often care for Paris—or rural emptiness on the other side; the season, as of the harvest, between overambitious teleological or eschatological reaches of time or the too shortsighted daily perspectives; the trade-union movements in politics; and so on. He spoke for the centered literary work, e.g., the novel, as against formalistic art on the one hand and journalism on the other; and it was supposed to be balanced between private concerns and public. As a novelist, he was a daring innovator, and yet he spoke again and again of his love for the French classic era and style: Pascal, Molière, Madame de LaFayette. He wanted to write a modern tragedy, and, in a fine essay, he saw tragedy as arising on its two august occasions, in Greece and Renaissance Europe, between an age of faith declining and a rising age of reason. Altogether, he was a sublime muddler-through, in the enlightened middle as it were. That is not a comfortable position to be in, especially when everyone else is taking sides as they usually do. You get hit by both parties at times, like a referee. Politics is not carried on this way and he can be said, in brief, to be largely apolitical despite his struggles to pitch into his time. McCarthy calls him "indifferent" in contradiction to the popular image of Camus as a moral leader, but that is excessive. No, he was a fiercely caring man, but in his own far-seeing and superior way. At times, of course, these higher syntheses drop into a dreadful opposite of nothingness, indifference in that sense, and Camus, with his recurring tuberculosis, certainly had his black or zero moments; his friend, Martin du Gard, even spoke of his misanthropy. But taking that with the sacrificial and deep concerns, still, all in all, including the sensitivity, the courage, the lucidity, the culture, the style, the sense of humor, he was probably what we Americans all along tended to think he was: beyond all intellectual fashions and ideological factions, the finest, most authentic voice of his age.

Camus's Sacred: The Growing Stone

Most educated people one encounters these days, in the leading countries of the West, tend to be vague about their religiosity—including the formal adherents to recognized doctrines.[1] But when one puts it to them, they are likely to agree, in my experience, with the proposition that, Gentile or Jew, they are, broadly speaking, rooted in three main layers of tradition: Hebrew, Christian, and modern (implying some modification of the other views, influenced by the Enlightenment).

What does this really mean?

Some clarification can be obtained by looking at the changing relation, over the years, of the two great axes of religiosity: the vertical, between God and mortal, and the horizontal joining communing people.

From the beginning, the direct relation to God is apt to be solitary, as when Moses went up Mount Sinai. It is full of ambivalence and paradox, the *awful* and *terrible* aspect of deity, beautiful and frightening, the problem of evil, the troubling relation of God and Satan. When Moses, or any other prophet, returns to the world of men and women, there is a tempering partial separation of the "metaphoric" paradox-poles of vision into this identity versus that, in the horizontal plane of fragmentation, analysis, reason, measured daily doings, "metonymy." This tempering can be seen positively—"golden mean," "sanity," and the like—or, conversely, as "mediocrity," "shallowness," etc.[2]

---

[1] In France, today, 81% of the people declare themselves to be Catholic; only 16% go regularly to Mass. In a solid commentary on the state of Catholicism in France today ("Après la visite du Pape," *L'Express*, October 16, 1986), Alain Besançon sees the same "confusion" and confirms my view of the unidimensional ("vaguement oecuménique humanitaire") rut which is the intellectual failure of modern Catholicism.

[2] Today, since Jakobson, we are apt to speak of the "metaphoric" and "metonymic" dimensions at play here. These terms, taken from rhetoric, are rather awkward, but they have become familiar and so are a useful reference at this point. But the more general

These two axes tend to be rather evenly balanced in the Hebrew layer. To be sure, Voltaire, Gibbon, Auerbach, et al. emphasize the vertical in the "stiffnecked" Hebrews, with their elitist claim to be "the chosen people"—to which Auerbach adds the deep, tragic, lyric thrust, for example, in the Abraham and Joseph stories[3]—but there is a great deal to counterbalance that tendency: the worldly Edenic and Adamic perspective—the seed of Abraham, in earthly time—as opposed to Christian otherworldliness, transcendental eschatology.[4] The shape of the Star of David, a certain prevailing stockiness and rurality in the Synagogue forms, the Menorah, the Succoth booths,[5] tolerance toward others as in the story of Ruth, the generally temperate gnomic passages of the Old Testament, there is much that is suggestive of the "other direction" here.

This approach to mandalic four-squaredness is perpetuated in early Christian style,[6] e.g., Romanesque—but the strong emphasis on the transcendent or sublime brings about the Gothic and, more abidingly and revealingly, the imbalance of the central symbol of Christianity: the cross of the crucifixion (reflected in the lateral structure of the cathedral). The node of it is located almost always at the level of Christ's head—sometimes just below—whereas in reality the vast psychic dimensions tend to equilibrium: the true center of man is located at the point "where he came in," at the navel.

Saint Thomas restores the centrality in his Catholic balance of faith and reason.[7] And modern Christianity in its Protestant branches moves very far in this direction. Hence, there is a certain sense of restored Hebraicism in, say, the evangelical doctrines and the neat and humble

---

terms, "vertical" (prevailingly holistic) and "horizontal" (fragmented), are more adequate. In reality, the aspects of whole and fragmentary shift between the axes. Thus, Jakobson himself—rather loosely—indicated the shift of the paradigmatic (involving whole-whole substitutions) to the syntagmatic (involving combination of sentence parts). But the shifts are many, indeed, in life as a whole.

[3]He contrasts this with the "sunny," good-natured, reportorial quality of Greek epic narrative, in *The Odyssey*. This is the main dialectic of his fine book, *Mimesis* (New York: Doubleday-Anchor, 1957). There is a certain lyric (and synthetic) strain in the Jews which Thomas Mann recognizes, in *Dr. Faustus* (New York: Vintage Books, 1948).

[4]Pascal, in his *Pensées*, chides the Jews on these grounds.

[5]The sculpture of Chaim Gross strikes one in this sense.

[6]The wonderful art of Leonardo and Matisse, for example, or Fouquet, seems to me to feature this child-block *carrure*.

[7]Needless to say, modern *unidimensional* doctrines which violate this balance, e.g., structuralist narratology, totalitarianism, secularism, all *ideologies*, are dreary distortions. Our Western world is foundering on an inability to recognize that "democracy" without a strong qualitative dimension equal to its fraternal thrust is nonviable.

pioneering churches of America[8] and particularly the Mormon creed. This spills into the modern with a more general openness to the non-Christian—not so much back to the Hebrew but, rather, forward to the broadly ecumenical—in Quakerism, Unitarianism, Ethical Culture, and the like.

It goes so far in this way of nonsectarianism, reason, secularist solutions to man's fate, that it tends to make common cause with the "horizontal religions" (Camus) that stem from the Enlightenment—utopianism, socialism, communism—and then the imbalance can be extreme indeed, the heart of our modern spiritual pathology.[9]

But, as I began by noting, it is entirely possible in this current phase to retain a piety to the earlier phases of our mainstream tradition, even as one moves to a *very* central (the node of the balanced cross) and wide-open position of modern self-critique and awareness. The specifics of dogma, starting with the Hebrew texts—e.g., Moses, or the other ancient prophets, as being in literal communication, *viva voce*, with God (through a sort of "hotline"); the precise location of Eden; a rigid creationism and foreshortened chronology, etc.—are no longer naïvely accepted by the thoughtful, but the *axes* are: *there is* Something or Somebody bigger than we, and we *are* bound in terms of It, as well as in terms of our diasporic (fragmented, analytic, regulated, rational, metonymic, material, industrial) doings.

In the Christian phase we learned that the balance, the spiritual "higher health," meant a recurrent humility (on the vertical axis), starting with the lowly stable scene, and a fraternal reaching out—to the Gentiles, eventually to most of mankind—well beyond the "Chosen." The imbalance in the cross pattern reflecting an ever-threatening spiritual pride (Dante saw it as the source of the deepest sin) was less decisive in the long run than this reversal to the bottom and an attendant *pivoting* to the "love of one's fellow man," the horizontal axis of essential Christian doctrine.[10]

Of course, these impulses are as operative as ever. Today we can see fairly objectively that the prophets—Isaiah, Ezekiel, and the rest—were talented visionaries, as great artists always are: altogether, in our long-

---

[8]Twentieth-century theologians Barth and Tillich extend that spirit in their emphasis on the fully redemptive nature of Eden.

[9]The quest for transcendence in a New World after 1492 certainly was influential in this direction: cf. all those later discoveries of America by the soul-sick (e.g., Chateaubriand).

[10]On their side, the Jews were moving to a more adaptive stance which favored their group survival, "smuggling themselves to the future" as Isaac B. Singer put it in his Nobel address. The Enlightenment furthered this trend massively (Haskalah).

flowing culture, they point compellingly to that Something or Somebody; the conception of Jesus was surely in that heritage; to say the least, those who imagined, or reported on, Him were inspired.

But our modern meditative centralities—one thinks of Mallarmé's "sacred spider" at the node of his web of universal analogy; of Valéry's location of Leonardo's genius at that same demanding locus of convergence—indicate that we need not commune with these old truths in a given church or doctrine. Emily Dickinson did so in her backyard, in Amherst, on her own poetic terms; Walt Whitman out on the roads of America; Hermann Melville on the world's oceans...[11] Eden can be anywhere on the map, so to speak: through the authentic artists or our own "privileged moments," we are reminded of that supreme goal and are encouraged to go on. Its *ultimate* nature, *toward* which we muddle through in a messy real world, is often represented by a distant star (usually the North).

That is what Mallarmé referred to in his oft-cited "You can't do without Eden" and "Toward... A CONSTELLATION" (*Un coup de dés*).

This perspective theoretically extends our three layers—Hebrew-Christian-Modern—indefinitely backward in time toward the Big Bang or Source (the first COUP) and a "matin oublié des prophètes" (*Hérodiade, Scène*) and forward into a future well beyond our current horizon. In this sense, Mallarmé's fundamentally religious view is open and quietly innovative. Unlike Victor Hugo, about whose ideas a new church was founded in Indo-China, one does not see any sign of an official Mallarmé cult, though he has never lacked for fervent disciples. But he does illustrate the notion of a dynamic Western faith still growing in our time.

One who came after him, Albert Camus—fifteen years elapsed between Mallarmé's death in 1898 and Camus's birth in 1913—despite the obvious differences in locale, Zeitgeist, temperament, family circumstances, build, and genre, strikes me as very close to him in important intimate ways. Camus does not refer to Mallarmé very often. But we know that he had a much-thumbed-through copy of the *Poésies*; there is a strong hint of him in his hero Joseph Grand. But that is not to our inner point, which is the parallel in religious perspectives.

The adolescent Camus, as we learn in Patrick McCarthy's solid biography, told a friend: "God is a question of beauty."[12] He is better known for his rejection of Christianity in *The Stranger, The Myth of Sisyphus*, and *The Plague*, but Camus, we now know, was a fundamentally

[11]Nothing in this suppler attitude prevents one from going respectfully into the places of worship or even joining up.

[12]Patrick McCarthy, *Camus* (New York: Random House, 1982) 18.

believing man. Throughout his life we see him, for example, edging toward the Franciscans—notably during his dreary stay in St. Etienne during the war—or, again, in an essay, showing warm sympathy for the published apologetics of a Catholic priest. In his later phase, he saw that only values rooted in "the sacred"—a modest, undogmatic form of belief but belief all the same—could offset the fanatic sectarian drives of the totalitarians, their "horizontal religions" which led to massive murder. In his doctrine of "limits" one infinite needed another, at right angles, to check it and bring about some reasonable balance in humanity.

In an interview published in *Lyrical and Critical Essays* (Vintage), he came out forthrightly with "There is something vulgar about the antireligious attitude." His remarks about Faulkner in the same volume are full of their shared sense of the sacred.[13] Cf. "I believe in the sacred."[14] In *The Rebel*, and before, he tended to shy away from his Hebraic-Christian and ancestral tradition, in favor of what he deemed to be a more temperate, Mediterranean sort of inner climate in the early Greeks. Camus was repelled by the harsh teleology of the Hebrews and Christians; he resented the *linear* aspect of their eschatology, "going somewhere" implacably, judgmentally, toward salvation, scanting the simultaneous moment of beauty now, in a sudden stab of salvation despite our sins. Such were the forgiving tender words of Jesus, absolving the fallen Magdalena. That is perhaps why in *The Fall* his Clamence expresses his "sympathy for the first Christian," but not for the later Christians who use the cross to climb up over others (including those in the Vatican who were playing footsy with the Nazis). In this he resembled Gide (to whose style he was generally beholden) and Dostoevsky, in his preference for Jesus over the instutionalizers such as Saint Paul...[15]

That slanting away from his ancestral mainstream toward the Greek sense of beauty (*Helen's Exile*) is, fundamentally, we repeat, in order to bring a vast vertical to bear on a murderous runaway horizontality in his time. The emphasis on Greek temperateness was to move in that same direction of overall balance, or what he called a "higher balance" (in the same essay), i.e., of the infinite main *dimensions* of existence (and not just the conventional *poles* of mind and body, etc.).

The fact that he did not find that kind of "mandalic" health in his own Judeo-Christian heritage is, I think, rather accidental; his youthful

---

[13]This is not so surprising: our finest minds are often avowed believers and churchgoers: Saul Bellow, John Updike, Anthony Burgess, Richard Wilbur, among others.

[14]Interview with Brisville, *Lyrical and Critical Essays* 364.

[15]On the other hand, Camus was close to the Jews. Personally, in North Africa, and in his many strong anti-Nazi utterances, e.g., in *The Fall, The Rebel*, etc.

revolt and his marginal relation to metropolitan France had induced him to look elsewhere for a while. Moreover, he had seen the breakdown of the heritage in his time and the failure of the Christian West to rise to the occasion. Indeed, the West was foundering on excesses of Faustian pride and manipulation, and the Church itself compromised itself in arrangements with Franco, Mussolini, and Hitler. We forgive him for this incompleteness and partiality because he made amends of the sort we noted earlier (and in many a humble admission) and, particularly, in his later bent. *The Rebel* remains, in the minds of many of us, the most sane and helpful approach to the basic problems of our age, along with Raymond Aron's.

After that came the splendidly mature writing in *The Fall* and *Exile and the Kingdom*. The latter collection ends with *The Growing Stone*, and here Camus gently approaches the sweeping religious perspective of Mallarmé, pushing back his three-tiered tradition to the primitive for basic telluric health, and tentatively forward (spirally) toward a modification of Christianity, which is modern, to be sure, but goes beyond contemporary modernity—certainly the atheistic brand of it as well as the naïvely socialistic—toward something original: questing, open, yet firmly believing and, altogether, rounded as a stone.

The Camus who wrote *The Exile and the Kingdom* was a man who above all needed to be reborn. That is the key theme of the collection.[16] He knew that unless he stripped off his success and sophistication, his French overcivilization, as he said in the preface to the re-edition of *The Right Side and the Wrong*, he would never write anything worthwhile again.

He yearned for the adolescent innocence, simplicity, piety (to his mother; to a few deep principles) that had gone into those early sketches. "O to be nothing" is the *cri de coeur* of a youthful essay, *The Stop in Oran* where he had already understood that need for baptismal self-cleansing, metamorphosis (Gide's "palingenesia"). The pristine purity was represented by a stone. That is a persuasive image throughout Camus. And so it is prominently in the title *The Growing Stone*. A stone, but "alive" and changing: this stubborn paradox at the heart of things is harder than the stone to crack; it was the stuff of the "absurd" in *The Myth of Sisyphus*, where a stone is the eternal burden of man, his useless torment and yet "his thing" (sic), his only hope: "I imagine Sisyphus happy." A sort of Kierkegaardian leap occurred there, in spite of Camus's implacable doctrine, and we were apt to feel good about it. That leap or

---

[16]*Jonas* features a need to start over; so does *La femme adultère* and, more grimly, *Le renégat*.

tilt occurred also later in *The Plague* when Camus allowed that there was "more to admire than despise" in a good heart like his hero's, Joseph Grand's ... or a schoolteacher's, etc. In the preface to *The Rebel* the tilt is very complex[17]—it takes place at the excruciating intersection of the absurd and the nonabsurd (values).[18]   But still it was the sign of a fundamentally good heart, in a "good egg" (sort of a biological growing stone), Camus, who refused to get "hung up" on one dimension, the nihilistic absurd, when he had seen the harm nihilism had done in his totalitarian time. In short, he learned to traverse it with another dimension, the "sacred" (source of values) in his later doctrine of "limits." And since the two infinite perspectives formed a new level of conflict within him, he yielded *in extremis* to his good human impulses and what he called a "revolt," irrational but meaningful, against mass murder regardless of the "logic" involved.

In *The Growing Stone*, the absurd paradox is not so fateful; it is linked to a primitive, semi-pagan, superstitious form of Christianity among the simple people in the Brazilian town where the scene is laid. They believe in a stone that seems to grow again where pieces are broken off. Other humble Christians have always believed, for example, in stone statues of the Madonna weeping. Camus knows naïveté when he sees it: he is not subscribing to this article of faith itself. Rather, he chooses it for his title because it is suggestive of the way faith itself grows.

The story begins with the arrival of d'Arrast, a middle-aged engineer —a huge yet profoundly inward man—in Brazil where he is supposed to supervise the construction of a flood-control project in the little town of Iguape on the coast. D'Arrast, we soon learn, is suffering under a heavy burden of guilt.[19]   He encounters a *sympathique* black sea-cook (*le coq*) who tells how he promised Jesus to carry a huge stone in a religious pro-cession if he were saved from a shipwreck, as he was. He asks d'Arrast if he has ever called out to Jesus for help. D'Arrast replies that he wanted to as the result of his having caused the death of someone—but he could not call out. The *coq* suggests that if d'Arrast comes and somehow assists him in carrying out his promise, he too—d'Arrast—may find consola-tion. This turns out to be prophetic. And we have already sensed that the stone to be carried will also "grow" in some way.

---

[17]See our "The True Camus" in this volume.

[18]In *The Absolute Paradox* (ch. 3 of *Philosophical Fragments* [Princeton: Princeton University Press, 1936]), Kierkegaard had come to just such a dimensional crossroad where he makes a special "leap" of faith (one might call this "quintessential").

[19]Something of the vague guilt-burden of Chateaubriand seeking salvation in the New World is at work here, we noted. And a common Romantic exotic element, underneath.

The night before the procession, the *coq* takes him to a barnlike building where a primitive ritual goes on until dawn: though he is aware of the folly of it, he joins in the frenzied dancing and exhausts himself. As the orgy reaches its climax, d'Arrast is ordered to leave. He has not "made it" in his return to the simple source, his quest for renewal. This nostalgia theme runs through the piece—there are strange calls in the forest and, though he is repelled by the raw nature, he feels that something is "waiting for him" there.[20] A lithe young black woman particularly haunts him, but he loses contact with her, too, leaving her behind in the ritual together with the others.

From a remark made by his black chauffeur, Socrate: "Chez toi, c'est la messe seulement. Personne ne danse," we sense that the genesis of religion, from dance to text, is *en cause*, as we grow toward newer forms (spirally in this case, via very old ones, "baptismally").

An airplane, a modern cross in the skies over the rain forest and parade, seems vaguely symbolic in the same genetic sense.[21] This one seems strangely flimsy, especially as pitted against all that crude nature.

The atmosphere of *misère*, utter destitution, among the poorest of these folk is brought out repeatedly. Yet they are proud. It is d'Arrast who is initially rejected, even before the ritual orgy, when he asks permission to inspect one of the typical huts in a lowly section of town. An old man at first says no, then gives in only under pressure from an official. The comely black girl appeared in this scene, too, but was as elusive as the bird she later portrayed in the ritual. There is no real *encounter*.

Finally, there is the calvary of the tired *coq*, urged on by his brother among others. Nearing his goal, the church in the central square of Iguape, he stumbles, is gashed in the shoulder by the slipping stone, falls, cannot go on anymore. D'Arrast tries to encourage him, sees it is hopeless and then, in a sudden impulse puts the weight on his own head and carries on for the *coq*. At a certain point, despite the alarmed cries of the waiting throng—"on to the church" (he later understands)—he *deviates*,[22] heads instead for the hut of the *coq* in the poorest section of town and, almost out of steam, drops the stone in the central cooking spot

---

[20]That is a familiar theme in late literature, e.g., Conrad's *The Heart of Darkness*. There is something, too, of a neoanimism as in Hugo (*La Bouche d'ombre*), Baudelaire (*Correspondances*), Proust (the soul-haunted apple trees).

[21]One might think of the statue of Christ towed by a helicopter through the skies over a neopagan Rome, in Fellini's *La dolce vita*.

[22]This deviation parallels the earlier one, to the Greek sacred, away from the Judeo-Christian; but this one is closer to the mainstream, even as it pushes farther back.

where it lies "half buried in ashes and dirt." The *coq* and his brother, along with some others—an old woman, the elusive girl—show up and find d'Arrast leaning against a wall of the hut filled with a surpassing joy. At first they sit down around the stone without him. Then the brother says to d'Arrast: "Assieds-toi avec nous." That is the end of the story. In some important sense he has "made it," despite his having slighted the local cult. What can this mean?

The stone, standing for their belief and burden, is dumped, true, but in a place of renewing fire and earth. It is *half* buried there: surely d'Arrast meant no total insult to their superstition and, a civilized Frenchman, he understood tact and compromise, a decent regard for the people whom he, in some deep sense, admired and wanted the approval of. Nor can we assume for a moment, despite *The Plague*, that this mature Camus, who had written so fervently (in *The Rebel*) against the "horizontal religions" of his time, meant to replace their old cult with some secular humanism and materialistic idea of progress à la Auguste Comte.

No, the truth here, like the title, is vibrant, alive, humbly returning to the old problematic absurd—problematic both inwardly, in its paradox, and outwardly, in its questionable truth as such—but now, as in the Trinity—or the "Word that was with God and was God"—in the form of sacred mystery: the mystery, here, of the old-new, of filial renewal, as when an Old Testament gives way to a New, with pious continuity and change.

A living rock—Petrus—and an ambiguity in Christ's own words, "On this rock..." arose at just such a juncture.

Camus is not offering us anything so pretentious as a "Gospel According to Albert" or a literal Newest Testament, in the lineage of the Mormons, for promulgation to a fresh cult, California style.

No, but like Mallarmé, he is giving us a suggestion of how belief is prolonged and modified, even in our indifferent era.

The figure of Saint John the Baptist arose prominently and centrally in the late work of both writers: the Precursor who, like an annunciatory index finger, erect or tilted to the future, *pointed to...* or *toward...*

Moses, too, went up to Vision, came down and pointed both to God and, horizontally, to Canaan... But he could not get there himself; one cannot, it seems, go so *high* and get so *far* in this life.

We are back to our mandalic equilibrium here, or "higher balance." In *The Plague*, already, Dr. Rieux was described as aged thirty-five, stocky, a doctor who was deeply thoughtful—it is hard to be more four-square than that. The dimension of stubborn doing, fighting a plague, was pitted against the dimension of faith and beauty: the communion with nature in the ocean, the poetic vocation—though appropriately humbled at this historic stage when, as Camus noted, "he had become more modest"—of Joseph Grand; even, subtly, in the excessively vertical religiosity of Paneloux, which is at least a real challenge. But now Camus has moved on to a new awareness: d'Arrast is a doer, an engineer, and he is helping the people of Iguape in that way and will continue to do so, we are made to feel. Camus unquestionably chose him because, far more gravely wounded and meditative than Rieux, he bore within him the other, plunging and soaring, perspective, of sacred faith, to help right the "higher balance" of an era which he knew to be frighteningly askew.

Baudelaire's *Frisson Nouveau*

In his *Projet de préface* for *Les Fleurs du mal,* Baudelaire flirted with the idea of demonstrating "Que la phrase poétique peut imiter (et par là elle touche à l'art musical et à la science mathématique) la ligne horizontale, la ligne droite... qu'elle peut suivre la spirale, décrire la parabole, ou le zigzag..."

The only hint he gives of how this is accomplished is "par l'accouplement de tel substantif avec tel adjectif, analogue ou contraire."

Not too much to go on here, or anywhere else that I am aware of, to afford some precise notion of the tricks of the trade he claims he can teach anyone in twenty lessons.

Well, the *Projet de préface* is often ironic, bitterly recriminatory; it is neurotically personal, in sum, and unfinished. This is already the late, ailing Baudelaire of *Pauvre Belgique...*

We are going to have to recreate aspects of his métier mostly on our own, relying on certain repeated effects in superior stretches of his poetry.

From *La Chevelure:*

La langoureuse Asie et la brûlante Afrique

uses the adjective-noun coupling he mentions in the *Projet,* but the trick he does not mention is that if you want to imitate a horizontal line you choose a long adjective like *langoureuse*—its shape underscores its spread-out, supine meaning—and couple it with a noun with a prominent *A* in it, because that is the acoustically flattest of all letters. There are many *a*'s in that line. Not as many as in his model Gautier's:

La caravane humaine au Sahara du monde

Or his pupil Mallarmé's:

Quand l'ombre menaça de la fatale loi

but still he gets that nostalgic sweep Ravel begins his orchestral-vocal *Asie*

48

with (from the *Schéhérazade* suite) using the suppler musical devices, in this case a sustained largo and crooning voice.

Le Jet d'eau, which Debussy also set (along with *La Chevelure*), uses that flat *a* in the first line very effectively:

> Tes beaux yeux sont las, pauvre amante

For a vertical line, when this lassitude is whipped up into frenzy, he naturally uses the bright sounds:

> L'éclair brûlant des voluptés
> S'élance rapide et hardie

And for the downward movement, when the excitement flags:

> Puis elle s'épanche, mourante

In the same way, Mallarmé will, for exactly the same intimate phenomenon, say:

> Comme mourir pourpre la roue
>   (*M'introduire dans ton histoire*)

What of the spiral, or nearby, the circle?

In his *Le Balcon* there is a much-appreciated "musical" effect:

> Car à quoi bon chercher tes beautés langoureuses
> Ailleurs qu'en ton cher corps et qu'en ton coeur si doux?

The "*en on oe i ou*," for example, sort of swishes around in the mouth in something like the spiral he alluded to. The vowel sounds, moving between front and back (*oe-i*) or high and low (*i-ou*) and between other poles of the key relations on the vowel chart (as presented by Pierre Delattre), touch all the bases, box the compass. There is a similar totalizing satisfaction in rhythm, when after a while it reverses its beat in syncopation or slips between ternary and binary, etc. Sort of a transcendent fair play, or drive to homeostasis in infinity, or plenitude. It is a microcosmic moment of the poem's fruition or ripeness:

> To bend with apples the moss'd cottage trees,
> And fill all fruit with ripeness to the core,
> To swell the gourd, and plump the hazel shells...
>   (Keats, *To Autumn*)

The important imagery of fruit in Keats, Baudelaire, Mallarmé reflects this process at another level. We will allude to this effect from the letter *o* in a moment.

Returning to the spiral: Joseph Campbell provides a cosmic, or macrocosmic, equivalent to Baudelaire's personally romantic plenitude in his remarks on the Tibetan religious word AUM. It goes through *au-ou-mm* plus a silence, hence is called the four-element term. That gives it a tetradic-mandalic quality akin to Mallarmé's key seasonal cycle and a similar pattern Baudelaire described in a metaphysical passage of his major essay on Hugo. AUM. It reminds one of the "*oomb, oomb, all-wombing tomb*" Bloom dreamed of mouthing on a maternal navel which would connect him back to Adam. Baudelaire's open-mouthed, awed *O* before his mistress is cognate:

> O toison... O boucles
> (*La Chevelure*)

This is "intimate globality." Swallow her whole, if possible, in infantile possessiveness. He sets about this systematically in *Les Bijoux*, including those *grappes de ma vigne*, female fruit.

> Vous me rendez l'azur du ciel immense et rond

He wants to absorb all, the macro, in this micro head of hair, which "gets a handle on it."

> De la vaporisation et de la centralisation du Moi. Tout est là.
> (*Mon coeur mis à nu*)

There is a similar paradox in:

> Il n'y a pas de pointe plus acérée que celle de l'infini
> (*Le Confiteor de l'artiste*)

La Chevelure ends with another cosmic-human womb-circle, "l'oasis où je rêve, et la gourde," as plump, no doubt, as Keats's.

Those simple candid *bons*, e.g., in *Le Balcon*:

> que ton coeur m'était bon!

are of this order, as are the *O*'s that begin and end the poem:

> O toi tous mes plaisirs! ô toi, tous mes devoirs

and:

> O serments! ô parfums! ô baisers infinis!

There too a space-time cross, of plunging and rising sun of love, ever-renewed cyclically, forms a mandalic roundedness at another level of the poem. That pattern is ubiquitous in him and offers the fullness of the characteristic Baudelaire tone, or universe, as a whole, the romantic-classic chiasmus Valéry and Peyre speak of. In this, at his best, he reminds me of his coeval Brahms, rather than Wagner.

Baudelaire uses letter-shape and sound to bring out poetically another powerful shape, pattern, and effect, the inverted cone, the *entonnoir* of a *gouffre* or *tourbillon*, a descent into the womb... In *Le Flacon*:

> Voilà le souvenir enivrant qui voltige
> Dans l'air troublé: les yeux se ferment: le Vertige
> Saisit l'âme vaincue et la pousse à deux mains
> Vers un gouffre obscurci de miasmes humains:

The capitalized *V* of *Vertige* sums up the effect: an intimate version of Poe's descent into the maelstrom, a rummaging in a petty whirlpool of old worn objects as in a maternal drawer of dangerous memory, linked with death and resurrection, the key image of Lazarus, as well as forbidden incest-return.

The "vieux flacon désolé / Décrépit, poudreux, sale, visqueux, fêlé" that is rummaged for is his own humbly reprobate, scorned essence derived as a *fleur* from *mal*. Orpheus from a suffering psychic underworld. Jeanne, his muse, his *douceur* and *poison*, is closely associated with this motif; his poetry will preserve her spirit, "toujours à respirer si nous en périssons" as Mallarmé put it in the *Tombeau de Charles Baudelaire*.

The *v* is fine for that baptismal adventure down and up, almost Dantean but much more inward, with a giddiness like the one in *Harmonie du Soir*: "langoureux vertige."

Charles Baudoin, in *De l'instinct à l'esprit*, confirms that the *v* is a spontaneous image, in his patients, for the female organ or womb, supported by the Eve-Vénus-vierge-vase-vagin-vulve cluster and a mystic tradition, e.g., the lower part of the Seal of Solomon, as the Kabbala saw it and later Joyce, Mallarmé, Pynchon. There is a wonderful series of *v*'s in *Hérodiade* reflecting the nakedness of the "inviolate virgin." The womb-shape of the *viole*—the musical instrument—gets associated powerfully with all this in *Hérodiade* fragments, *Don du poëme*, *Une dentelle*, and later, Picasso.

> Vous dotez le ciel de l'art d'on ne sait quel rayon macabre. Vous créez
> un frisson nouveau. (Hugo, lettre à Baudelaire, 6 octobre 1859)

With this, we realize even more how inadequate spatial and geometric forms are to stand for the moods of poetry, though they offer skeletal approximations. The *o* is a bare, poor equivalent of amorous, open-mouthed awe and total appetite. A *v* scarcely hints at the overlapping levels of psychic return to the depths. And so on. Likewise, a *frisson* is, minimally, a rhythm in space-time, but it is so much more than that. Here, too, there are endless levels in universal analogy, from the earliest waves released from the Big Bang up through the various forms of psychic shiver in emotions, to the sound waves of advanced music and words. The quality or mood of shiver varies immensely, being pleasurable or painful according to the dosage of negative and positive charge in it, with all sorts of subtle nuances. Baudelaire's *frisson nouveau* brought his own frequencies, his own *petite sensation* (Cézanne's reference to his own unique tone; he adored Baudelaire, of course). We get a clue of what Hugo's *tympans* picked up from the word *macabre*. There is that in Baudelaire, to be sure, but it hardly does justice to our Brahmsian artist, has nothing to do with his finest poems such as *La Chevelure*, *L'Invitation au voyage*, *Le Cygne*, and only marginally with great ones like *Les Petites Vieilles*. The power and beauty of those works goes far beyond the special vein of sensibility we are dealing with here but, nevertheless, the word *macabre* provides a hint of a very resonant and characteristic effect, one which he shares with other representative artists of his time. The word is not adequate, but the *br* in it is highly suggestive:

Take a wonderful poem like *Chant d'automne* (Jérôme and Alissa's favorite):

> Bientôt nous plongerons dans les froides ténèbres;
> Adieu vive clarté de nos étés trop courts!
> J'entends déjà tomber avec des chocs funèbres
> Le bois retentissant sur le pavé des cours.

No doubt about the *brr*, and *frr* in *froids* helps too. It is the scared-running moment between warmth and cold which is shocking and exhilarating as a roller coaster or scenic railway. That is what a *frisson* does for us: it turns the delight-bringing shock into humanly tempered (through alternation) rhythm, like a laugh or a sneeze. The infinity-opening extremeness of emotion and the humanizing tempering are polar —reversible—moments of the one artistic expression. But, as we noted, there are all kinds of tones for this process, as there are in the modes of laughter. This is not Hugo's *macabre*, better suited to Poe, or Baudelaire's *Une martyre*. Nor is it Verlaine's

L'ombre des arbres dans la rivière embrumée

which Debussy set. The latter is close to Debussy's *brum brum brum*, with his famous "drowned pedal" in *Reflets dans l'eau*. We see the warm-cold, light-dark dialectic of a shiver, visual, in Pissarro's river landscapes or Monet's *La Grenouillère*, for well-known examples. There, the black ripple shadows have a decisive quality which adds to the *heurté* effect of a good resistance, like cold intervening in our summer comfort, and that makes for a robust shiver, if we are up to it; it is *bracing*. The *heurté* is being used to refer to the classic remarks Walter Benjamin made about Baudelaire's *Tableaux parisiens* and prose poetry, taking off from the *heurté* in the preface of the *Spleen de Paris* and the line "Trébuchant sur les mots comme sur les pavés" (*Le Soleil*). In a study of the prose poems (edited by Mary Ann Caws and Hermine Riffaterre), I linked those paving stones over which one stumbles piquantly with the "rides profondes et nombreuses" of the *petites vieilles* in *Les Veuves*. It is the sort of interference of metonymy—the jumbled city—amid metaphoric lyricism that makes for advanced poetry like this.

Something like that occurs in *Chant d'automne* which is on the whole delightfully alive, like Mallarmé's *Le vierge le vivace et le bel aujourd'hui*. That texture of life is in the fibres of the porous "bois retentissant sur le pavé des cours": fibres-vibre-vivre. Vibrancy, as opposed to flat inertia, is the minimal stuff of life, and the impressionists made it theirs and everybody's. *Enivrez-vous* is in the cluster. "Ivre, il vit" (Mallarmé's *Les Fenêtres*). In Baudelaire's *Les Fenêtres* (which came, curiously, after Mallarmé's), we peer across a synaptic gap of space into a window where "vit la vie, rêve la vie, souffre la vie" in the form of a "femme ridée." The poet feels a wonderful stir of sympathy: "fier d'avoir vécu et souffert dans d'autres que moi-même"; "cette réalité... m'a aidé à vivre."

All of that *fait époque*, is in the tone of the finest art of that period. If we seek, like Baudelaire, for correspondences, this *br, fr, vr, cr*, and rolled *r* (or *rr*) thrill and its equivalent rhythm-structures, in Debussy, Ravel, and the impressionists, is like an archetypal strand joining the arts of the period.

We spoke of a synaptic gap, which is related to the *heurté* resistance effect. That is what an arc-light does, in a *réverbère* in a vibrantly human city, Paris.[1] Hence, Mallarmé saw an essence of Baudelaire in it and put a *réverbère* at the heart of his sonnet on him. How nervously alert in sleepy morning chill are *L'aube spirituelle* and *Le Crépuscule du matin*, in particular:

---

[1] It is the resistance of the transistor—literally "trans-resistor"—which helps to tame electric current into useful impulses for modern technology. As in the transformation of excessive emotion into rhythmically tempered shiver, laughter, etc. In both cases there is a shift from wholeness to fragmentation, or ta-ta-ta as in the metaphor-metonymy pair, through a crucial pivoting, which also characterizes the relation of electricity to magnetism, according to James Clerk Maxwell. Or light turning to warmth, light turning to love. And vice versa.

> La diane chantait dans la cour des casernes,
> Et le vent du matin soufflait sur les lanternes.
> ...
> L'air est plein du frisson des choses qui s'enfuient,
> ...
> Les pauvresses, traînant leurs seins maigres et froids...
> ...
> Le chant du coq au loin déchirait l'air brumeux:
> ...
> Les débauchés rentraient, brisés par leurs travaux.
> L'aurore grelottante en robe rose et verte
> S'avançait lentement sur la Seine déserte,
> Et le sombre Paris, en se frottant les yeux,
> Empoignait ses outils, vieillard laborieux.

Brr, n'est-ce pas?

You will find variants on that burlap texture in Debussy's *Voiles*, with its water-ripplings and sail flutterings, like the "petite voile frissonnante" in *Le Confiteor de l'artiste*. Or brusque wind-brushings over heather, *bruyères*, in another piano prelude.

Close to the *Crépuscule* vibrancy is the atmosphere, *bien sûr*, of *Les Petites Vieilles*. It begins with a series of *plis* of rhythm:

> Dans les plis sinueux des vieilles capitales
> Où tout même l'horreur tourne aux enchantements...

This is *fleurs* from *mal*, *aufgehoben* by the resistance of the sordid city, which, as T. S. Eliot noted, turns, in Baudelaire, to "poetry of the first intensity." Those *plis* are related closely to the cobblestone and wrinkle metonymy we mentioned earlier. There is a special thrill in "Ces monstres disloqués furent jadis des femmes." They are "monstres brisées. Sous des jupons troués et sous de froids tissus / Frémissant au fracas roulant des omnibus."

Even the word *tendresse*, the kind Baudelaire wrings from this suffering, participates in this *frisson nouveau*.

> Mais moi, moi qui de loin tendrement vous surveille
> ...
> Je goûte à votre insu des plaisirs clandestins...

The *de profundis* shriek, "Ruines! ma famille" sums up this poetic charity, this *agape*, this heartbreaking love. The poem ends with "la griffe effroyable de Dieu."

Part III of *Les Petites Vieilles* was developed into his finest prose poem, *Les Veuves*. There we find the familiar intensity of texture:

> dans ces rides profondes et nombreuses, dans ces démarches si lentes ou si saccadées, il déchiffre tout de suite les innombrables légendes de l'amour trompé... de la faim et du froid humblement, silencieusement supportés.

The repetition of *nombreuses, innombrables* is revelatory: this is prose poetry consummated in the lyric depth of the emotion and the metonymic staidness of number, those repeated wrinkles and stories resisting usual appeal and sublimated into something superior and Baudelairian. The *br* effect, the *frisson nouveau*, is built into the words, just as the marriage of light and water is consummated in the literal imbrication of "l'or dans la moire" (*La Chevelure*); *moire* contains the *or*, just as *lampe* and *palme* coalesce in Mallarmé's morning-shivery *Don du poème*, where "l'azur stérile a frémi."

Such a willed repetition is found in the "population innombrable de nombres" (stars) in the essay on Hugo. The depth is in the immediately following and summing-up "Mystère."

Finally, I puzzle why Baudelaire did not exploit the resonance of months like *septembre, octobre, novembre, décembre*. Poe did, in *The Raven*:

> Ah, distinctly I remember, it was in the bleak December...

And *Ulalume*:

> It was night in the lonesome October...

Mallarmé later wrote, exquisitely, in *Soupir*:

> Vers l'Azur attendri d'Octobre pâle et pur...

Of course this is a quibble, of no importance at all. But it helps to remind us that the aesthetic we are talking about runs through a sustained golden age and the investigation could easily go on.

Intimate Globality: Baudelaire's *La Chevelure*

First, Eden and the disaster of loss. Then the grace of existing anyway, going on in the belief in a paradise someday regained. And along the way, a beacon of reassurance. Incomparably, *La Chevelure*.[1]

The poet remembers:

> Je n'ai pas oublié, voisine de la ville,
> Notre blanche maison, petite mais tranquille (XCIX, 99)

His mother and he, alone together. Then one day a strange man came, and everything changed:

> L'Enfant déshérité s'enivre de soleil,
> Et dans tout ce qu'il boit et dans tout ce qu'il mange
> Retrouve l'ambroisie et le nectar vermeil.
>
> Il joue avec le vent, cause avec le nuage,
> Et s'enivre en chantant du chemin de la croix; (Bénédiction, 7)

This ousted child, grief-stricken and eventually consoled by the beauty of the world, this intimacy and globality, is the nub of Baudelaire. What of the well-known contempt for nature and nature's queen? Read *La Chevelure*. Before our wide-open and misted eyes what was named "abominable" is redeemed and worshipped in his own good time.

Nature and the memory of the mother are properly speaking angelic, Shekhina. Their light, sky, winds, milky clouds, and remembered light in her eyes, her milk. Weaned, the child still has her voice, perhaps reading to him as Marcel's mother did, with "toute la tendresse naturelle," This outer and inner rivery flow is the melody that carries the boy child and

---

[1] *Les Fleurs du mal,* XXII, in Baudelaire, *Oeuvres complètes,* I, ed. Claude Pichois, Bibliothèque de la Pléiade (Paris: Gallimard, 1975) 26-27. Page references to other poems from *Les Fleurs du mal* are given in the text.

that he carries within him as he ventures out toward life. Extension of umbilical cord, milk-stream, and apron strings, this Ariadne thread of maternal grace can sustain a man even to the other end of his existence: in the foxholes of the Second World War, wounded soldiers were heard calling "Mama." Till the end, shamelessly, repeatedly in his letters to Caroline, Baudelaire called out to her.

La Chevelure begins with an "O." The child takes in everything through its mouth, the open mouth of adoration, breathing it all in. Like the "wooden O" of *Henry V*, the woman's hair is a world. Baudelaire is a rounded poet, with romantic depth and classic breadth: global. The poem ends, like its close companion piece *Le Balcon*,[2] with the feminine river (horizontality) of time and memory, the *abiding* mother-spirit: "Longtemps! toujours!... souvenir," crossed by the rising and plunging profound sensuality of his feeling: "dans ta crinière lourde... l'oasis où je rêve, et la gourde."

> O toison, moutonnant jusque sur l'encolure!

Through her hair, a woman is Daphne-like, a tree coming right out of nature, down to elemental mineral roots (hair is hard; but it grows softly and gracefully). It is totalizing, in this sense; not the more ordinary vegetable nature which Baudelaire often found easier to reject (as in land-scape painting), the biological flow. But this milder current of *tendresse* is redeemed too, we shall see, in her *tresses*.

Hair is a vital projection of a woman's intimacy,[3] reaching out to the child—when the mother bends over, it descends as a graspable way of climbing to Her, Rapunzel—and extending that ogival growth of surreal hairlike veins where we grew in her (the *ramures* of the walls Meaulnes remembered in the lost sheepfold; the similar ones in *Les Paradis artificiels*; the tree of *Hide and Seek* by Tchelitcheff where children's faces emerge among the branches...). It is her *total* vitality—"Fortes tresses"—both staying and flowing, up and down:

> Et sous un ventre uni, doux comme du velours,
>   Bistré comme la peau d'un bonze,
>
> Une riche toison qui, vraiment, est la soeur
>   De cette énorme chevelure,

---

[2] In *Le Balcon* (36), the time dimension is in "Ces serments, ces parfums, ces baisers, infinis, / Renaitront-ils...?" The deep spatial dimension is in "un gouffre interdit à nos sondes."

[3] Maeterlinck's (and Debussy's) Mélisande mingles her hair with tree branches in the love scene when she appears at the window of the tower.

> Souple et frisée, et qui t'égale en épaisseur,
> Nuit sans étoiles, Nuit obscure![4]

This *human* nature which goes on and sustains, mingles animality and divinity, pungent presence and infinite mystery.

The two *o*'s in *toison* and in the rest of the line bear out the roundedness. The animal hints in "toison" and "moutonnant" are on the lower pole of sensuality, the (here, dark) cloud suggestions in both (clouds typically "moutonnent") are the other, transcendent extreme. As in Verlaine's *L'Échelonnement des haies* where the "ciel comme du lait" echoes the "brebis" on the meadows below, or Mallarmé's *Don du poëme*, where azure and milk (mother-wife's) interpenetrate, the high-low vibrancy of full poetic (daemonic) metaphoricity is at play.

jusque: the hair fills his horizon, spills over in generosity of being.

> O boucles! O parfum chargé de nonchaloir!

Perfume, the sense of smell, more rooted in animal sensuality than manipulable sight, is gratuitous usually, out of the ordinary practical way.[5] So it is effective for involuntary memory—those album scents that seize and remain as we pass a hidden garden—as Proust realized when he couldn't get the smell of varnish from his agonizing stairs, leading away from *Maman*, out of his suffering system. But here the memory-presence is blissful: the soft *g* and *ch* caress. *Parfum exotique*, close in mood and location to *La Chevelure*, features ten or more *ar*[6] effects: the cluster includes *parfum, clarté, art, air, clair, transparence, jardin, Paris, paradis* and through the broad effect of the *a* (middling on the sound-scale, between *i* and *ou* or *on*) brings out a feeling of serenity, feminine calm as in the line "Des femmes dont l'oeil *par* sa *franchise* étonne" (25) or "Mes yeux, mes *larges* yeux aux *clartés* éternelles" (*La Beauté*) (21). A sort of wide-screen effect. The *r*, in the right context, is the most liquid sound in French: "L'ombre des arbres dans la rivière embrumée" (Verlaine). The relaxed quality of this slow flow is in the direct meaning of *nonchaloir*; the effect of *oir* there (as in *soir, boire...*) is akin to the *ar* and close in sound (*a, wa*).

---

[4]"Les Promesses d'un visage," *Les Épaves*, XI, *O.c.*, I: 163.

[5]Sartre found something "trop parfumé" in Baudelaire. That is why Sartre was not a Baudelaire or Proust; he wasn't that open to the *mundus muliebris*, not that honest about himself and Her power over him.

[6]See Cohn, *A Critical Work*, Vol. I, *Modes of Art* Stanford French and Italian Studies (Saratoga: Anma Libri, 1975) 73-74.

Nonchaloir, though it negates warmth in its etymology, exudes it here ("Nier A c'est montrer A derrière une grille" [Valéry]), for "l'éternelle chaleur" is one of the key dimensions of the poem; not (vertical) light or extreme heat, but feminine sustaining warmth, going on from memory to future time.

> Extase! Pour peupler ce soir l'alcôve obscure
> Des souvenirs dormant dans cette chevelure,
> Je la veux agiter dans l'air comme un mouchoir!

This is a childishly direct, willful gesture: what one loves wholly one wants to be utterly free to dispose of, without compromise or trade-off. Mallarmé's equally affectionate and primitive faun begins: "Ces nymphes, je les veux perpétuer," In both cases the *v* is delicately suggestive of the willful pout tending toward oral possession.

The liquid effect of *soir* (and *obscure*) have been alluded to. The three *p*'s (plosive) are slightly explosive dartings forth of (almost butterfly-like) "souvenirs"—*p*'s tend to *papillonner*.[7]

The *souvenirs* go *back* into the night of time as they do *down* into that dark hair, in a common relation of dimensions.

chevelure: caressing *ch*; overtones of *velours* (soft darkness), and *cheval* (animal mane). The word is long enough to undulate, helped by the dipping *u*. The crossing of male brightness (his focused delight, the jewels of the last strophe) and female fluid warmth is subtly in the main rhyme (*encolure-obscure-chevelure*), i.e., the vividness of the *u* sound versus the flow of the *r*.

mouchoir: freshly daring modernity, humble concreteness; all is saved for poetry eventually; the sublime is all over the map. This is the second of the metaphoric (paradigmatic) substitutions in the sort of algebraic development Valéry spoke of as the main line of poetic structure (the first was the *toison* but there are subtle other allusions so there is no point in counting).

agiter: the child is male and acts, willfully, stirs up the quiet beauty of woman-nature as little Rimbaud did in *Aube*, "en agitant les bras." He is the little *boute-en-train*. This becomes the "Look Ma, no hands" act of creating, below.

> La langoureuse Asie et la brûlante Afrique,

---

[7]"Épanouie, pétale et papillon géants" (referring to Loïe Fuller), Mallarmé, *Oeuvres complètes*, Bibliothèque de la Pléiade (Paris: Gallimard, 1970) 308.

Look how endless one alexandrine line can be made to feel (as in "Mes yeux, mes larges yeux aux clartés éternelles" [21])! The long, luxurious "langoureuse" has something to do with it; the broad *a* even more as in Gautier's "La caravane humaine au Sahara du monde."[8] A word like *Asie* accordingly—with its vast expanse in one mat color on the map, its exotic distance Oh so far from France—is made for that dreamy, crooning, sweeping largo of Ravel's "Asie... Asie..." beginning his *Shéhérazade* suite.

> Tout un monde lointain, absent, presque défunt

Way off, as Rimbaud too dreamed of a mythical Asia, there is a mysterious other world where life is lovelier, calmer, Edenic. It is so asymptotically far toward the Source ("of the longest river," as T. S. Eliot said), it *almost* disappears into it. Baudelaire's ideal, summed up by J.-P. Richard, is a *barely* moving hammock, harking back to that first *bercement* of all (see below), in early *life*, not still death.

The diphthongs (or digraphs) of *lointain* help us feel the filtering effect of distance. There are almost no bright sounds in this line, rather the dampened quality of nasal *un, absent, défunt*, the discreet mute *e*'s of *presque*.

> Vit dans tes profondeurs, forêt aromatique!

The sharp *V* and focused *i*—as in "vit la vie, rêve la vie, souffre la vie" of *Les Fenêtres*—may make one feel converging pathways like perspective lines in a distance, paths in the hair *plunging* (*V*) toward disappearing unity, at the roots. (But that is very subtle, hard to be convincing about.) For, clearly, the broad sweep has become one with a vertical, *profondeurs*, in that overall mating of dimensions, which is the core of polypolar epistemology (e.g., Einsteinian space-time and the romantic-classic pair in Baudelaire's "globality").

It is as if we traverse a *forêt* of mystery to get to that other world, disappeared over a horizon ("absent"). A forest is made of trees (circumflex), a ghostly suggestion in her hair, which he linked to the inner maternal tree of growth.

> Comme d'autres esprits voguent sur la musique,
> Le mien, ô mon amour, nage sur ton parfum.

Those other spirits include Baudelaire's at other times; in *La Musique*, he sets sail on the ocean of music as on that of her hair, and he is *bercé*:

[8]See *Modes of Art* 76-77.

La musique souvent me prend comme une mer! (68)

Who does not sense the overtone of *mère*?

Pater rightly saw his whole aesthetic era "aspiring to the condition of music," which is more freely open to play, unhampered by the arbitrary little shapes and sounds of writing. German subjectivism and Wagner, via Baudelaire, had a major role in the rising general aesthetics (and synaesthesia, *Gesamtkunstwerk*, interpenetration of the various arts) replacing a classical poetics. Visual art, of course, rises similarly in poetry, especially with Baudelaire (it is slightly less free—see Nietzsche's disinction between musical Dionysian and visual Apollonian "images"— more fragmentary, linear, or metonymic). So sound (*musique*), touch (*nager*), smell (*parfum*), and sight (*voguer* and *nager*) commune here, as in strophe four.

> J'irai là-bas où l'arbre et l'homme, pleins de sève,
> Se pâment longuement sous l'ardeur des climats;
> Fortes tresses, soyez la houle qui m'enlève!

The theme of ocean-hair and distant beauty continues. And just as the hair was water and tree (*forêt*), joining the woman back to her vegetable and elemental sources, the Edenic faraway place joins man and tree in the natural fraternal relaxation of warm climes. In *Parfum exotique*:

> Une île paresseuse où la nature donne
> Des arbres singuliers et des fruits savoureux;
> Des hommes dont le corps est mince et vigoureux,
> Et des femmes dont l'oeil par sa franchise étonne. (25)

The tree has water in it (*sève*), and both are in the woman's veins and growing, vitally nourished hair (*fortes tresses*). The double *ss* of *tresses* is fine for the waves; *soyez* has a silky overtone (*soie*) which goes with the "watered" silk of *moire* below; in *houle* the liquidity of wave is in the languid *l* which lolls and caresses in French poetry:[9] "mais langoureusement longe / Comme de blanc linge ôté" (Mallarmé, *Petit Air I*); the overtone is *roule*; the dark *ou*, as in *amour* (above) is appropriate to this darkly sensual love-ocean in Jeanne's dusky Caribbean hair.

> Tu contiens, mer d'ébène, un éblouissant rêve
> De voiles, de rameurs, de flammes et de mâts:

Here the male stir is at work, active events and things liven the ocean into bright points and flashes. The *dazzle* is that stir, rising, amid the

---

[9]See *Modes of Art* 79-80.

passive "dream." *Flammes* is flags (*oriflammes*) but also a suggestion of a bright flicker and swarm of fire in water (see below). But the *mer-mère* is still all-powerful and *carries* him off. She "contains" the world for him.[10]

> Un port retentissant où mon âme peut boire
> A grands flots le parfum, le son et la couleur;
> Où les vaisseaux, glissant dans l'or et dans la moire

This *port* is the threshold of the ocean, a place where you have and don't have and thus have more, like Christmas Eve, or the bench just *outside* the hidden garden, where Mallarmé preferred to sit: virtuality. In *L'Invitation au voyage* we see this port again, where the masts bob impatiently full of potentiality. Everyone knows that the send-off is fuller than the voyage...

Baudelaire is *just outside* his mistress... that loving long last look, before the plunge, Swann gave to Odette in the carriage... This midplace is the place of art, *Aufhebung*. Presence marries absence, which aerates it, lifts it, leavens it; *néantisation*, the glorious *bouffée* of nineteenth-century French poetry, Debussy, and impressionist painting; *perfume* naturally recurs as an airy theme here. And in the happy ethereal stir, promiscuously mingle all the senses:

> Les sons et les parfums tournent dans l'air du soir
> ("Harmonie du soir" 47)

Heavenly light mates with feminine water, the alchemist's (and Shakespeare's) transcendent absurdity, union of opposites: *l'or et la moire*. The canny use of language brings a union in the words: *or* is in *moire* physically, imbricates just as the *palmes* of outdoor light and creation mingles in the *lampe* of indoor light and creation in Mallarmé's *Don du poëme*.

> Elle est retrouvée!
> Quoi? l'éternité.
> C'est la mer mêlée
> Au soleil.
> (Rimbaud)

The *gl* of *glissant* and *gloire* is a throat-convulsion of pleasure: "Gloire du long désir" (Mallarmé, *Prose*). Baudelaire talks about that constriction and release of the creator's throat in "Le Peintre de la vie moderne" and in his review of *Madame Bovary*.

---

[10]For a study of *contiens*, see Cohn, *Toward the Poems of Mallarmé* (Berkeley: University of California Press, 1980) 263-64.

Ouvrent leurs vastes bras pour embrasser la gloire
D'un ciel pur où frémit l'éternelle chaleur.

Again, the broad *a*—so clearly purposeful in the "clumsy" repetition
some critics harp on (forgetting their Pascal): *bras* and *embrasser*—gives
the dominant feminine tone of wide "embrace" of nature, ocean that
carries like a life-flow of maternal strength. Even the *gloire* has the *a*
sound... as does *moire*, going with the *chaleur*.

In contrast there is a series of bright sounds—*pur, frémit, é*—reminding one of "Maint diamant d'imperceptible écume" (Valéry, *Le Cimetière
marin*); this is the light of the sky steeply up there. The male acuteness
and the female flow are mated, the two dimensions are *crossed*, just as the
or married the water (*moire*) before. Once again, this is the cross of globality, plenitude, rounded Baudelaire, as at the end of the poem and the
beginning, here in the mid-strophe (4 of 7).

Je plongerai ma tête amoureuse d'ivresse
Dans ce noir océan où l'autre est enfermé;

The head is a male intervention in the feminine hair-ocean; being in love
with drunkenness, as Augustine said he was with love, is the burden of
the prose poem *Enivrez-vous.* That "squaring" of emotion implies a complex dialectic of the *homo duplex* Baudelaire saw himself to be (e.g., in *La
Fanfarlo*), someone who can stand off from his loving or drunken self
and see and desire it ("Je me voyais me voir," Valéry, *La Jeune Parque*).
That squaring (tetrapolarity) is indeed the posture of the classic-romantic
who wrote (e.g., *Les paradis artificiels*) both coolly and passionately.

The *ivresse, caresse*, and *paresse* in these strophes are in the key tone of
tresses, with their wavy double *s*.

The next line has the micro-macro paradoxical vibrancy of "De la
vaporisation et de la centralisation du *Moi*. Tout est là": this is the global
version of diastole-systole and other more partial pulsations. This perspective opens *Le Voyage*:

Ah! que le monde est grand à la clarté des lampes!
Aux yeux du souvenir que le monde est petit! (129)

Cheveux bleus, pavillon de ténèbres tendues,
Vous me rendez l'azur du ciel immense et rond;

The roundness of the head of hair bolsters our feeling that *pavillon* refers
to "pavilion" (tent) and not "flag"—indeed that is the first dictionary
meaning of *pavillon.* Those old tents had round crests and walls hanging
down as if on both sides of a face; these would be the *ténèbres tendues*,

the darkness of her hair stretched down like wall-hangings. In his small essay on Gautier, Baudelaire quotes:

> Ensemble nous dormirons
> Sous mes cheveux, tente sombre.

Surely he had read and been impressed by the appropriate *organic* metaphor at the time he wrote *La Chevelure*. I don't see a horizontal, or otherwise, flag shape at all, in this calm hair compared to an ocean. That would be only in a walking and probably breeze-harried woman and is rather funny.

Other critics have seen the *pavillon* as I do: e.g., Antoine Adam. He didn't even question it. But Yves Bonnefoy got curiously vexed at it...

One sees that blue of darkness in certain lights.

> Sur les bords duvetés de vos mèches tordues
> Je m'enivre ardemment des senteurs confondues
> De l'huile de coco, du musc et du goudron.

The pungency of Jeanne's hair takes him down to dusky sensuality: *goudron*, for example, is in a heavy register both by its sound (*ou* is low on the acoustic scale and the nasal is lower) and its color as well as its smell and general feel. This register figures in *Correspondances* with similar allusions. In Plato's *Symposium*, love moves unimpededly—through Diotima—from high to low, and that is the way D. H. Lawrence, for example, saw feminine emotion.[11]

Mallarmé's *Tombeau de Charles Baudelaire* hymns that fluidity with the *mèche louche* which one breathes like a "tutelary poison" even if it kills us; or, as Baudelaire says in his equivalent moment of extreme ambivalence (going beyond this sensual one): "Ô Mort... Au fond de l'Inconnu pour trouver du *nouveau*" (*Le Voyage* 134). Elsewhere he speaks of her as "douceur, poison" (*Le Balcon* 36). But ambivalence runs throughout the collection, starting with the very title and ending with the *boue-or* of (the unfinished) *A Paris*.

> Et mon esprit subtil que le roulis caresse
> Saura vous retrouver, ô féconde paresse,
> Infinis bercements du loisir embaumé!

The oceanic mother is so powerful, all-encompassing in this honest adoration that the little male appendage to her—the sort of afterthought of nature that the male actually is—is threatened with nothingness or insignificance; hence, all of those anthropological rituals in which adolescent

---

[11]For example, in his treatise *Psychology and the Unconscious*.

males have to purge themselves, through painful and fearful initiation, of all mother influence, as they become warriors, huntsmen, builders, etc. The little that worshipful Baudelaire claims for himself, equivalent to that male assertion, is the art of his "esprit subtil" which commemorates Her. His honest sense of dependency is stated in the fact that it is her maternal *bercements* that are the matrix-stuff of his writhing-writing rhythmic poetic art. Mallarmé repeats this humble dialectic in his *Tombeau d'Anatole* and his two *Éventail* poems.

A Renaissance poet like Ronsard got his mild own back, in this same sense, against Woman in his "Quand vous serez bien vieille." One might see in the thought of the female decrepitude and death a subtle note of revenge: thus, in *Une Charogne*, Baudelaire more assertively, and less beautifully-humbly, says: "J'ai gardé la forme... De mes amours décomposés" (31). That was a weaker moment like all the misogynistic, and unconvincing, ones scattered through his poetry and prose. *This* is the real Baudelaire, the global one, who, in a passage of the *Journaux intimes*, describes a wonderful Instant of total sympathy between man and woman. I think of Brahms's *Alto Rhapsody* in such a moment.

The nonassertive, nonlinear nature of this dialectic is reprised in the oxymoronic play between *féconde* and *paresse*, between motion and rest. In nearby *Parfum exotique* the same thing happens, statically and ecstatically:

> Une ile paresseuse où la nature donne
> Des arbres singuliers et des fruits savoureux;
> Des hommes dont le corps est mince et vigoureux,   (25)

This is a world of suspended opposites, an electric high-charged poetic reality recalling the motion-in-rest of a cradle (or hammock).

But here the feeling is rather of happy on-going life, which is the properly female dimension, as in the "Longtemps! toujours!," below. The tar and the coconuts are smells and images of a lively port, a bustle and stir and dipping sensuality.

> Longtemps! toujours! ma main dans ta crinière lourde
> Sèmera le rubis, la perle et le saphir,
> Afin qu'à mon désir tu ne sois jamais sourde!

There is a hint of paid-for love here, which Edward Ahearn[12] has commented upon, but oh so light! One certainly cannot take seriously

---

[12]See E. Ahearn, "'Simplifier avec gloire la femme': Syntax, Synecdoche, Subversion in a Mallarmé Sonnet," *The French Review* 58.3 (1985) 345-59.

the idea that he is paying her off with all those jewels literally strewn in her hair. Likelier is the feeling of caress, a repeated loving touch, as her reward. And it is possible that the gesture brings jewel-like reflections in the dark mass. Again, I feel the humility, the beseeching, of adoration and necessity:

> N'es-tu pas l'oasis où je rêve, et la gourde
> Où je hume à longs traits le vin du souvenir?

The *lourde*, above, and the *sourde* and *gourde* are heavy sounds, as we noted, befitting the hair weight and color (*r*, as in *amour*, adds soft fluidity to the darkness). And *gourde* is very feminine, like a womb or well of sensuality where one can drink of original deep life. That plunging-male dimension at the end crosses the line of time in "Longtemps! toujours!" prolonged in the final note of *souvenir*, which flows along the umbilical river of memory going back to Her as Source.

Oasis is similarly circular and originary, an Eden of final, and beginning, repose. We are back to the first "O" of globality—*O toison!*—with this concluding intimacy.

As in *Le Balcon*, so close in mood, there is a question mark ending all this. The deeper the need and the bliss of Eden, the greater the anguish of loss. This is partly faced by the doubt and question, homeopathically and wistfully. Perhaps the tiny possible irony of his jewel-bestowing may be seen in this self-protective light. But what is this little weakness compared to all that faith and love?...

Baudelaire's Beleaguered Prose Poems

Epistemological criticism is defined by four cardinal points: (1) an absolutely free epistemological theory; (2) an equally profound belief in meaning in the world and its authentic texts; (3) a comparable respect for the normative (sanity, history, conventions, classical forms); and (4) a concern for clarity and elegance of presentation.

"Polypolar epistemology" can be defined as a relation of multiple dimensions, each a polarity—such as the Cartesian cross—but absolutely (in the pure phase of thought) free and flexible. All four (or six, etc.) poles—and the point of origin as microcosm, together with the macro-totality encompassing it all—and the two (or more) dimensions are fully interchangeable; they "jump around" underneath.

As you move into normal, logical thought, through operational distinctions between the dimensions—vertical versus horizontal, holistic versus fragmentary, metaphoric versus metonymic, and so on—you get linear patterns such as the separation of space and time, of beginning and end, of form and matter, spirit and body, up and down, as well as the irreversibility of time and incest prohibition. All these allow *sense* (etymologically from the word for "direction" as is French *sens*), ordinary meaning.

The philosophical move toward sophisticated freedom is made through powers of paradox, going beyond the usual binary paradox to "paradox squared" (tetrapolarity) and so on (polypolarity). This *dimensional* thinking is parallel to that in music, where tones are related through division (or multiplication) of strings.

As tetrapolarity moves into becoming, a new concept, "antisynthesis," must be added to Hegel's dialectical triad. This entity has to do with such phenomena as backward movement in time (hypothesized of electrons by Feynman et al.), Nietzsche's "Eternal Return," and Kierkegaard's "absolute paradox," Mallarmé's deconstructive "n'abolira le hasard," various "setbacks," and so on. An application of this theory to a study of Baudelaire's prose poems now follows (other expositions and applications appear in my books).

In the familiar preface to his *Petits poèmes en prose*, Baudelaire states as his aim the

> miracle d'une prose poétique, musicale sans rythme et sans rime, assez souple et assez heurtée pour s'adapter aux mouvements lyriques de l'âme, aux ondulations de la rêverie, aux soubresauts de la conscience... C'est surtout de la fréquentation des villes énormes, c'est du croisement de leurs innombrables rapports que naît cet idéal obsédant.

> [miracle of a poetic prose, musical without rhythm and without rhyme, sufficiently supple and jerky to be adaptable to the lyrical movements of the psyche, the undulations of reverie, the jumps of consciousness... It is especially from the frequentation of enormous cities, from the crossing of their innumerable relations, that this obsessive ideal is born.] (281)[1]

This passage puts well what he in fact brings off in the best of the prose poems—for example, "Les veuves." The metaphoric depth of poetry—the "musicale" or the "mouvements lyriques de l'âme"—does combine in a vibrant fusion, "miraculously," with the metonymy of the "heurté" aspect, the jumbled variety of reality in a big city (and the prosaic or analytic rhythms implied in "conscience"). The ruggedness of texture is represented in "Les veuves" by the "rides profondes et *nombreuses*" and the "*innombrables* légendes de l'amour trompé, du dévouement méconnu, des efforts non récompensés, de la faim et du froid humblement, silencieusement supportés" (297; emphasis added). I emphasize the plural aspect here—number—in connection with metonymy, although in these passages the fusion is already there. Similarly, Walter Benjamin brought out the "heurté"—rugged or jerky—quality by alluding to stumbled-on cobblestones set unevenly in the Parisian streets ("On Some Motifs"). One feels a certain parallel between the wrinkles and the dirt-separated cobblestones, together suggesting the flavor, in realistic poetry, of the city, in this general horizontal direction.

In "A Poetry-Prose Cross" I demonstrate that the meeting or crossing of epistemological dimensions underlying Jakobson's terms tends to effectuate a certain imagery: windows (e.g., *croisées*) are scattered generously throughout the similar pieces of Bertrand and Mallarmé as well —as in "Les fenêtres," "Le mauvais vitrier," the framed picture one feels in "L'invitation au voyage," or the carrefour in the park of "Le fou et

---

[1]All translations are mine. Page references are to Baudelaire, *Oeuvres complètes*, ed. Claude Pichois (Paris: Gallimard, 1975).

la Vénus" or "Les veuves." Baudelaire, in his preface, speaks of the "villes" and the *croisement de leurs innombrables rapports*" (281; emphasis added). And in many of the poems, the number four dominates: for example, "L'étranger," where the tetrapolarity of the rejected family is followed by a series of four refused entities (friends, country, gold, and a routine sort of beauty). Significantly for our thesis, there is at the end a quintessential affirmation—the above-it-all clouds—parallel to the Kierkegaardian leap from the midst of a tetrapolar dilemma (in "The Absolute Paradox").

This tilt or resolution, offsetting any "antisynthetic" (fourth term deconstructing a Hegelian synthesis) movement, is what leaves almost all the prose poems with a positive tone, a bias for art, contrary to the opinions of many critics of today. In "Le *confiteor* de l'artiste" the little shivering sail at the center of such a crossroads stands for this vibrant zero-infinite quintessence, provisionally, and foretells the suggested reconciliation and victory of art at the end. Many other pieces have this tetradic pattern. In "Les dons des fées" there are two series: "Les Dons, les Facultés, les bons Hasards, les Circonstances invincibles" and "les Jours, les Heures, les Minutes, les Secondes" (the number is doubled into eight in the series of "Fées, Gnomes, Salamandres, Sylphides, Sylphes, Nixes, Ondins, Ondines" [309]). In "Les vocations" there are "quatre enfants" who discuss their desires. The "quatre hommes" of "Portraits de Maîtresses" are "ni vieux, ni jeunes, ni beaux ni laids."

T. S. Eliot was of course right: through this ("squared") chiasmus structure Baudelaire does raise the sordid and helter-skelter city to poetry of the "first intensity" (341).

He follows an old lady through the streets with the sort of fascinated devotion one recalls in Poe's *Man of the Crowd* (or for that matter the stubborn efforts of Proust to fathom, or be, the flower in front of which, according to Hahn, he sat for hours). The same happens in "Les fenêtres." At other times, he merely casts a "curious" glance over a motley crowd at an outdoor concert. But again the (vertical) figure of the noble "vieille" emerges right out of the "foule" or relatively indifferent (horizontal) ground, and the feeling of crossing, of organic fusion or exchange as in poetic-realistic impressionist painting—perhaps a crowd scene of Manet or Renoir or Pissarro—is strong.

He wondered why the old lady couldn't pay for an admission to the concert and merely hung on the outskirts with a little boy she held by the hand. He guessed it was because she wanted to keep her modest means to pay for some little gift to the child, maybe a toy. And he ends thus: "Et elle sera rentrée à pied, méditant et rêvant, seule, toujours seule; car l'enfant est turbulent, égoïste, sans douceur et sans patience..." [And she will have likely gone home on foot, meditating and dreaming, alone, always alone; for children are turbulent, egotistical, without sweetness and without patience...] (299). His fascination with the "vieille" likely has something to do with a typical theme of pity on the part of men, the same kind that goes into the extreme pathos of "sacrificial women" such as in *La bohème*, *Madame Butterfly*, *La traviata* (both the operas, of course, and the texts behind them). I have spoken elsewhere of the "Madame Butterfly sympathy" for the deserted woman in Rimbaud's "Mémoire" (*Poetry of Rimbaud* 19). It is a poignant old theme indeed. Baudelaire's Andromaque in "Le cygne" is, to be sure, much younger, but the sorrowing identification is similar; competent critics have seen the ghost of widowed Caroline behind her.

Baudelaire's extreme attachment to his mother needs no documentation. It may be harder to accept that she is connected with the "vieille" here and in other poems of Baudelaire, but his emotions—such as charity—did tend to such extremes. He did not readily respond to just any other but, naturally for a genius, when he did go out, he tended to go far, toward *ruines*, *ma famille*, or toward outcasts, *les éclopés de la vie*. The feeling for the old woman would embody both a special pity, such as Flaubert's for Félicité, and a sort of sacrificial evening of scores with the mother who had betrayed him by marrying a stranger. Something like this happens, it has been remarked, in Camus's *L'étranger*.

In a memorable passage of the *Journaux intimes*, Baudelaire describes a scene in which he weeps together with Jeanne Duval (undoubtedly it is she) in an instant of something like total sympathy (1202). These moments are rare for anyone and perhaps especially for one who like Baudelaire felt and expressed such separateness from the opposite sex (along with the moments of reconciliation which, however, were apt not to be so much total sympathy as rather self-indulgent enjoyment, as has often been observed—not that they were not sincerely heterosexual, despite a current corrosive view). But the point is he does make it in this trice to a profoundly moving "intersubjectivity" or "encounter" with the other, as Martin Buber and Gabriel Marcel would put it, and this is the personal "miracle" of which the prose poems such as "Les veuves" are the artistic equivalent.

This high instant of presence, of overriding tone, is what he unequivocally set his sights on in the collection and what he achieved in a few wonderful cases and approximated in others. And this, I submit, totally invalidates the deconstructive approaches to these masterpieces in various pieces of recent criticism. To be sure, these eager studies bring much talent to bear, but unfortunately they display even more a compulsive ingenuity that shoots right past the true targets in a mechanical trajectory. Whereas a mature critic knows when to change directions—a few examples are usually sufficient to establish a point, whereupon an imaginative mind wants to move on and round out a complex investigation— these *modernes* get stuck in their scheme and establish an elaborate new kind of pedantry.

One reason for this, I suspect, is that they tend to read Baudelaire with hindsight, through a Mallarméan perspective. Now, my regard for that perspective is second to none and I have devoted most of my energy to it, but at some point in my work on this unsurpassable poet I realized a sort of danger of automatism in the wide-open epistemology where paradox, as I noted in *L'oeuvre de Mallarmé*, "invades all forms of thought." Indeed, in explicating the *Coup de dés*, or *Igitur* or most of the *Poésies* (and *Divagations*, passim), one had almost constantly to observe that rule; no one, not even Kierkegaard or Nietzsche, is more ironic and inexhaustible than Mallarmé in this respect, and the critic is forced to extreme mobility and ironic awareness. But Baudelaire is not at all at that level, even in his most mature work, though he does move up to it intermittently.

In this way, an exaggeration of Baudelaire's epistemological complexity, as well as the one-sided emphasis on negation—even in the *Petits poèmes en prose* where, indeed, a "cold wind" of aging, sickness, and disenchantment blows intermittently, as opposed to the plenitude of tone that he still reaches, at times perhaps unprecedentedly (as fine readers like Soupault and Jouve have felt)—these newer critics miss the mark by a wide margin, as I now will try to demonstrate on a text they have particularly misused, "Le *confiteor* de l'artiste."

> Grand délice que celui de noyer son regard dans l'immensité du ciel et de la mer! Solitude, silence, incomparable chasteté de l'azur! une petite voile frissonnante à l'horizon, et qui, par sa petitesse et son isolement, imite mon irrémédiable existence, mélodie monotone de la houle, toutes ces choses pensent par moi, ou je pense par elles (car dans la grandeur de la rêverie, le *moi* se perd vite!); elles pensent, dis-je mais musicalement et pittoresquement, sans arguties, sans syllogismes, sans déductions.

> [A sheer delight it is to drown one's look in the immensity of the sky and the sea! Solitude, silence, incomparable chastity of the azure! a little sail shivering at the horizon and which, by its tininess and isolation, imitates my irremediable existence, monotonous melody of the sea-swell, all those things think through me, or I think through them (for

in the greatness of reverie the self is quickly lost); they think, I say, but musically and pictorially, without quibbling, without syllogisms, without deductions.] (284)

This is the metaphoric dimension the preface alluded to, with the "musicalement" echoing the "musicale" there (music and visual art are more openly and fluidly metaphoric than literature is and characterize more and more nineteenth-century aesthetics, as we all know). There is a dialectical tension between the plenitude of "délice" and "isolement" versus "irremédiable existence," corresponding to the "fleurs" and "mal" of the collection in verse, but here as there (in this deep dimension) is a resolving tone leaning to the positive, aesthetic joy. It is the same with any serious music, that final tilt despite *lacrimae rerum*: beauty as high culture usually knows it.

But the mood is interrupted by a suffering that is equally familiar, as often following such extremes of delight. And then Baudelaire ends the piece with an ambiguous remark: "L'étude du beau est un duel où l'artiste crie de frayeur avant d'être vaincu."

Barbara Johnson, in her *Défigurations du langage poétique*, sees this as a deconstructive conclusion. Is she right? I do not think so. Nor is it, despite the ambiguity, the sort of undecidable (paradox, irony) that the deconstructionists always regard as the high point of art and find everywhere *comme par hasard*. No, the moment of suffering does not at all, on the one hand, finally negate the strong note of artistic aliveness in the first and determining section—it is much longer, more impressive, sustained, felt, than the few lines devoted to the reaction, which really ends when he apostrophizes "Nature, enchanteresse sans pitié..." and so on to the end, for nature in this context is tantamount to the supreme principle of beauty he still believes in. She is a "rivale toujours victorieuse." There is no hint of irony here but rather a pathetic appeal to an awesome mistress-muse and to life itself, inevitably redolent of his own mother, as are those many poems hymning the power of the feminine ("La beauté," "La géante"). And the ambiguity of the end tilts, once again, toward a quintessential resolution that affirms faith in art. For even if the artist cries with fright and is "vaincu," what can that mean except that he is overcome by beauty itself as a man is in the throes of love with life-affirming and procreative or creative effect?

No amount of ingenuity will ever persuade me of anything else in Baudelaire's intention and achievement here. This prose poem is not as typical of the genre at its best as is "Les veuves": rather than a metonymic going out into a city, there is a somewhat didactic excursion into suffering and negation, which does deconstruct the poetic flight but only for a moment. Thus the horizontal is reabsorbed, resolvingly, into the vertical-horizontal synthesis of the genre finally, just as the city's negation and ugliness is caught up in the overall tone of "Les veuves" through a savory complexity of wrinkled, elegiac sweetness and compassion, perhaps like a fine old wine, or an intimate winterscape by Pissarro or Monet. In "Le *confiteor* de l'artiste" the clearly impressionist effect is different, to be sure, rather like a breezy and light-brimming Monet oceanscape at first, with a menacing cloud later dimming it all, but with the light promising to break out again for another go at artistic awareness. Contrary to the critics in question, there is no hint of pulling down his previous poetry, in disenchanted, bitterly ironic old age, even though this "cold wind" does blow through other prose poems, such as "Perte d'auréole" and "Chacun sa chimère." And the collection holds a number of dark-toned, grimly realistic pieces, but there is nothing programmatic about them, no collective effect of burning what he had adored. The grim pieces are merely bad-tempered vignettes, parallel to some somber poems in *Les fleurs du mal*, such as "Une charogne" or "Le squelette laboureur": that they are in prose and hence more realistic proves nothing at all about a subversive intent. They are really not very interesting and are hardly to be dwelt on except for tendentious purposes. One feels sure that Baudelaire thought little of them and that his apologetic remarks in the preface may well refer to them in particular. He was getting old and ailing, and he did tend to knock off works hastily to fill in a collection—for the *Fleurs du mal* as well, it is known.

"Le galant tireur" is wryly cynical rather than grim: a man shoots the head of a doll off, replacing a desire to kill his wife, and so informs her in a twisted bit of gallantry. Hardly worth stopping at except for the incredible ingenuity that Jeffrey Mehlman ("Baudelaire with Freud") and Johnson apply to it. Johnson makes an immense lot of the phrase "*tuer* le Temps." Over a long series of pages, she charts its supposed infolding, *en abyme*, ironies. All that adds nothing; Baudelaire is merely referring as he often does to Time (often capitalized for that usage: in "L'horloge," "La chambre double," etc.) as a monster that kills us in the end; here, too, he calls it "ce monstre-là." The italicizing of "tuer" does no more than point up the overtone of the setting, the shooting gallery where dolls are "killed." Of course, paradoxes (such as the Freudian-Lacanian one of cultural *Aufhebung*—the nothing-something of the phallus resulting from the castration threat in the oedipal crisis) underlie this as they do all language, all signifiers. And, yes, there is even a Mallarméan meta-ambiguity in the relation of (vertical) figural and (horizontal) literal, parallel to our contemporary awareness of the deeper relation of metaphor and metonymy, and going back to Mallarmé's polydimensional ironies as in "Il y a et il n'y a pas de hasard" (and "Artifice que la réalité") or forward to Derrida's *clôture*. But either it is an unconscious, subjacent complexity or, if Baudelaire was aware of it, it has to do with a free play of syntax fairly characteristic of his verse poems, hence hardly a new attitude negating those poems. For example, in "Le cygne" the paradoxical relation of figure and ground, figural and literal, is present in "tout devient allégorie," and the play between past and present, poet and city, self and other, is very lively. In "Le voyage" to see desire as an antinomy between the sun and the earth, as a "grand arbre," is to postulate an organic fusion and reversibility like Yeats's "great rooted blossomer... how can we tell the dancer from the dance?" These fluidities of thought are scattered throughout Baudelaire's verse poetry from the earliest.

Mehlman, commenting on the same prose text and finding just as much epistemological to-do, concludes not only for the new disabused Baudelaire's superiority over the merely poetic old, but in a moment of triumph, recalling the aging Hegel's, he sees *himself* soaring above all artists like the Nietzschean *Übermensch* ("Freud with Pain"). This mood is prolonged in a tendentious reading of "Une mort héroïque," where the critic finds an open-minded superiority in the Prince, over the poor rejected artist Fancioulle. In this, Mehlman turns against his quondam mentor Mauron. But Mauron, in his *Le dernier Baudelaire*, is much closer to the *Stimmung* and the truth of his poet. Psychology doesn't have the mobility of epistemology, but Mauron manages well anyway, mostly because, unlike the newer critics, he had a solid sense of the essential. (Unfortunately, elsewhere, he is carried off wildly by his hobbyhorse of dead-mother imago, particularly in the case of Mallarmé.)

"Une mort héroïque" is complex, and the Prince does represent a challenging entity, deconstructive if you will, prosaic and murderously cool and analytic in the mood of the detective story since Poe. He is the eternal-revenant father authority (like Hamlet's ghostly sire), an ingredient that Baudelaire or any other artist never finally can do without, as goad and dialectical partner.[2] Up to the decisive moment! Then an artist naturally sides with the artist (especially if he is as deeply tragi-comic as Fancioulle is—compare the old *saltimbanque*) and with art, just as he did in "Le *confiteor* de l'artiste" and really everywhere else, even in "Perte

---

[2]This haunting figure is everywhere in great literature: Balzac's Dr. Bianchon; Flaubert's Dr. Larivière; Stendhal's Republican Gautier or Altamira; Proust's father. He is often mediated by a contemporary older boy friend as in *Le grand Meaulnes*, *Tonio Kröger*, or *The Last Pilgrim*.

d'auréole," where he doffs his halo (as Mallarmé did later, speaking to his friend, Dauphin), yes, but as a strategy familiar in geniuses, perhaps particularly those who are struggling against old age and fate—compare "*Petits* poèmes en prose" (emphasis added) or titles like *Divagations*. But when Baudelaire made a self-deprecatory remark in Belgium and the Belgians took him at his word, the true Baudelaire rose up in resentful wrath and poured contempt on them.

"L'invitation au voyage" is another basically glowing piece, bathed in serene lowland light and middle-class luxurious reality with furniture (and even cooking). Johnson makes much of the use of metonymic devices such as a series of phrases using *comme*, which Baudelaire would never have employed in the poetry in verse. This is true, and these devices do impart a somewhat dry and flattening effect, but not decisively; the understatement is not deconstructive but rather experimentally lyric, and it may indeed raise the poetic presence, just as the enumeration of exiles at the end of the fully poetic "Le cygne" does, including the throw-away last line "et bien d'autres encore." I repeat, that is poetic understatement as effective as Laforgue's or Pound's and just as risky: the proof is that many critics find it plain flat. But to me, caught up in the irresistible mood (much in the poetic is indeed contextual, part of a code if you will) set by that incredibly poignant and stirring poem most of the way, that throwaway enumeration is the gesture of one who has something deeper to say than even his art at its best could convey. Just the opposite of deconstruction in intent. The maneuver provisionally moves that way (a *reculer pour mieux sauter*, or "stoop to conquer") but does not stop there. In other words, the repeated *comme* is parallel to the "innombrable" metonymy of "Les veuves," raised into the poetic miraculously, as pop art with its rows of tomato cans or Marilyn Monroes manages to do at its luckiest, or camp, or Joyce's "Plumtree's Potted Meat" sign on the Dublin streets. The examples from modern art, roughly starting with Nerval and Sainte-Beuve, are endless.[3]

Almost everyone agrees that "Les fenêtres" is a high point of the collection and of the modern tradition generally. The young critics seize on the somewhat disabused final sentence to try to pull the whole thing their way, but they get nowhere. As in the "*Confiteor* de l'artiste," the tone is too well established, and the ending is just a pinprick in the new manner, adding almost dutifully a dry flavor to a moment of sincere sensibility bursting with life, yearning, Parisian, wistful poetic presence at the brim. Rimbaud ends most of his poems in *Illuminations* with the

---

[3]See my *Modes of Art*, "From Poetic Realism to Pop Art" (144-52).

same sort of minor deflation, mostly a strategy for dealing with terminal pomposity.

The same full-circle dialectic applies to the following jaunty remark in Baudelaire's preface: "il n'a ni queue ni tête, puisque tout, au contraire y est à la fois tête et queue, alternativement et réciproquement... Enlevez une vertèbre, et les deux morceaux de cette tortueuse fantaisie se rejoindront sans peine" (282).

Some readers see this passage as a validation of the currently important vogue of the fragment in critical theory, but it is mainly just a light-hearted suggestion to the editor, Houssaye, that "Nous pouvons couper où nous voulons, moi ma rêverie, vous le manuscrit." There is no connecting unity in the collection, but not because that is any artistic *gain*, it is just a fact; the unity is in each poem.

If anything, Baudelaire is being self-deprecatory here; clearly, unlike the modern theorists, he believed in overall harmony and architecture and tried for it when it seemed appropriate, as it did in *Les fleurs du mal.*

One might add that to hypostatize the fragment is just as sterile as its opposite, a pretentious claim to completeness. Proust indicates the richly human middle ground here when he states that obscurity is to be neither courted nor eschewed ("Contre l'obscurité"). Along this middle course— not just the clung-to "undecidable"—the artist muddles through toward something as fully present and real as it is remote.

No, totally unlike the subsequent practitioners of the *aléatoire* in composition—Duchamp, Cage, Boulez, Pollock—Baudelaire was incapable of hoping for anything to come of the randomness of this sequence in *Le spleen de Paris.* If prose tempted him, it was not because its looseness, as opposed to poetry's constrictions, was conducive to mere chance, but rather because it could lead to an even higher (and subtler) control, as Mallarmé, Proust, and Joyce demonstrated. Prose offered him opportunities of "metaphoric" openness and fluidity parallel to music or visual art in this sense. The critics are following the same will-o'-the-wisp of something for nothing that has led to our contemporary emptiness, such as the childish belief that a drug-induced stupor can produce masterpieces.

Other pieces in the collection are worthy of our attention if only because the skeptical critics avoid them in a telling way. "Chacun sa chimère" is a case in point: it is skirted as being insufficiently undecidable. There is an indecision or ambiguity in the "condemnés à espérer toujours" of the procession of artist figures (recalling "La Caravane" of Gautier and "Le Guignon" of Mallarmé), but the final image is of Baudelaire himself unambiguously weighed down by this "rat-race" of his species and, more generally, of mankind. *A quoi bon?* No undecidable there, and it doesn't deconstruct anything; rather, it tears down everything—it is just an old Job-like lamentation about existence, anybody's who hopes. It is one big sigh and not very rewarding. (Note that there is no synthesis followed by a deconstructive antisynthesis, but a jump to a negative "quintessence").

"La belle Dorothée, on the other hand, is all smiles and sunlight, graceful feminine nature, and totally useless to the contemporary thesis about the *Petits poèmes en prose*. It is, accordingly, ignored as a sheer embarrassment. I must allow that it is not typical of the genre: it is too relaxed on the reality side, being rather exotic, without much resistance from existence, as is felt to be true of lush tropical nature generically.

The rest of the prose poems offer all sorts of interest but none particularly for our rescue operation. The prose poems are usually well worth saving from the modernist onslaught (including Breton's). Not that all or even many are true masterpieces—some contemporary critics have exaggerated their power altogether. *Les fleurs du mal* is much richer in density of achievement—particularly the *Tableaux parisiens*, which are often close to the prose poems in realistic magic. But one senses too how Baudelaire, tiring and unhappy, played around with this new form, in some resurgence of old ambition—the hoped-for miracle—but often to settle some rankling scores, to try out understatement (not always "taking off"), to write out some minor curious experiences almost journalistically or half-journalistically, sketchily, summarily (or too lengthily), with all sorts of tentative expressions playing around his vital core of intensity and vulnerability. One is at last grateful for the successes and even the half-successes: "Les bons chiens," for example, where he speaks characteristically of his "muse citadine," is rambling and overly personal but points in passages to the best the new manner can do.

The critical fads and approaches will slip around him and fade in time: this lucid, suffering, exquisitely sensitive, and indispensable Baudelaire will remain.

The Mallarmé Century

It is only in fairly recent years that we have begun to appreciate the fuller scope of Mallarmé's genius. Not only was he the chief figure of a school but also of what gradually, under the guidance of Edmund Wilson in particular, we have come to see as a golden-age literary period of the ending nineteenth and beginning twentieth century: Symbolism. (René Wellek has added his scholarly touches and given his blessing to this full-blown entity of late.) Further, around 1940-1950, it began to dawn on a few that Mallarmé was the pivotal personality of what is amounting to a whole century of Western thought; literary thought primarily, but so thoroughly literary that it comes closer to being a spiritual revolution, involving practically all the arts and humanities.

In the introduction to his revised *Mallarmé*, Guy Michaud writes:

> On peut affirmer sans nulle exagération que Mallarmé, un demisiècle avant de Saussure, jetait à sa manière les fondements d'une linguistique structurale, qu'un siècle avant Lévi-Strauss et Gilbert Durand le "démon de l'analogie" le poussait à chercher ce qu'on appelerait aujourd'hui des isomorphismes entre les structures du langage, celle des mythes, celles de notre esprit et celles du monde, afin de saisir "l'ensemble des relations entre tout" et qu'un siècle également avant Barthes, il définissait à peu près le langage poétique comme une langue plurielle, d'une nature autre que celle du langage ordinaire. (Hatier-Boivin, 6)

As Léon Cellier observes in his opening remarks to the *Colloque Mallarmé* (Nizet, 1975): "Une telle orientation [la linguistique] faisait de Mallarmé le patron tout designé de la nouvelle critique, et, si l'on peut dire, un collaborateur de *Tel Quel*" (12).

Who might be a rival of Mallarmé for this central position? Ezra Pound, as Hugh Kenner proposes in *The Pound Era*, is an obvious candidate, but his significance tends to dwindle with time and, particularly, space, i.e., an international or comparative literature perspective. So it is

probably going too far to name an entire epoch after him. He was unquestionably a distinguished poet who exerted a key influence on diction:
through his tough-minded realism and plainness of speech, his understatement and hardness of line, he dialectically raised the presence of
imagery, a typically post-Laforguian and American effect. At the same
time, there is much that is mannered in him, superstitious of European
culture (even if he called it "kulcher"). Someone noted recently that the
newer French poets maintain a rural accent distinct from American
urban sophistication; we, Pound with us, can afford less to be natural,
running, like James and Eliot, after European deeply-historical refinement (though occasionally, Pound with us, we are ostentatiously ourselves). Pound's critical influence on Eliot was impressive. But, as Harry
Levin remarks in "The Wasteland from Ur to Echt," Pound never really
made it into the big forms as compared to Eliot, Valéry, Rilke, Joyce,
Proust; the *Cantos* lack a compelling coherence, and the political attitudes are obtrusive, not-thought-through, even sophomoric. Pound himself, as quoted in William Chace's *The Politics of Eliot and Pound*,
admitted not long before he died that the meaner aspects of his pro-
fascist stand were silly.

It happens that Pound read the *Coup de dés* early, in the 1897 *Cos-
mopolis* version, as he informed the de Campos brothers of São Paulo in
a series of letters from 1955-1959.[1] In the last one he mentions "les
expériences initiées par Mallarmé avec un coeur pur." Previously he had
"ignored Mallarmé" in his essays on French poetry, as Eliot says in his
preface to *The Literary Essays of Ezra Pound*. With that we can drop
Pound from our purview. Kenner himself is highly respectful of the revolution Mallarmé wrought, comparing him, like Edmund Wilson, to
Einstein.

In *Axel's Castle* (1931) Edmund Wilson laid the groundwork for our
perspective, particularly in America, but Mallarmé, who is seen as a *fons
et origo*, remains a rather shadowy figure in this book. Let's face it:
Wilson was temperamentally incapable of doing full justice to Mallarmé
or, for that matter, to Proust or Valéry. Wilson, like Sartre, was too
much of a moralist, in the ordinary sense, and a social critic, slightly
Marxist, at that. And besides, much of the fuller Mallarmé flowering
occurred after he wrote. Still, we Americans owe him a considerable debt
for this inspired attempt as well as his generous overall critical
performance. If Mallarmé remains vague in *Axel's Castle*, that is hardly
surprising in any case since we are only now beginning to understand

---

[1] See Haroldo de Campos, "Pound Made (new) in Brazil," in *Ezra Pound* 1 (Paris: Les
Cahiers de l'Herne, 1965).

him at all fully. What was Mallarmé's basic contribution? Very summarily, we can say this: Western thought and literature evolves through an increasing dialectical emphasis on negation and/or nothingness. Along this route we might mention, swiftly, Descartes's radical doubt and *tabula rasa*; Hegel's pure negation (which is the essence of an identity) and the modern absurdists and dark-toned existentialists insisting, like Sartre, on Nothingness. Today, with Derrida, we are apt to speak of a "deconstructive" philosophical mood of which the phrase "emptier than thou" has become wryly characteristic. In this sense, Kierkegaard exerted a radical negation, a critique, on Hegel's panlogicism, and in a little-read work entitled *Philosophical Fragments* there is a chapter entitled "The Absolute Paradox" which points straight to the Mallarmé revolution, more specifically than Nietzsche (who is however, in his frenzied ironies and critique of Western constructs—including time—very much in the general picture).

In "The Absolute Paradox" Kierkegaard describes a basic paradox—the problem of evil in a good God—and then, in a desperately honest maneuver, instead of resolving it, *squares* it, plunges deeper into the problem. We might call this "paradox squared" or "paradox of paradox," but at any rate we now have, instead of a bipolar paradox such as Zeno's (between continuity and discontinuity) or the free-determined antinomy, a four-polar one, which we can call "tetrapolar." It is easy to see how a persistently anguished and self-contentious spirit could plunge further into "polypolarity," but we have problems enough already with this one crucial step, this *salto vitale*.

In the center is a zero or infinite (as in the Cartesian coordinate axes), which is the source of further paradoxical dimensions and/or of fallible resolutions. Catholics may think of the hands conjoined in the quintessential amen after the Father-son vertical axis and the Holy-spirit horizontal tracing a cross on the upper body; the hands can be separated opening things anew (in a characteristic Italian *è*), theoretically.

For the purposes of our historical perspective, what counts is the depth of Mallarmé's dive into the zero point of "origin" (which term as we have just implied is problematic, i.e., the modern problem of origins) which goes farther than Kierkegaard's, since the latter settles for a "leap" to God at this "quintessential" point. Mallarmé opens things up more uncompromisingly, in texts like *Igitur*, the *Coup de dés*, and a fragment entitled "Le Rien" published in the *Revue de l'Histoire Littéraire de la France* (October-December 1964) with notes by J.-P. Richard. He not only goes farther down and in, but he manages to formulate the experience more lucidly; he comes up with the archetypal human drama of knowing and being most compellingly and lastingly. It was, first, the so-human, childish "coeur sans défense" *tentativeness*, his uncluttered availability, his utter unwillingness to be duped by any imposed consolatory construct—Camus has familiarized us with this in the term "leap"; the youth like the slang "cop-out"—and, second, the ambitious conception of a totalizing *Grand Oeuvre* that caused Maurice Blanchot to single him out as the key figure on the threshold of the twentieth century as Hegel was for the nineteenth (see *L'Entretien infini* 621). And it will cause Barthes to say, in an "Interview with Stephen Heath," "all we do is repeat Mallarmé. And we do very well when it is Mallarmé that we repeat." Derrida certainly looks to Mallarmé for his deeper deconstructions of Hegel, for example, in his invented term "la différance" which involves a horizontal vibrancy of time (deferral) and a vertical one of distinction in space, the two paradoxical axes vibrating irresolvably together as in Mallarmé's sketches for an ideal Drama in *Le Livre*. This can be seen in various ways: for example, if the basic Hegelian pattern is the triad, which he discusses and defends in the closing pages of *The Logic*, and if we put this in the simplified popular form of thesis-antithesis-synthesis, it is the settling for a final synthesis as the limit of this system which makes Hegel vulnerable to the deconstruction of Derrida (Kristeva, etc.), as they add, initially, a fourth pole to the three. In this sequential approach to the tetrapolarity (which has affinities to Nietzsche's Eternal Return), I proposed the term "anti-synthesis" for the fourth pole, in my *Oeuvre de Mallarmé* (1951). I still think it is useful, but although Derrida refers to it in *La Dissémination* it has not attained general currency.

Another way to look at the tetrad is the "symphonic equation proper to the seasons" which Mallarmé announced in *La Musique et les Lettres* as the armature of his future Great Work and which is incarnated in his sketch for that Work, the *Coup de dés*. Here we are on better-known terrain: the opening of a new literary space with the *Coup de dés* through an added vertical dimension, analogous to the harmonic dimension of music. As is well known, the *Coup de dés* is read partly like a musical score, with parallel lines, intermittently, along with the normal monolinear text. The page tries to become a simultaneity, and Mallarmé's aesthetic can be called "constellatory": the words relate to each other in all directions almost as freely as stars do in gravitational space; hence, for example, "les mots, d'eux-mêmes, s'exaltent de mainte facette reconnue la plus rare ou valant pour l'esprit, centre de suspens vibratoire... réciprocité de feux distante...," etc. ("Crise de vers").

It will readily be seen that this new vertical emphasis is a movement toward holism (simultaneity), which it achieves in vibrant combination with the traditional horizontal linear dimension of the text. The vertical impulse is already a movement to the origins, baptismally, so to speak, for a rebirth, a new consciousness, a revolt bringing a new wholeness of fresh being, originality in a rich sense. But, paradoxically, it is through renewed dialectical commerce with the horizontal, which defers and completes it, that the fuller literary simultaneity, or total vision, occurs in time. And this is the eventual stance of the Mallarméan symbol, of symbolism, today, as seen by Guy Michaud and others. The modern linguists are apt to use metaphor and metonymy for the two axes. Again it is evident that the initial plunge into simultaneity in the structural language-system of Saussure, followed by reintegrations with the dia-chronic in subsequent linguists, e.g., Jakobson, are in this pattern.

The well-known *suggestion* of Mallarmé is an extension of this new global reality, i.e., the constellatory field of force on the page involves the overtones of words (echo-sounds, "puns," anagrams, etc.) in a *Jeu su-prême*. The faint overtones, suppressed in previous *ad hoc* discourse, emerge to the attentive playful ear as they marry each other in pure musical-verbal space. Or the delicate myriad events on the page attract each other through "universal analogy," to put it in a Baudelairian way.

The eventual impact of all this is simply enormous, from Marinetti through Apollinaire's *Calligrammes*, cubism, concrete poetry, structural-ism, the new novel, where do we start or stop? Mallarmé's plunge into this intimate drama at the heart of reality was, sort-of, like cracking the atom. The modest, discreet little man went down into a tiny evanescent dot of pure phenomenon that, on our controlled days, continues to fission productively and, on festive days, explodes into a dazzling fire-works that illuminates the century artistically and intellectually.

Mallarmé was conscious, positively and negatively, of the drastic impact of his spiritual revolution and at times saw himself as a Saint John the Baptist preparing the way for a messiah: the mysterious and awesome tones accompanying the apparition of Saint John, in the frag-ments of *Hérodiade* written not long before Mallarmé's death, together with passages of the *Coup de dés*, are quite indicative. But, in a way, this was self-protective strategy. If only metaphorically—there is no use blinding oneself to the possibilities of ridiculously pretentious exaggera-tion here (Mallarmé himself kept his sense of humor at such junctures, as in the passage of "Crise de vers" which warns about taking oneself for God); and I am not for a moment suggesting that we erect Mallarmé into a cult-leader—if only metaphorically, I repeat, Mallarmé is more

usefully seen as the discreet, obscure, almost unread, arcane, secret figure
that haunts Wilson's early pages and many another allusive and reveren-
tial text including Valéry's, a sort of literary *deus absconditus*, a modest
near-nothingness from which, like the *lux candida*, all the colors and
phenomena seem to emanate. As in Pound's cited remark ("coeur pur")
or Valéry's "Mallarmé le plus pur... de tous ceux qui ont tenu la plume,"
there is something stubbornly appropriate at work here, and I suggest we
work with it for a while.

To Valéry, he was easily the Father-spirit and a mysteriously transcendent one. Valéry was his favorite son, no question. He preserved the
pure vision like an intact egg, and passed it on at the nothing-core of his
Introduction à la méthode de Léonard de Vinci, where all the spokes of
dazzling doing radiate like Mallarmé's famous web at the center of which
he saw himself as a "sacred spider" (one thinks of Bergmann's God-
spider in *Through a Glass Darkly*: it goes back farther also, to the Vedas).
He often spoke of Mallarmé with utter piety: "I don't know what I
would have become without him" and the like.[2] Valéry seemed to make
him incarnate—in the limited sense of more ordinary presence, horizontally, so to speak—getting into the Academy, becoming an official
figure almost like Hugo, playing around with commissions and the
ladies. I do not mean to deprecate Valéry at all, he is conceivably our best
twentieth-century poet. But, as I have tried to show elsewhere, the established critics—Raymond, Bowra, Winters, even Burke—have gotten this
key relationship all wrong up until fairly recently when the tide has
turned radically in this respect. I said Valéry *seemed* to make Mallarmé
incarnate: the important point here is that Mallarmé is both *more mental
and physical* than Valéry in his creative moments—like the *faune*, demigod above, goat below—and is a more poetic poet in this sense. The
extreme vertical psychic dimension—daemonic, eternal-romantic—mag-
netizes the horizontal—normal, eternal-classic—into a new globality of
musical space, and in terms of the immense tension between poles and
axes it spirally resolves provisionally, like galaxies or crystals into a sort of
healing tissue, *aufgehoben*, crystallized on the page so solidly that, to use
MacLeish's time-tried language, it "walks off of it," not meaning but
being. Mallarmé is the more original (partly but not mainly because he
preceded) and necessary of the two. Valéry was a maker, *homo faber*,
more classic or neo-classic, scientific or technical (Mallarmé never would
have referred to a poem as a "machine"), more ordinarily melodious and

---

[2]At a Mallarmé session of the *Association Internationale des Études Françaises* a few sum-
mers ago, Valéry's daughter was there with the same close-set blue eyes and the same
rapt expression when the master's name was mentioned.

less crystallized, more histrionic, *bel canto*, linear operatic and operational, etc. As Thibaudet put it, Mallarmé's images slowly emerge like
stalactites from the tragic life-matrix. That is why Bachelard, in *L'Eau et
les rêves* sees Mallarmé as *the* poet of elemental imagery, why Ponge, with
his bias for things, sees Mallarmé as his direct forbear.

Of course there are advantages to Valéry's position, and he needs no
defending. He wrote more, and he invented timbres and transitions of
his own. He had an admirable sense of limit, which Victor Brombert, in
a Valéryan essay in *Hudson Review* rightly sees as linked to his poise and
grace and, one might add, survival into old age. Mallarmé risked more
and was closer to the pulse of things. His unprecedentedly sensitive,
responsive use of language, his diction, clearly is extended by his disciple:
few can read the *Narcisse* poems without being at least subconsciously
aware that the same phonostylistics are at work as in the *Faune* which
Valéry (who had, according to Mondor, a weak memory) knew by heart.
Likewise for *Hérodiade* and *La Jeune Parque* (also in terms of theme,
imagery, etc.). A perceptive reader like Gide, in his *NRF* anthology,
could see that. Now I can hardly go over the many facets of the reci-
procities of this remarkable duo here. I just want to observe that the
mainstream of modern sensibility passes through these two points and
the subject is still wide-open and immensely appetizing. No one, so far as
I know, has done real justice to the relation of Mallarmé's deepest
thought to Valéry's more-scientific formulations, such as his thermo-
dynamic metaphors.

For example, in the well-known CEM from the *Cahiers*—standing for
corps, esprit, monde—the triad is evidently vulnerable to a tetradic critique. In some places, as in the third of the *Petits poèmes abstraits*,[3] Valéry
moves to a tetradic perspective as Hegel also does at times and equally
unsteadily. In the case of Valéry, the two poles of mind and body oscil-
late between two positions, positive and negative. But this does not reach
the lucidity and centrality of the pattern in Mallarmé's theories and texts.
All this needs to be put into perspective by someone who will take the
trouble to rethink Mallarmé and not just rely on his difficulty, and the
related ignorance of most critics and readers, to persuade the public that
the more accessible Valéry invented the wheel. An understandable yet
very real bad faith has been at work here for too long. But as in the case
of the poetry the tide will turn here, too, as it has begun to do with
Derrida and the *Tel Quel* group, and a number of thoughtful critics
around the world. It is Mallarmé who is now considered to be the

---

[3]See Ursula Franklin's brilliant study of Valéry's prose *aubades*, published by the University of Toronto Press.

turning point by some leading thinkers—Blanchot, Sartre, Foucault, Barthes—and it is only a matter of time until the others get around to accepting this and showing how it is spelled out in detail.

Similarly, if Valéry's emphasis on interpretive relativism and demythified ideas of literary "production" make him the father of the new criticism, as Ralph Freedman (in *Modern French Criticism*, ed. Simon) and René Girard (disapprovingly, *passim*) see it, this has to be reconciled to Barthes's truer view which goes back to the source. Here again, the key point is that Mallarmé goes farther in both directions than his disciple: he is both more open and closed, in terms of meaning, both more objective (like Poe) and subjective or personal, in terms of creation. His world is infinitely wild yet meaningful, mobile yet stable. Thus he said to Ghil, "On ne peut se passer d'Eden," and to Jean Royère, "Le monde sera sauvé par la littérature." Despite the endless odds he himself proposed, he *believed*. Far out enough there was a constellation, *peut-être*, an Edenic point *toward* which, *VERS*. Though you could never get there, it was there, glimpsable, or out there somewhere and magnetic to faith. That is why Mallarmé is always *present* (to use Mikel Dufrenne's favorite aesthetic term), an exquisite poet, and because he believes we believe and are willing to go on for years looking for better meaning in and through him (if anyone's view is as good as another's, why bother?). Although Valéry was really better than his doctrine here, *malgré lui*, still this provides at least some hint of why René Char thinks of him as a *faiseur* compared to Mallarmé. Bonnefoy similarly. And this is why Nathalie Saurraute in her article "Valéry et l'enfant d'éléphant" (*Temps modernes* 16 [1947]) sees Valéry as somewhat academic, neo-classic, and gives a considerable boost to a fuller, comparatively seminal role for Mallarmé from that time on. A year later, Pierre Schneider wrote a parallel piece for *Yale French Studies*, entitled "Notes on the Exquisite Corpse." Valéry's flirtation with right-wing attitudes during the Dreyfus affair had some bearing here, but Valéry was no Pound and we ought not to dwell on this momentary naïveté which could befuddle Proust, too, at times. At any rate, Mallarmé came out of this trial smelling like absent roses: he usually sympathized with underdogs, including Dreyfus (according to Thadée Nathanson, writing in *La Nef*, in February, 1949) and was altogether *chic*.[4]

[4]Anyone planning further work on Mallarmé-Valéry ought to start with the article by James Lawler in *Yale French Studies* 44. Mallarmé's one antisemitic reference (in his Villiers lecture) was to a pleasantry of his deceased friend, Villiers, about Catulle Mendès: it is very mild and mitigated by the circumstances. As Bettina Knapp documents in her *Céline*, it is incredible how many great French writers were virulently antisemitic on occasion. The contrary is rare.

Near to Valéry, among those identified as being in the symbolist wake by Edmund Wilson, is Proust. I have tried to do some justice to the relationship in my article "Proust and Mallarmé" in *French Studies* 24.3 (Oxford). Although Baudelaire's more anecdotally human wrestling with evil reassured him more fraternally, warmly, and was linked with the important theme of memory, still, in terms of ambitious artistic vision, in scope, coherence, and depth, Mallarmé's impact on Proust was unsurpassed. Mallarmé springs up under his pen at crucial moments of his wavering career-strength, for example, in *Contre Saint-Beuve*: Mallarmé stands there for a steadfast faith in art, along with Flaubert, as Proust hesitates to plunge into the ocean of the "cold feary father" along which he Oedipally passes in that dream sequence of *Du Côté de chez Swann*. A comparable obsession is in his preface to *Tendres stocks* by Paul Morand, where he contrasts Stendhal's personal exploitation of art to Mallarmé's position. Proust, who showed up at the *mardis* on occasion and was a sort of rival for the attention of Méry Laurent, absorbed the Mallarméan climate in all sorts of ways; this is mainly a matter of the general aesthetic which we outlined earlier and which had become dominant by the end of the nineteenth century when Proust was beginning to write in earnest.

Then there was Gide, who attended the *mardis* faithfully and wanted to become to the novel what Mallarmé was to poetry; a symbolist novelist. He partly did, as Ralph Freedman shows in his *The Lyrical Novel*, with the *en abyme* vertical concern of *Les Faux-Monnayeurs* in particular and a certain tender transparency of style, fresh and pristine as *Apparition*, at his best. Gide kept the faith all the way: despite some leanings in the new, horizontal, Rivière direction—the novel of adventure, *engagement*, etc.—he resigned from the *NRF* in protest against a *lèse*-Mallarmé piece by Marc Bernard. Near the end of his long life, writing for a Joyce exhibition catalogue (La Hune, 1949), he saw the master, like Joyce, like Beethoven, as one who had *dared* not only in his strong early years but, more courageously, at the end. And he spoke of the *Coup de dés* with rare penetration: "one of the extreme points to which the human spirit has ventured."

Alain-Fournier, that ephemeral field-flower of French finesse and intimate sensitivity, owed much to Mallarmé's atmosphere, along with Debussy. But we must move on, regretfully. Rivière, his brother-in-law, sought his independence from the "hothouse" of symbolism and set a tone for a whole string of devil's advocates; but he knew better, and there are expressions of amends later. The usual tactic of the "brood of mockers" is to set up strawmen, lesser, paler symbolists like Régnier, and assume Mallarmé is floored when they are knocked down. But they are a minor diversion.

Claudel came near to being Mallarmé's favorite for a while; until that singularly brutal letter in which he announced his allegiance to Rimbaud, who was closer to his peasant temperament. Still, despite his lumpish religious bias, Claudel always appreciated Mallarmé's total questioning ("qu'est-ce que cela veut dire?"). His use of language and his analysis in *Les Mots Anglais* worked powerfully on Claudel, who evokes this in his *Entretiens* (avec Amrouche). But Claudel's prejudices always end by spoiling things: his "Catastrophe d'Igitur" is a monstrous distortion. To make the author of the sun-drenched *Après-midi d'un faune*, the Monet-like *Nénuphar blanc*, or the nature-worshipping *La Gloire* into a poet—even primarily—of the indoors is singularly obtuse and mean-spirited. Even the *Coup de dés* is a cosmic oceanscape, storm-swept, like *A la nue accablante tu*. Claudel was a good poet in a Whitmanesque way, but almost no one takes his ideas seriously any more; Camus called him *un esprit vulgaire*, and there may be something to it.

Off to Ireland and Yeats, who learned to admire Mallarmé early from Gosse and Symons and admitted an influence on his *Wind among the Reeds* (see his *Ideas of Good and Evil*). Later, he veered away to folk speech and legends—Mallarmé in his Wagner essay felt that legends weren't right for his French genius—plus Irish politics and rag-and-bone humble imagery, dry realities in the direction of T. E. Hulme, Laforgue, Pound, Eliot, the Imagists. But in later years he reminisced admiringly about Mallarmé, and on the whole I think Wilson and others were right to see him in the symbolist lineage primarily. He liked ambitious vision, mystic universal analogies along with his precisions and intimacies. He was wonderfully naïve in this sense, not at all your facile debunking sophisticate; neither, come to think of it, was the best Laforgue, who objected to a compulsive defensive irony in Corbière and regarded Mallarmé as a sort of Buddha, loved him for his autumn moods and his generosity of soul. Laforgue was aiming in that general direction with his longer poems like *L'Hiver qui vient* when he died, too young.

Which brings us naturally to Eliot. He classed Mallarmé with his cherished "metaphysical" poets in a 1926 article (*NRF*), high praise indeed. But he initially went the Laforgue route and attacked Valéry's poetics on this score in his preface to the *Art of Poetry* (Vintage). Yet at the end, as Hugh Kenner agrees, Mallarmé is a powerful presence in the *Four Quartets*, which to me are the ripest expression of Eliot's towering talent. These things are well known, and I brush on rapidly past that "familiar compound ghost" from *Burnt Norton,* citing the line about "purifying the dialect of the tribe."

Joyce? He copied some of Mallarmé's *Poésies* into his Trieste notebook; Mallarmé's "Hamlet" haunts pages of *Ulysses,* and there are echoes of the *Faune* as well. David Hayman, in his *Joyce et Mallarmé,* has shown the parallels between the two aesthetics and the two supreme visions of the *Coup de dés* and *Finnegans Wake.* There are some direct echoes of the former in the latter. Thomas Hanson has found some other convincing vestiges of the *Coup de dés* in *Ulysses,* according to his recent article in *Yale French Studies* 54 ("Mallarmé's Hats"). Philippe Soupault told Hayman that Joyce had owned a copy of the final Poem. More enigmatically, an acquaintance informed me that, according to Beckett, Joyce "froze" at the mention of Mallarmé. What does that mean? It could betoken awe, pique, who knows what? Something in any case.

Once again, Wilson's insights were sound. Joyce, as Harry Levin claimed in his little book on Joyce (which won Joyce's approval) is a combination of symbolism and naturalism, though I prefer symbolist-realist. Surely he owes a lot to the symbolist heritage: for example, he is known to have admired Valéry's *Ébauche d'un serpent* exceedingly; Adrienne Monnier so informed me personally in 1950.[5]

Even Faulkner is somewhere in our picture: his early poetic efforts, *A Greening Bough,* are touched here and there by reminiscences of the *Faune.*

Moving to the poets proper, the influence of Mallarmé's pioneering poetics on figures such as Stefan George, Rilke, Apollinaire, Ungaretti, Guillen, Ponge, Emmanuel, Bonnefoy, and Michel Deguy is well established and hardly needs going over here. Wallace Stevens deserves special mention since he has been called the "Mallarmé in Hartford" with some aptness. The globality and transparency of Mallarmé, his wintry purities, his musical allusions, much else has passed fruitfully to the American. Ungaretti interests me here for personal reasons: not long before the Italian master died, he honored me with a series of letters in which he stated how profoundly Mallarmé had influenced his thought and poetry. These letters were published in *Forum Italicum* 6.4 and 8.1, with a commentary by Giovanni Cecchetti; they will be republished in the collected correspondence being issued by Mondadori, with the notes. Mallarmé was one of Ungaretti's two prime masters (the other being Leopardi). Among his closest friends was Jorge Guillen, perhaps the greatest living Spanish poet, who was my teacher at Yale and whom I remember with

---

[5]She also said that Joyce spoke an "adorable" French and that he showed little interest in the work of others, e.g., Larbaud. She thought him altogether an excessive figure.

admiration and affection. About a year ago he wrote me as follows: "Mallarmé! Il reste toujours à sa place, au premier rang de la poésie moderne. Vous me parlez d'un cours sur le symbolisme. En effet, notre origine à tous est là."

Concerning the theater, Haskell Block, in his *Mallarmé and the Symbolist Drama*, writes: "Mallarmé's observations on the theater... are as stimulating and pertinent today as when they were written, and we may find them at the origin of much of the reflection on the drama in our time... For Mallarmé, the theater is coexistent with the whole of experience, a momentary revelation of the mystery of existence, a clue to its ultimate meaning..." (134). Lugné-Poe and his *Théâtre de l'Oeuvre*, Maeterlinck, and Claudel were his immediate heirs; but Hoffmanstahl, Yeats, Strindberg, Lorca, Ghelderode, and Beckett are part of the extended heritage, according to Block. The related streams of the "theater of silence," the new metaphysical depth and stark absurdist reality, the poetic language emerging from such steep hushes, all this is in the symbolist wake. In *Waiting for Godot* we may recognize Didi-Gogo, Pozzo-Lucky as a "tetrapolarity," the spare sort of dramatic armature Mallarmé aimed at in his essays on theater, a stripped modern *mystère*, haunted by an older cross. Rosette Lamont finds a similar impact on Ionesco's plays.[6]

Walter Sokel, the leading Kafka authority, considers his man to be a symbolist, if only because of the verbal origin of meaning. Sokel deems Mallarmé, along with Joyce, to be central to our time. When René Wellek, in a speech at Stanford, defined the symbolist literary period (now a chapter in *Discriminations*), I suggested to him, during the question period, that an era really could be fully distinguished only in relation to what followed it, and I asked what, in his opinion, on a comparable scale, came after. He thought for a moment and answered, in approximately the following words: "the allegorical movement, represented by Kafka." Although he did not specify further, the Kafka-Bataille-Blanchot-Beckett-Broch "absurdist" line may have been what he had in mind, related to the formulation of J. Guglielmi in *Synthèses* 258-259: 69-71: "Au centre du tetraède Lautréamont-Roussel-Kafka-Joyce brille l'impersonnelle lucidité mallarméenne." But I don't see that stripped stance as a rounded movement comparable to symbolism. Besides, all the later figures are still steeped in symbolism, haunted by it; they seem rather in a "neo" relationship to it. Kafka is too puzzling, marginal, and abstract to constitute a convincing *Zeitgeist*, even with partial assists from the above-mentioned people.

[6]In *Ionesco: A Collection of Critical Essays* (Reading, Mass.: Prentice-Hall, 1973).

One notes that the great Kafka and symbolist critic Walter Benjamin, to quote Hannah Arendt (preface to *Illuminations*, Schocken Books): "places at the center of his essay, 'The Task of the Translator,' the astonishing quotation from Mallarmé in which the spoken languages in their multiplicity and diversity suffocate, as it were, by virtue of their Babel-like tumult, the 'immortelle parole' which cannot even be thought, since 'thinking is writing without implement or whispers, silently...'." And Arendt sums up Benjamin's critical aim as being to "think poetically," in the context of Mallarmé.[7]

With Kafka we can pass to the new novel. The following opinion by Karlheinz Stierle is fairly representative: "Among those who inspired the latest nouveau roman, Mallarmé with his poetics of 'fiction' is probably the most essential" (*Yale French Studies* 54: 115). We observe, in passing, that the poetics of "fiction" is outlined in our earlier remarks on his aesthetics (the zero-based openness, paradox, etc.); the term "fiction" (as "le procédé même de l'esprit") is used in this sense in the *Notes*, published in the *Oeuvres complètes*, toward a linguistic theory (which was really an epistemology, *pure* theory).

Sarraute has already been mentioned for her article on Valéry. In a similar vein, a character in *Les Fruits d'or* (1963) says: "C'est aussi grand que Mallarmé... c'est bien plus fort que Valéry" (104). Robbe-Grillet, following a speech he gave at Stanford in 1963, told me that as a prose-writer he felt he was in Flaubert's lineage but that had he been a poet he would look back more directly to Mallarmé. I showed my puzzlement by citing "On ne peut se passer d'Eden" and asking him if he subscribed to that, which he obviously didn't. He looked as uncomfortable as a devil on whom holy water had been thrown and soon left the gathering. Years later, I wondered if his cinematic "l'Eden et après" (which could be translated "Eden so what") had anything to do with that wet-blanket episode.

The Cuban writer Severo Sarduy has adopted Mallarmé's mobile-page idea, from *Le Livre*, in the form of a loose-leaf novel. Carlos Fuentes communicated with me to check on a reference to the circularity of a

---

[7]Kafka's symbolism is more abstract, less "present" than Mallarmé's, and it is colored by Jewish ethics, as Sokel agrees. A new book by Henri Pierresens, *La Tour de Babel*, continues Benjamin's Mallarméan concern with the *Ursprache* as magnet and impossibility; Mallarmé was not the first in this line, but he was certainly prominent for our era: both Valéry and Claudel, referring to his *Les Mots Anglais* in particular, see this concern as the core of his esthetic, or part of it. Genette's chapter on Mallarmé in his *Mimologiques* shows remarkable misunderstanding of Mallarmé's position here (see my article, "Mallarmé contre Genette," *Tel Quel* [Spring, 1977]).

work in Mallarmé's writings. Borges, Sollers, Haroldo de Campos, other *Tel Quellistes* are in this fictive lineage.

As for the critics, Thibaudet owes his great reputation to his trail-blazing *La Poésie de Stéphane Mallarmé* as much as to anything. And what would the dean of French criticism, Blanchot, be without Mallarmé? All his theorizing about the Great Work turns on Mallarmé's theory and practice. Bachelard, as I noted, singles out Mallarmé as *the* poet of elemental imagination (in *L'Eau et les rêves*); he authored a fine essay on his dynamic imagery in *Le Point* (Lanzac, 1946). Poulet's *Studies in Human Time* features two major essays on Mallarmé, who brings out his worthiest efforts. Poulet switched his views from one to the other essay; in the meantime, he had discovered the polydimensional thought of Mallarmé, particularly in *Igitur,* and so evolved with the century in this direction. Mauron's psychocriticism grew out of his work on Mallarmé. Richard came *enfin*; his masterwork, one of the critical monuments of our time, is certainly his *Univers imaginaire de Mallarmé.* But crossing into structuralism, Derrida (along with Genette) takes Richard to task for being a bit old hat, settling for synthetic resting places like *le bonheur* or fixed imagery such as *le blanc, le pli* which Derrida keeps implacably moving like all his uncompromising universe of thought (see *La Dissémination,* Part II). Barthes was the bellwether of the newest criticism; he goes back to Mallarmé for support in his struggle with Raymond Picard; Part II of *Critique et vérité* leans very heavily on the master. And as we noted, he believes that "all we do is repeat Mallarmé" in our century and he is grateful for the fact. The semiotician he admires most, Julia Kristeva—I am also among her admirers—puts Mallarmé at the center of her most ambitious book, *La Révolution du langage poétique.* Her husband, Philippe Sollers, has written key essays on a Mallarmé for our time. Derrida, loosely associated with their group and probably the most influential philosopher-critic writing in France today, is very much in the tradition of Mallarméan thought. *La Dissémination,* particularly Parts II and III, is much taken with the thought-play that I have called "polypolar," and he refers often to his great ancestor. In a different vein, *Glas* probably could not have existed without *Les Mots anglais,* e.g.: "G... une aspiration simple... le désir comme satisfait par 1, exprime avec la dite liquide, joie, lumière, etc." Derrida quotes this as part of a network of associations which he finds running seminally through the writings of Genet. I am convinced that the *glaïeuls* of Mallarmé's *Prose (pour des Esseintes)* and the "gloire du long désir" from the same have important bearing on this influence (Genet is intimately linked with Mallarmé's aesthetic in Sartre's study of the former).

Sartre, in his preface to the Gallimard pocket edition of the *Poésies*, says of Mallarmé: "Héros, prophète, mage et tragédien, ce petit homme féminin, discret, peu porté sur les femmes mérite de mourir au seuil de notre siècle: il l'annonce. Plus et mieux que Nietzsche il a vécu la mort de Dieu; bien avant Camus, il a senti que le suicide est la question originelle que l'homme doit se poser; sa lutte de chaque jour contre le hasard, d'autres la reprendront sans dépasser sa lucidité." At times, for Sartre (according to the back of the Gallimard edition of Mondor's *Eugène Lefébure*) he was the greatest French poet. But Sartre's emphasis on praxis and *engagement*, virility and dynamism, his neo-Marxism, mar his literary judgments more and more as he goes on. His bias for a horizontal movement toward a working-class, utopian future brings forth pat, predictable notions, both in the preface and the Genet study, about Mallarmé's bourgeois status, his passivity, his nineteenth-century limitations à la Baudelaire, Flaubert, Proust. He is too self-involved as contrasted to the wildly dynamic and politically-*révolté* Rimbaud. All this is quite shallow and arbitrary, based on stereotypical half-truths. For example, Rimbaud's lyric world depends on static epiphanies, hierarchized metaphors, universal analogy, symbolism, in large part. What is "l'aube exaltée ainsi qu'un peuple de colombes" if not a simile, and metaphoric in essence; what is the drunken boat if not a multileveled symbol? And where is the man going who said "on ne part pas" and described action as a "way to waste some energy"? Who really cares about Rimbaud's inchoate politics or his ignorant, immature, often loutish attitude toward women? His fantastic genius is elsewhere.

Sartre's essay on Mallarmé says nothing new but exhibits his usual sure touch of compulsively virtuoso, *normalien* brilliance. It misses the tone of Mallarmé, the magnificently concrete, present poet, by a wide margin, as Bonnefoy agrees. Sartre has never penetrated into the depths of Mallarmé's thought, the new dimensions of paradox and the more thoroughly charted and structured cosmos which emerges from it. He abdicates before the *Coup de dés*, considers the *Grand Oeuvre* to be a "mystification." All he knows is some generalizations he could have gleaned from Mondor's *Vie de Mallarmé* plus a few posthumous texts. Sartre once wrote a whole manuscript on the *Poésies* and lost it on a train, according to Simone de Beauvoir. I doubt that we have missed much. In 1950 I took a chapter of my unpublished *Oeuvre de Mallarmé* to the offices of *Les Temps modernes*; Merleau-Ponty expressed keen interest but said he couldn't use it since Sartre was working on Mallarmé. Obviously not much came of it... Still, Sartre is a powerful Somebody and an important *point de repère* for our twentieth-century view.

In 1949 Hugh Kenner, then a graduate student at Yale, came over from the English Department to see me. He had bought two copies of my just-out *Mallarmé's Un Coup de dés*, one for himself and one for his mentor Marshall McLuhan. McLuhan, according to Kenner, had written a terse message, upon receiving his copy: "Go see Cohn." I had no idea who Kenner was and only the vaguest awareness of McLuhan, gleaned from the pages of *Commonweal*. Kenner informed me that McLuhan was preparing a book on the *Poésies*. I informed Kenner that I was preparing one myself. For whatever reason, McLuhan seems to have abandoned his project, but there is no doubt that the general aesthetic and outlook of Mallarmé worked on him considerably and through him a large body of Western opinion.

Several years ago, I opened a copy of *La Quinzaine Littéraire* and came upon this in an article by Pierre Bernard: "Toute la typographie moderne vient de Mallarmé... Mallarmé ouvre à la typographie moderne une nouvelle dimension: l'espace. La révolution typographique vient de Mallarmé, affirme Jacques Damase dans une clairvoyante introduction... Cette révolution se poursuivra avec les poètes et les peintres: Tzara, Marinetti, Apollinaire, Kandinsky, Mondrian, Braque, Léger. Il y a un domaine où le structuralisme a toujours existé: c'est bien l'écriture et la typographie. Mallarmé a changé la structure de la page, il a brisé la marge, rompu la ligne." As I noted earlier, modern criticism—from Thibaudet through Poulet to Richard and Barthes—is mainly in a symbolist tradition. All branches of structuralist thought extend this heritage, as the foregoing article on print implies: for example, Haroldo de Campos, in his *Mallarmé*,[8] observes that Mallarmé's use of anagrams, and the critical work thereon, long precedes Saussure's and Starobinski's work.

In *From Symbolism to Structuralism* (Harper Torchbooks, 1972), James A. Boon links Lévi-Strauss to our perspective: in a chapter entitled "Mallarméan mythologiques" he draws convincing parallels, implying at least indirect influence on this highly cultured man who obviously enjoyed and occasionally commented in print on the major symbolists. In *Anthropologie structurale* he refers to Mallarmé's phonostylistics. His friend Jakobson had moved to add a diachronic dimension to the mono-linear Saussurean language structure and so worked toward the two-dimensional structure (or polydimensional), vibrantly interrelating the two axes, which is characteristic of later structuralist thought, including Lacan (who modifies Saussure's linear syntax in a parallel way, in "L'Instance de la lettre dans l'inconscient"). Lacan acknowledges his debt to Jakobson here. The best-known paradigm of this new awareness is the

[8](Editora da Universidade de São Paulo, 1974) 121.

famous metaphor-metonymy armature, further developed by Lacan in his new structuring of the ego, etc. Lacan, who is sometimes called a union of Mallarmé and Freud, writes much like the former and occasionally refers to him. Jakobson's classic essay on "Linguistics and Poetics" puts itself squarely in the Mallarméan heritage in respect to phonostylistics. In a recent letter, Jakobson sides with him against Genette and announces a forthcoming volume which will treat this subject *in extenso.*

Then there is Foucault in *Les Mots et les choses* (316): "la grande tâche à laquelle s'est voué Mallarmé, et jusqu'à la mort c'est elle qui nous domine maintenant, dans son balbutiement elle enveloppe tous nos efforts d'aujourd'hui pour ramener à la contrainte d'une unité peut-être impossible l'être morcelé du langage... A cette question nietzschéenne: qui parle? Mallarmé répond et ne cesse de reprendre sa réponse, en disant que ce qui parle, c'est en sa solitude, en sa vibration fragile, en son néant le mot lui-même—non pas le sens du mot, mais son être énigmatique et précaire..." One recognizes here not only the vast perspective that Mallarmé opens up in Foucault's mind but also in Lacan's neo-Freudian emphasis on the endless chain of signifiers, the symbolic chain, revealed particularly in the *ça parle* of the suffering unconscious. Foucault sees this open question and fragile Mallarméan answer leading, after the death of God, to the death of man, as a reassuring "this," a subject, as of modern anthropology. Derrida, awed by this same run-away perspective, is frightened by the prospect of a future monstrosity, in his contribution to *The Structuralist Controversy* ("Structure, Sign, and Play"). We shall return to this horizon-scanning in a moment.

According to André Levinson,[9] Mallarmé totally renewed the dance with his series of articles in *Divagations*. No more clutter of plot, no coy sentimentalities, but pure *play,* a *Jeu suprême* on the clean-swept stage. Nijinsky's ballet version of the *Faune* does not strike quite this tone but is worthy of passing mention, especially as it leads us to Debussy. His *Prélude à l'après-midi d'un faune* is generally considered to be the turning point of modern music.. It never really abandons traditional tonality but tests it to its utmost fluidity. In a remarkable article in *La Revue Musicale,* Paul Dukas observed that with Debussy, poetic *language,* singularly, introduced new timbres and effects into *music* (see Arthur Wenk, *Claude Debussy and the Poets,* California, 1976). As Leonard Bernstein in his fetchingly hammy way exclaimed in his TV series on modern music, "The Unanswered Question," after listening to a rendition of the *Faune:*

[9] "Mallarmé, métaphysicien du ballet," *Revue Musicale,* November 1, 1923, 21-23.

"Some crazy modern music!" And he demonstrated some connection with the text that inspired it. Has anything more reminiscent of Eden *ever* been composed? Ravel said he's like to die listening to it. He too set some Mallarmé poems to music, poignantly; so did Milhaud and Sauguet. Boulez has made Mallarmé his hallmark and tries to go Debussy, who haunts him, one better in closeness to the master, but I preferred the earlier, sweeter stage of things musically.

Mallarmé was the friend of many wonderful artists: Manet (whom he defended loyally in print), Monet, Renoir, Morisot, Degas; he knew Pissarro; Rodin came to his *mardis,* was at his funeral, and said sadly afterward: "How long will it take nature to make another spirit like that?" For Mallarmé, impressionism was "an effort to find again the ancient naïveté by superconscious means." That, in an article in *Les Mardis* entitled "Stéphane Mallarmé and the Artists of His Circle,"(The University of Kansas Museum of Art, misc. pubs. no. 61), sums up very well Mallarmé's attitude as expressed in his fine remarks on his contemporaries. He influenced Gauguin, who wrote from Tahiti: "my dream is not tangible, contains no allegory; a musical poem has no need of libretto, as quoted from Mallarmé." Mallarmé returned the compliment to Gauguin: "Il est extraordinaire qu'on puisse mettre tant de mystère dans tant d'éclat."

Redon, who was commissioned by his poet friend to illustrate the *Coup de dés,* was called "the Mallarmé of painting" by Maurice Denis. Others in his lineage were les Nabis: Serusier, Denis, Vuillard, Bonnard, Felix Valloton, Maillol, Verkade, Duchamp. Also Munch, who knew him, drew him, and developed a stark symbolist-expressionist style of his own, vaguely related to Bergmann's.

Henri Peyre, in his *Connaissance de Baudelaire,* tells us tantalizingly that Picasso first came to Paris largely because of Mallarmé. In "Picasso's Musical and Mallarméan Constructions," Ronald Johnson demonstrates Picasso's indebtedness to the *Coup de dés* for his dice theme and his general open aesthetic (*Arts Magazine* 5.51, March 1977). Kenneth Rexroth, who thinks the *Coup de dés* is the greatest poem ever, sees it leading to cubism: Picasso, Braque, Gris, and an allied movement in verse including Reverdy (see his translations of Reverdy, preface, *New Directions,* 1969). Some further connections to cubism are sketched in my "Mallarmé's Windows" (*Yale French Studies* 54). All this influence on highly present, sensual, often exquisite painters, musicians, poets, and page designers, nicely offsets the arid one-sided impression left by thinkers like Sartre and Foucault, with their rather brittle, cold, abstract, structuralist, or quasi-scientific half-truths.

The other half depends on the Mallarmé who said: "on ne peut se passer d'Éden" and "il faut penser de tout son corps" and "la nature existe" and "le monde sera sauvé par la littérature." He was consciously rooted in totality and, very far off in space-time was at one with it, through a sort of triangulation between himself, the objective world, and that remote It which, at the very least, like Saul Bellow in his Nobel address, he could claim with some conviction to have "glimpsed" in the greatest art. That is what his "c'eût été la vérité," "on aurait pu," "ce serait," and the like, mean, a hint of meaning in that modest yet real sense. He kept that beauty and faith for us well into the twentieth century so far. It is with this double, or whole-seeking truth—the unprecedented questioning *and* the unprecedented glow of the "Oui" (*Quand l'ombre menaça*)—that the century keeps resembling Mallarmé and promises to go on doing so, if it is lucky. Mallarmé, in "La Musique et les Lettres," outlined the epistemological core, or armature, of his future Great Work, of which the *Coup de dés* is a dazzling sketch—a glimpse— in these now well-known words: "la symphonique équation propre aux saisons." *O Saisons*! Mallarmé was a man for all of them.

Keats and Mallarmé

Keats and Mallarmé: the paired names spontaneously vibrate with a warm reciprocity, and one senses their nearness without any foreknowledge of whether the French poet was aware of the English one's existence. Still, to this day, very little has been done to explore their actual relationship in print. A single reference in Mondor's biography mentions *Endymion* as a possible source for the *Faune*; in his general study of Mallarmé, Kurt Wais traces some images of "Mes bouquins refermés" back to Keats's *Fancy* or *Sleep and Poetry*; Antoine Orliac, in his *Mallarmé tel qu'en lui-même*, observes some parallel aspects of their temperament and art; but, with one exception, there is nothing very specific.

Orliac rightly points to their joint fixation on Hamlet, their shared weight of sensuality, and their equal ambitions for art. The only specific reference has to do with a passage from Keats's correspondence which, without any proof, the critic claims Mallarmé must have read: "It seems to me that everyone can, like the spider, weave his own substance, his own airy citadel..." Orliac connects this with the famous passage in Mallarmé's 1866 letter to Aubanel, in which Mallarmé sees himself as a "sacred spider": "I wanted to tell you simply that I have just put down the plan of my whole Work, after having found the key to myself, capstone, or center, if you like, in order not to mix metaphors—center of myself, where I cling like a sacred spider, on the principal threads already issued from my spirit and by the means of which I will weave *at the points of juncture* marvelous lace, which I devine, and which exist already in the breast of Beauty."

This is suggestive; however, Mallarmé refers, unlike Keats, to a "sacred spider," which links his image to a mystic tradition going back to the Hindu Vedas. (I suppose we could put aside Swift's well-known metaphor for the same reason.) But even if Mallarmé did not read Keats's letter, Orliac was approaching here something quite essential in their real relationship. More on this in a moment.

It is surprising that some other, even more striking, points of contact have escaped critical notice: the theme of absence in "unheard melodies," which haunts the silent instruments of *Sainte* and many another Mallarméan image; the corollary theme of "disinterestedness," which finds its perfect expression in the "steadfast" star and the calm sea below, as it will again in the pure constellation of the *Coup de dés*. This anonymity in Keats's epitaph, "One whose name was writ in water," is reflected in "A la nue accablante tu," where nothing is left from a man's passing but the meaningless motion of waves. The distinction between poet and dreamer in *The Fall of Hyperion* has its counterpart in *Toast funèbre*. The curious *tribu* of the sonnet to Poe may go back to those bards of *Endymion* who left "great verse unto a little clan." Most compelling, and again virgin of mention, is the shared, infantile milk imagery: Keats, twice in *Endymion*, uses suckling as a metaphor of bliss; he wrote Fanny Brawne of his attempts to "wean himself" from her; and he refers to the imagination as being sucked from the "teat of the heart" by the mind. Such images are central to Mallarmé's art—*Les Fenêtres, Hérodiade, Don du poème*—as we have detailed in various studies.

Mallarmé himself has spoken of Keats only in his anthology, *Les Beautés de l'Anglais: Prose et vers*, a fragment of which has been recently published in Mondor's *Autres précisions sur Mallarmé et inédits*. It is brief but pithy. I give here all that was printed, noting that there is an indication of omitted portions: "Keats died in his twenty-fifth year from the shaft hurled by a hateful critic. Leigh Hunt and the scarce entourage of the sick young man for a long time were the only ones to admire him, together with Shelley who entombed this memory in an imperishable elegy... Beside some occasionally confused pilings-up of riches, such as might erect a child hurried by a brief destiny, there is in the unfinished work of Keats many a poem, pure, ardent, musical, where the most splendid imagination of the present wears at once the solemnity and the grace of antiquity." This puts Keats high indeed in Mallarmé's estimation and confirms the opinion I expressed on page 276 in *Toward the Poems of Mallarmé*: "This [ancient] image of a web or cross, passing through the 'rose-croix' of Dante, leads to Keats, the English poet of the nineteenth century nearest in spirit to Mallarmé: 'the wreathed trellis of a working brain' (*Ode to Psyche*); compare 'Cette poésie... trellis délicat et net tendu sur un azur connu... longues fleurs sortant de l'enlacement' (Letter to Albert Mérat, May 6, 1866, two months before the letter on the spider's web)."

The image of the web runs in varying forms throughout Mallarmé's writings. It is worth mentioning here because it is involved in a direct link between these incomparable two, traceable to a passage in *Sleep and Poetry*. I italicize the key passages:

> ...though no great minist'ring reason sorts
> Out the dark mysteries of the human soul
> To clear conceiving: yet there ever rolls
> A *vast idea* before me, and I glean
> Therefrom my liberty; *thence too I've seen*
> *The end and aim of Poesy.* 'Tis clear
> As anything most true; as that *the year*
> *Is made of the four seasons—manifest*
> *As a large cross,* some old cathedral's crest,
> Lifted to the white clouds. Therefore should I
> Be but the essence of deformity,
> A coward, did my very eye-lids wink
> At speaking out what I have dared to think.
> Ah! rather let me like a mad man run
> Over some precipice; let the hot sun
> Melt my Dedalian wings, and drive me down
> Convuls'd and headlong! *Stay! an inward frown*
> *Of conscience bids me be more calm awhile.*
> *An ocean dim, sprinkled with many an isle,*
> *Spreads awfully before me. How much toil!*
> How many days! what desperate turmoil!
> Ere I can have explored its widenesses.
> Ah, what a task! Upon my bended knees,
> I could unsay those—no, impossible!
> Impossible!
>   *For sweet relief I'll dwell*
> *On humbler thoughts...*

Here we have not only the "symphonic equation of the seasons" which Mallarmé, in *La Musique et les lettres,* put squarely at the center of his conception of his Work[1] and which shows up again and again in his sketches ("Le Livre") as a cross-pattern (or what may be called "tetra-polarity") but, further, the basic idea of *Prose (pour des Esseintes)* which I have identified, in various studies, as an interim report on why the Great Work was not forthcoming: the idea of the "*patience*" (or Keats's "calm") needed to accomplish the staggering task, the image of the isle of beauty rescued from the ocean of life, all is first in Keats. Here is the way Mallarmé began to put it:

---

[1]For an extensive study of this "equation" and of the work, see my *L'Oeuvre de Mallarmé: "Un Coup de dés"* (Paris, 1951) and *Mallarmé's Masterwork: New findings* (The Hague, 1966).

> Car j'installe, par la science,
> L'hymne des coeurs spirituels
> En l'oeuvre de ma patience...

In an essay entitled *Catholicisme*, Mallarmé links this "hymne," or Great Work, with the equation of the four seasons as follows: "Here recognize, henceforth, in true drama the passion, to enlarge the canonic conception or, as was the case with the festive aesthetic of the Church, and its revolving flashes of hymns, a human assimilation to the tetralogy of the Year."[2]

Returning to *Prose*, the vision as it was received by the astonished and overwhelmed Mallarmé is now put in the Keatsian metaphors of island and ocean:

> Oui, dans une île que l'air charge
> De vue...
> Parmi mon jeune étonnement
> D'ouïr tout le ciel et la carte
> Sans fin attestés sur mes pas,
> Par le flot même qui s'écarte...
> L'enfant abdique son extase...

We may translate roughly as follows:

> Yes, on an island that the air fills
> With view...
> Amid my youthful astonishment
> At hearing all the sky and the map
> Endlessly attested as I walk
> By the very [ocean] wave [meaningless chance
>   existence] which withdraws...
> The child abandons his ecstasy...

This last is exactly the return to "humbler thoughts," out of the same need; for, as with Keats, the vision "grandissait trop pour nos raisons" (*Prose*). And just as Mallarmé in his preface to the *Coup de dés* says that there is no reason to exclude such vast and ambitious subjects from "la Poésie—unique source," so Keats, with his "vast idea" before him, had proclaimed in precisely the same spirit, "thence too I've seen / The end and aim of Poesy."

In Book III of *Endymion*, Keats, scorning the empty pomp of kings and conquerors, hymns the ethereal powers to which the poet has access:

[2]An early image, in *La Symphonie littéraire*, prefigures the link between the rhythm of a hymn and that of a rose window: "un hymne... Le rythme de ce chant ressemble à la rosace d'une ancienne église..."

...there are throned seats unscalable
But by a patient wing, a constant spell,
Or by ethereal things that, unconfin'd,
Can make a ladder of the eternal wind,
And poise about in cloudy thunder-tents
To watch the abysm-birth of elements.

These powers dwell in the various elements; in Book III the search of the youthful hero, Endymion, for his love (the Moon, but by extension creative power) takes him through the realm of water, the ocean. There, in the depths, he sees

Rudders that for a hundred years had lost
The sway of human hand; gold vase emboss'd
With long-forgotten story
         ...mouldering scrolls,
Writ in the tongue of heaven, by those souls
Who first were on the earth...
  ...
     .... then skeletons of man...

This has some of the feel of Page 4 of the *Coup de dés*, where ancient man, as a hardy ancestor of the young poet-figure who slowly evolves (and includes him), is seen as a white-haired master of a symbolic boat with his "anciens calculs, la manoeuvre avec l'âge oubliée... jadis il empoignait la barre." On the next Page, his underwater skeleton is portrayed, "durs os perdus entre les ais."

Later, Endymion comes upon a sort of summation of the ancestral figures in the form of a sage, an old man of the sea, with white hair, wearing a magic cloak on which are woven all the archetypal forms of ocean movement (this is developed throughout the *Coup de dés*; incidentally, Joyce was planning a book in this vein just before his death). Like the master in Mallarmé's poem, he had been moved to hubris, a total *coup*, and was thereby doomed to a thousand-year spell under the water. For Keats, he has the ancient quality of a father spirit; Shakespeare is without doubt very much involved, recalling the oceanic father of "Full fathom five" and Prospero, who drowns his magic book.

The sage tells his story. One day he had witnessed a shipwreck where all hands were lost:

When at my feet emerg'd an old man's hand
Grasping this scroll, and this same slender wand.
I knelt with pain—reached out my hand—had grasped
These treasures—touched the knuckles—they unclasp'd—
I caught a finger: but the downward weight
O'erpowered me—it sank.

In the scroll, he read:

> In the wide sea there lives a forlorn wretch,
> Doom'd with enfeebled carcase to outstretch
> His loath'd existence through ten centuries,
> And then to die alone. Who can devise
> A total opposition? No one. So
> One million times ocean must ebb and flow,
> And he oppressed. Yet he shall not die,
> These things accomplish'd:—If he utterly
> Scans all the depths of magic, and expounds
> The meanings of all motions, shapes and sounds;
> If he explores all forms and substances
> Straight homeward to their symbol-essences;
> He shall not die.
>   ...all these labors ripened,
> A youth, by heavenly power lov'd and led,
> Shall stand before him; whom he shall direct
> How to consummate all.

Although the story here is involved with personal love and the resurrection of dead lovers, the basic scheme is that of a spiritual succession in a great poetic task: from some distant and vague grandfather figure to an old sage who from over the centuries in turn hands down his torch to young Keats. (How moving the passage where Endymion-Keats starts to draw back from the crushing responsibility, whereupon "the grey-haired creature wept"!)   The imagery of the drowning master passing on the task is very similar in Mallarmé: "la main crispée... legs en la disparition... à quelqu'un / son ombre puérile" (5). The hubris of "total opposition" repeats in Mallarmé's "opposition au ciel" (7). The whole idea has been confirmed by Vigny (*La Bouteille à la mer, L'Esprit pur*) and complicated by echoes from many other sources, including Shakespeare directly, and Milton—for Mallarmé's aim was to sum up all previous attempts—but the Keats-Mallarmé link here is, I think, quite noteworthy.

The kinship with Keats extends from these deep "syntactical" affinities, and perhaps influences, to the imagery which emanates from the common source. The fusion of sparkling intellect and plunging sensuality, this is surely the main point. In the *Faune*, the mood of pagan eroticism organized by sophisticated precision is Keatsian indeed, as had been sensed by previous commentators who mentioned *Endymion* as a possible locus. But, on the whole, what the *Faune* owes to Keats is a more pervasive matter. I suppose a general familiarity with the former on the part of the reader: the noontide-drowsy sylvan creature who dreams of rediscovering a pair of enlaced nymphs; who doesn't know whether he was awake or asleep when he glimpsed them; who thirsts for wine and, to console himself altogether, recalls that he once glutted on grapes—or rather, more poetically, on the light that shone through their empty transparent skins.

Now, Mallarmé was too delicate to life lines, but the overall similarity of atmosphere, as we read the following fragments from Keats and from Mallarmé's own *Faune*, is striking enough:

> ...ripe was the drowsy hour;
> The blissful cloud of summer indolence
>> (*Ode to Indolence*)

>> ...l'air
> Assoupi de sommeils touffus

>> ...so sweet as drowsy noons
> And evenings steeped in indolence
>> (*Ode to a Nightingale*)

>> ...full of dewy wine,
> The murmurous haunt of flies on summer eves.
>> (*Ode to a Nightingale*)

> Tu sais, ma passion, que, pourpre et déjà mûre,
> Chaque grenade éclate et d'abeilles murmure
> Et notre sang, épris de qui le va saisir,
> Coule pour tout l'essaim éternal du désir.

> In cool mid-forest...
> Or I have dreamed...
> And awaking up...
> Dids't find a lyre...
>> (*Hyperion*)

> Aimai-je un rêve?

> Then glut thy sorrow
> ...burst Joy's grape against his palate fine...
>> (*Ode to Melancholy*)

> Ainsi, quand j'ai des raisins sucé la clarté,
> Pour bannir un regret...

Sleep and Poetry itself abounds in hints: the image of the Pan-like poet sleeping in the grass, eating wild strawberries, chasing nymphs to "touch their shoulders white / Into a pretty shrinking with a bite"; "from a thick brake, / Nested and quiet in a valley mild, / Bubbles a pipe." The equivalents in Mallarmé were a "morsure mystérieuse due à quelque auguste dent" and the bubbly effect of the syrinx, "point d'eau que ne verse ma flûte."

In the *Ode to Psyche*, there is much of the impressionistic imagery of the *Faune*:

> I wander'd in a forest thoughtlessly,
> And on the sudden, fainting with surprise,
> Saw two fair creatures, couched side by side
> In deepest grass, beneath the whisp'ring roof
> Of leaves and trembled blossoms...
> They lay calm-breathing, on the bedded grass;
> Their lips touched not, but had not bid adieu,
> As if disjoined by soft-handed slumber,
> And ready still past kisses to outnumber...

This has the feel of the spied-upon, delicately joined yet separated—by "le mal d'être deux"—pair of nymphs, the host of kisses ungiven—"la touffe de baisers..."[3]

The French poet managed to live longer and put the "*patience*" to work for his art. He is closer to us in time and was able to profit not only from Keats himself but all that came after, notably Baudelaire, in the way of concision or, to use Keats's own formula, "loading every rift with ore." What Mallarmé says of his young predecessor is fundamentally just, as usual: he did seem to be piling up too much too fast, as if he knew he had so little time. And yet, looking past these excesses and prolixities and the occasional neoclassical rhetoric, most of us are inclined to agree with Mallarmé that Keats's was "la plus splendide imagination d'à présent." From the region where he might be beating his luminous wings in vain—but which we prefer to think of as liberally provisioned with apples from the moss'd cottage trees and beakers of the flowing south— one can easily imagine Keats returning the compliment.

---

[3]Much more could be done along this line. For example, perhaps the description, in the second stanza, of flowers "Blue, silver-white" gave some impetus to the mood of *Apparition*: "De blancs sanglots glissant sur l'azur des corolles." Or, "Vénus, qui, le soir brûle dans le feuillage" (*Hérodiade*) compared to "What leaf-fringed legend haunts about thy shape of deities" (*Ode on a Grecian Urn*); or Hérodiade's "je ne veux rien d'humain" compared with Lamia's "What taste of purer air hast thou to soothe my essence?" Or the "dazzling spokes" of the bridal car in *Lamia* compared with the splendid *roue* of *M'introduire*.

Mallarmé and/or Barbara Johnson: A Decidable

Barbara Johnson republished an essay on Mallarmé: "Les fleurs du mal armé: Some Reflections on Intertextuality" in *Stéphane Mallarmé*, edited by Harold Bloom, 1987.[1] Like everything I have seen of hers, it is impressively ingenious and well written. On the other hand, it misses what I take to be the essential Mallarmé at a number of key points.

First, the anagrammatic presence of "Mallarmé" ("m'alarmaient") in a note of Baudelaire is possible, but only of marginal interest. She uses it to point up a relation of intertextuality and "oedipal" rivalry between the two, which is already apparent without that minor hypothesis. But she sees this relationship as operating in texts of Mallarmé in a way that violates the very spirit of his aesthetic, which is remarkably *self*-involved, *self*-sufficient, ambitiously *totalisant*.

It is true that in his *Symphonie littéraire* Mallarmé revealed he was awed and cowed into impotence by great ancestral—or "parental"—figures like Baudelaire, belied by the very text in which he makes this claim as well as by all his subsequent fecundity. Johnson rightly sees the paradox at work here: the "baptismal" death and rebirth that is his characteristic maneuver. That "death" sometimes takes the form of impotence or silence, as she notes, and is often figured by the blank page with its whiteness. But what she totally omits is the "reborn" power of that whiteness itself as proliferating poetic imagery, in the form of the "whiteness chain" that Derrida made widely known.

That whiteness, in sum, is not just a negating moment but the beauty that springs from it:

As a projection of the depths of *l'Abîme*—compare *écumes originelles*: (9), Eros—it is a sort of universalized milk (or *soma*); woman's milk

---

[1] (New York: Chelsea House Publishers, 1987). The essay originally appeared in *Lyric Poetry: Beyond New Criticism*, ed. Chaviva Hosek and Patricia Parker (Ithaca, N.Y.: Cornell University Press, 1985).

105

properly speaking, *jaillissement* of stars as in the Milky Way, or thought, male expression such as poetry, or seed, and so forth...

In sum, the blanchi refers to something like the birth of Love in Hesiod's *Theogony*: from the sperm-foam of Zeus floating on the waves is born Aphrodite.

A pure springing of beauty, as a snowfall delights the heart of a child, it will spread through universal analogy to all the possible springings of light or whiteness or Form such as wing, sail, *cheveux chenus*, goose feather, plume on Hamlet's bonnet, lightning flash, stars in the milky way, and again, thought...

This quoted text is from, originally, my *L'Oeuvre de Mallarmé: Un Coup de dés* (1951)[2] and was reprinted, translated, in *Toward the Poems of Mallarmé*, appendix A.[3]

In his *La Dissémination* (which Barbara Johnson translated into English), Derrida not only makes extensive use of this "chain," but he uncharacteristically revels in its poetic sensuality, as he does also in an essay on Blanchot.

Accordingly, it is rather disappointing to see someone who obviously was very attentive to Derrida treating the theme so unpoetically, so schematically, in order to nail down a deconstructive point. This she does, first, with the early poem *l'Azur*:

The fact that the word is repeated four times at the end of the poem would seem to indicate that what haunts Mallarmé is not simply some ideal symbolized by azure itself but the very word "azure" itself. Even a casual glance at nineteenth-century French poetry reveals that the word "azure" is par excellence a "poetic" word—a sign that what one is reading is a poem. The repetition of this word can thus be read as the return of the stereotyped poetic language as a *reflex*, a moment when initiative is being taken by the words *of others*, which is one of the things Mallarmé will later call "chance." Azure, says Mallarmé, "becomes voice." The text ends: "I am haunted: cliché! cliché! cliché! cliché! (Johnson 216)

Of course, the text says no such thing, and Barbara Johnson is herself being predictable. This was an early poem, and in any case Mallarmé uses the word over and over again even in later poetry (as does his favorite disciple Valéry: e.g., in *Palme*): *Don du poème*, one of his finest sonnets, features the word, as does *Hérodiade*, *Hommage à Puvis de*

---

[2](Paris: Librairie Les Lettres, 1951).
[3](Berkeley: University of California Press, 1966). Also the expanded paperback edition, same press, 1980.

Chavannes, L'Après-midi d'un faune. The last poem, of which he was manifestly proud and which he rewrote several times—would he have allowed a cliché in it, one he had *rejected* in the earlier poem? There are thirteen uses of the word in his poetic oeuvre. He obviously *loved* it. A friendlier reading of his work offers the likely reason: it is very rich phonostylistically[4] and, even more, because it is part of the milk network in a subtle way that needs some explaining.

In my study of *Le Démon de l'analogie,*[5] I try to demonstrate that Mallarmé is haunted by the word *pénultième,* largely because of the tight and ambiguous *u* sound, which is obsessively repeated in the text:

> je fis des pas dans la rue et reconnus en le son
> *nul* la corde tendue de l'instrument de musique...
> luthier vendeur de vieux instruments, pendus au mur...

It is in the *plus-plume* echo that runs throughout the oeuvre; what is more centrally Mallarméan than that *plume?* In *Mallarmé's Prose Poems,* I note (12):

> that *u* is the real germ of *logos spermatikos* here, precisely because of its subtle ambiguity between male, acuteness of sound, and female, womb-shape.

> Pas d'autre mot qui sonne comme cruche. Grâce à cet *u* qui s'ouvre en son milieu. (Ponge, *Cinq sapates*)

In connection with "le plumage instrumental / Musicienne du silence," from *Sainte,* I wrote, in the same study of *Le Démon de l'analogie:*

> Here the main effect is the silent tension-and-release of musical "milk" from a maternal muse (*musique-muse-suce-jus-écume*) or the corollary tension between rounded source (or lips) and kinetic (linear) flow. (*Mallarmé's Prose Poems* 14)

---

[4]The following phonostylistic effects concord closely with those described in the *Letter Table* of *Toward the Poems of Mallarmé* (265-80). In *azur,* the *a* is appropriately vast, calm (even as, Baudelaire claims in *Le Confiteor de l'artiste,* "there is nothing sharper than the infinite," referring, precisely, to the *azur*); the *z* is the effect of "woven blue" that Richard Wilbur uses in his *Merlin Enthralled:* (*Things of this World,* 1956). The *u* is the taut, sensual "sucking" nub of it that makes one mouth the word obsessively (Emilie Noulet comments on this remarkable French *u* in one of her studies). The *r* is fluid, harmonious, tender, "summery." So the word was still irresistible to Valéry, in *Palme:*

> Patience, patience, patience sous l'azur...

Can one imagine a better choice? One doesn't throw away a great word: one *makes* it *new.* A lesson our era finds hard to learn...

[5]In *Mallarmé's Prose Poems* (Cambridge: Cambridge University Press, 1987).

The old-young figure of the poet in *Les Fenêtres* literally tries to mouth the beauty in the window-panes which are brimming with the milky azure:

> Et la bouche, fiévreuse et d'azur bleu vorace,
> Telle, Jeune, elle alla respirer son trésor,
> Une peau virginale et de jadis! encrasse
> D'un long baiser amer les tièdes carreaux d'or.

This recalls the sucked-out grape skin ("sucé la clarté"), communion with the total light-source in the *Faune*, and, further, the whole theme of windows as communion, playing on the ambiguity of *glace* (who has not used ice-slivers as *sucettes?*). The *u* in *sucé* and *azur* plays in the merry-go-round of the *Jeu suprême*.

In... the literally milky *azur* of *Don du poëme* (which the baby-poem hungers for, right after the central image of the *sein*: compare "le ciel comme du lait," Verlaine, *L'Echelonnement des haies*) the *u* effect is very positive, sensual. (*Mallarmé's Prose Poems* 15)

Note that the *azur* is called "le vierge azur" in *Don du poëme*, echoing the "d'azur bleu vorace... son trésor, / Une peau virginale"; which is clearly the skin of the mother's breast (Mauron notes that *trésor* is always the breast in psychoanalytic experience). *Vierge* has the fierce tension of the long-lost young beauty, e.g., the *pure* absence-presence of the Lady in *Le Nénuphar blanc*. Granted, there is some ambiguity about the azure's hungering the poem's lips—one can read it as meaning that the sterility of the sky makes the "baby" hungry, the way cold air might. But the other meaning is in a more pervasive network, one that haunts the oeuvre, as it did in *Hérodiade*:

> Si tu me vois les yeux perdus au paradis
> C'est quand je me souviens de ton lait bu jadis.

Then there is the "eternal milk" in the gorgeous young breasts pointing up to the sky in *Le Phénomène futur*. And so on, obsessively. It is the far more poetic reading, that "milk of paradise" (Coleridge, *Kubla Khan*) associated with the young musical beauty, the "damsel with a dulcimer."

Johnson's reading, on the contrary, is forced and programmatic; she says:

> the newborn poem might die of "azure" which, as we have seen, represents the weight of poetic history.

We have seen no such thing, rather the opposite. That "weight," for her, is the stereotypical character of the word. Why would Mallarmé have marred his exquisite sonnet with such a schematic negation? He struggled to make every part of his poems render the overall effect: the unity of tone he often spoke of in his critical pronouncements (learned largely from Poe).

Now, Johnson sees the whiteness as essentially feminine in Mallarmé. But nowhere does she connect it with that fertile "chain" or stream of imagery that runs right up into the "blanchi... voile... plume...écumes originelles... constellation" of the *Coup de dés*:

> tartine de fromage blanc, les lys ravis, la neige, la plume des cygnes, les étoiles, et toutes les blancheurs sacrées des poètes... (*Réminis-cence*, first version)

Nowhere does she touch on the milk image that is ultimately a part of that "flow" and pervasively an expression of maternal feminity in Mallarmé.

Another major flaw has to do with the swan image that, as we just saw, is part of the whiteness chain.

In the splendid sonnet "Le vierge, le vivace et le bel aujourd'hui," Johnson again picks up the oedipal theme of intertextuality. For her, the *cygne d'autrefois* is the precursor, Baudelaire. But the text reads:

> Un cygne d'autrefois se souvient que c'est lui
> Magnifique mais qui sans espoir se délivre
> Pour n'avoir pas chanté la région où vivre
> Quand du stérile hiver a resplendi l'ennui.

It is absolutely clear that the swan-poet here is not an ancestor but the author of the sonnet himself, remembering his youthful dreams of flying away to utter freedom and paradise, a region where one could truly "live" —as poets since Plato, at least, have always dreamed. Those earlier hopes were the "vols qui n'ont pas fui," all his, inevitably, humanly, dashed dreams of perfection.

Just because Baudelaire himself wrote a swan poem, which Mallarmé undoubtedly read, and which we are naturally aware of as practiced readers of French poetry, is no reason to force his rivaling presence into what is obviously a tightly *individual* existential struggle, creature against totality. (Nor, incidentally, can one see how Swann is also a "predecessor-figure"; he is not really a rival of Marcel, rather something like a loved older brother who represented a relaxation from oedipal rivalries: Vinteuil, Bergotte, and Elstir are the paternal figures, clearly).

The swan image has a much likelier source and bearing in our poet. In his juvenile poem *Loeda*, the swan is a god-beast, as in the original legend, with whom the artist easily identifies (as later with the half-god, half-goat, the *Faune*). The female beauty with whom he is sensually, and internally (animus-anima, cf. the androgynous theme in his "Hamlet" and the *Coup de dés*, etc.) *confused*—"ils ne forment qu'un corps"— becomes his swan-princess *Hérodiade*, a "mask" of the poet, reminiscent, again of his lost female loves (mother, sister, whoever), as is the female alter ego in *Prose*. Later, he looks back at that "sweet bird of youth" and its untaken flights, its pristine song, that golden voice that tries to struggle up in the *Ouverture ancienne* and that he hears, enviously, in the golden blare of Wagner, surging up from "mistress clarities." In the *Ouverture ancienne*, he already was looking back, in a sort of Platonic "Reminiscence" (*Meno*) to those lost purities from another life, in time, in Memory:

> ...o quel lointain en ces appels celé...

This supreme Nostalgia does remind me of Baudelaire, but rather of the image that, although embedded in the *Cygne*, has little to do with the bird there:

> Ainsi dans la forêt ou mon esprit s'exile
> Un vieux souvenir sonne à plein souffle du cor!

That horn of Reminiscence is in the Tristan story as well and runs through Vigny's *Mort du loup* and Verlaine's *Le son du cor s'afflige* (with gone echoes of that old virile agony in the *Chanson de Roland* and its oliphant). The swan and its song are, primarily, that long-lost para-disiacal beauty, as in the horn-theme, associated with spiritual death or martyrdom in an age-old struggle of creation or salvation.

In *Les Phares* Baudelaire thinks of the chain of ancestral artists and associates their linked voices as "Un appel de chasseurs perdus dans les grands bois!" But there is nothing like that other-relatedness at all in Mallarmé's isolated creature, full of scorn and utter independence. *He* is the swan, "c'est lui." No other. Or, at most, it is his ancestral *self*, as in the *Coup de dés*, "son ombre puérile," the child who was father of the man, whom Mallarmé often invokes, as in *Les Fenêtres, Las de l'amer repos*, and the *Tombeau d'Anatole*. Anatole was part of him, the drowned "enfant" of *A la nue accablante tu*, spirally, intimately, the within-self-son. But even Anatole is *de trop* here. The poet goes it alone.

Of course, Baudelaire meant a great deal to him and he does pay him high homage in the *Symphonie littéraire*. On the other hand, both that text and the sonnet addressed to him keep a certain distance. Well, the main point is: though we professors can't help hearing the echo of Baudelaire—rather faint at that—there is simply no way to read the sonnet as meaning anything other than that the swan itself remembers its youth. For how could the swan as dead Baudelaire, in Mallarmé's poem, remember now—"aujourd'hui"—that it is "he, magnificent"? Clearly, it is the *living* old swan-poet *recalling*, along with the golden promise, the fact that "magnificent" as his dream and aspiration were—as *he* was in that sense—he hadn't flown away to another world.

To her credit, Barbara Johnson's analysis of the male-female dialectic in Mallarmé is convincing, and I agree with her feminine challenge to his, after all, prevailingly male viewpoint. If this is "feminism," it is so at a high level, highly "individuated," as Jung would say. The well-known essay on "Mallarmé as Mother" was, on the contrary, futile: who needed to be told that there are parallels between poetic creation and mothering?

In *Mallarmé's Prose Poems*, a footnote argues that she had reduced the embryonic *universe* of *Le Démon de l'analogie* to a linear, thin, deconstructive *scheme*. She makes him out as denying poetry. But Mallarmé never did—not even in the *Coup de dés* that he proudly entitles *Poëme* and whose preface ends with "la Poésie, unique Source"—and surely not in all those major poems that followed the *Démon* in time. Come on! Poets have their deep doubts, and they evolve dialectically through prose, but they are *poets* first and last.

His remarks on Poe make clear that he had no patience for linearity, "armature" (that he wanted hidden amid the white spaces), schemes, ideology. What he aimed at always was a world—"le monde est fait pour aboutir à un beau livre" (*Sur l'évolution littéraire*). / "Quel génie pour être un poète!... Simplement la vie, vierge..." (*Sur Poe*); "le monde y tient; un livre..." (*Solennité*).

Rescuing a Sonnet of Verlaine

[handwritten: for the Lucretian reading of it by Michel Serres]

L'espoir luit comme un brin de paille dans l'étable,
Que crains-tu de la guêpe ivre de son vol fou?
Vois, le soleil toujours poudroie à quelque trou.
Que ne t'endormais-tu, le coude sur la table?

Pauvre âme pâle, au moins cette eau du puits glacé,
Bois-la. Puis dors après. Allons, tu vois, je reste.
Et je dorloterai les rêves de ta sieste,
Et tu chantonneras comme un enfant bercé.

Midi sonne. De grâce, éloignez-vous madame.
Il dort. C'est étonnant comme les pas de femme
Résonnent au cerveau des pauvres malheureux.

Midi sonne. Jai fait arroser dans la chambre.
Va, dors! L'espoir luit comme un caillou dans un creux.
Ah! quand refleuriront les roses de septembre!

This touching, humming, summery poem from Verlaine's *Sagesse* has been familiar to many of us since adolescence, when he came upon it in textbook anthologies or whatever. Does it really need another elucidation? Probably not, but "*on a touché au vers*," in modern criticism like that of Michel Serres, who has offered a Lucretian reading of it in his usual genetic way. Well, one may agree with fusions of science and art in such approaches generally, but there is a terribly important question of emphasis, dosage, tone. I think Serres, who is usually stylish and interesting, hit extremely wide of the mark in this instance, and his misreading points to a great deal that is wrong in contemporary criticism.

The poem does imply a descent toward the origins of life in nature, womb, infancy, but the accent is not on numbers, *pace* Serres, or even the multiple, or his familiar "bruit de fond" (and "acousphènes") and the like, which are rather too cold for art and certainly Verlaine's.

112

I'd say the poem steeps "baptismally" in utter humility and humble rural beginnings, with Christian undertones—at least subtle ones—befitting Verlaine's complete abjection and spiritual rebirth, after his prison experience, expressed notably in *Sagesse*. We recall the simplicity and childlike faith of "Le ciel est, par-dessus le toit" from the same collection, or "Je suis venu, calme orphelin."

The nativity scene in a stable—*sermo humilis*—is to the point of the straw shining in the farm-shed here. The constant theme of Verlaine's yearning for the peace, the lost paradise, in the mother or her presence —he had a remarkably intense relation with her, we know—has an important clear overtone in Mary, the fountain of feminine grace which pervades, nostalgically, the sonnet, and has to do, for example, with the drinking of water from the well. The roses at the end of the poem are, as in traditional symbolism, hers, "full of grace." The whole of *Sagesse* is permeated with her presence: "Je ne veux plus aimer que ma mère Marie" (II, II).

Midi sonne, in a Catholic country, is well understood—this end-of-cycle moment of repose, of reconciliation, of Being—from a comparison with Claudel's finest poem, "La Vierge à midi," at which calming instant he weeps with her "grand pardon," her generous maternal gift of self: "Parce que vous êtes là pour toujours, simplement parce que vous existez..."

The sheer Being is the whole point as in Verlaine's "Le ciel est, par-dessus le toit" (the comma brings out the isolated purity of the *est*); "Mon Dieu, mon Dieu, la vie est là"...

Claudel, of course, owed an immense debt to this Verlaine, and said so. Don't we all?

Hope which shines in the lowly stable like a wisp of straw, then, is the miracle of faith (in life, in love, in Being going on, which is woman's essence to a needy male) rising out of despair, *de profundis*, and out of the most ordinary everyday experience or wild, random ("fou") nature in the raw countryside. True life "flows from the source," like mother milk or a glass of water from the well.

Serres sees the wasp buzzing erratically as an originary chaos from which number will arise, then the subtler rhythms of art, in a developmental scheme. But true art like Verlaine's doesn't follow linear patterns of progression: it tends to be circular, like the whole and fluid patterns of the metaphoric dimension, the visionary and imaginative realm, altogether. The tone is primarily that of static "epiphany" in the Joycean sense: the divinely maternal, the sensuous, earthy, childish, primitive, rural, natural. As in Plato's *Symposium* or D. H. Lawrence's view of feminine temperament, there is little split between high and low, past and future...[1]

So Serres's emphasis on number in connection with *Midi sonne*—the advent of the alexandrine with the stroke of twelve—misses the simple peaceful tone, maternal in that sense, reconciliatory with her and the world in this still end-of-cycle moment (as in Valéry's "midi le juste" in the contemplative air of *Le Cimetière marin*).

Serres raises a major question when he sees number as being prior to language. This is an entirely arbitrary and one-sided scientific view. I see no reason to settle for anything other than an undecidable here, as Mallarmé did with his polar pair of music and letters, stemming from a vibrant mystery including them both. I see no grounds for accepting original "structures" (I do not quite like the word) which are more analytic than synthetic, more numerical than pre-linguistic.

I quote from "The Structure of Ancient Wisdom" by Harvey Wheeler (*Journal of Sociological and Biological Structure* 5 [1982] 223-32):

> Although Giorgio de Santillana thinks that numbers came before letters (de Santillana, 1961) and Mary Danielli holds that mandalic ideograms predated both (Danielli, 1974), it is generally assumed that naming and counting have almost equally remote symbolic and notational origins. The earliest Sumerian texts show that skills in these two idioms were taught in roughly coordinated sequences...

Wheeler gives many examples, including one from Leibnitz. But it is really a matter of common sense to throw up one's hands in a sort of "fifty-fifty" gesture in all such problematic cases (heredity-environment, freedom-necessity, order-disorder...) where a dialectic goes off into infinite regress, chicken-and-egg, to deep mystery rather than any specific historical documentation. Since Mallarmé and his "fiction" epistemology, we tend to keep such matters open, problematic...

Serres is likewise unconvincing on the notion of a progression from an even to an uneven rhythm. He sees a neat scheme of evolution from the regular *bercement* to the last line which features a *sept* and a rose pattern which he claims to be pentagonal and an eleven-syllable line following an "Ah." This is far-fetched and forced. A *bercement* is regular but it is not at all monotonous; it is, rather, incantational, magic, as artistic as anything—one thinks of the wonderful "Berceuses" like Stravinsky's in

---

[1]The quiet tetrapolar pattern of this epiphany—like a *croisée*—is at play here as in typical Symbolist poetry (e.g., Mallarmé's *Les Fenêtres*).

The Firebird. On the other hand, advanced music is very regular, as well as not. No, there is a circle, or spiral, here, not a scientist's line of progress.

So Mallarmé in his *Tombeau d'Anatole* saw a maternal *bercement* as the matrix of his poet's rhythm; before him, Baudelaire, in *La Chevelure*, wrote:

> Et mon esprit subtil que le roulis caresse
> Saura vous retrouver, ô féconde paresse,
> Infinis bercements du loisir embaumé!

There is here, as in the Mallarmé text (or his two *Eventail* poems), a notion not so much of poetic *evolution*, but rather a paradoxical, ironic (oxymoronic) play, interchangeably between up and down, fecundity and laziness, etc.

Similarly, the "pas de femme" of our sonnet have nothing to do with an advance from rhythm to music; they are a pure lovely phenomenon in themselves, as Mallarmé knew in *Le Nénuphar Blanc*: "Subtil secret des pieds qui vont, viennent..." with a fiercely tender, erotic undertone, as in Valéry's canny *Les Pas*, accompanying a basically maternal tone: mother-sounds bringing comfort, or retreating in the night... The whole poem, as Henri Peyre comments, seems to be addressed by a mother to a sick child. But the poet's own viewpoint is intermingled: it is out of his own suffering self that this *pietà* is imagined. So there is a good deal of narcissistic feeling, self-accusation and self-pity, as so often in "le pauvre Lélian." The epiphany of a sacrificial child is really his. To whom—a third party?—is addressed "De grâce, éloignez-vous, madame?" That is unimportant: it gives the familiar feeling of a caring woman tip-toeing or walking out from a room as a child falls asleep...

A similar unsureness is in the last line: who says it? Small matter: the feeling is of the elegiac poet, as so often in Verlaine, yearning for a lost innocence in his sinning older years, which is the tone of "septembre" in part, the autumn of life as of the year. And the rose, *pace* Serres, is not a "pentagon," really, or not here; it is *the* symbol of woman and specifically the Virgin Mother. It ends the poem on another *round* note, that of plenitude and reconciled "womb" of Eden (or beyond), as in Dante; the roundness of the *o* on the page has to do with this, as in Baudelaire's *Le Balcon*, addressed to a maternal muse; it begins with *O* and ends with a plunging into the globality of sky and ocean. Similarly, *La Chevelure*, likewise addressed, begins with "O boucles" and ends with images of "l'azur du ciel immense et rond," "océan," and "oasis." Note all the *o*'s as in Verlaine's roses.

Much of what Serres said can be *included* in an adequate commentary;[2] but the tone could hardly have been farther from the intimate musicality and intuitive art of Verlaine, which includes all sorts of drowsy echoes (dort-dorloter, arrose-rose, résonnent-sonne) and down-home visual effects, and altogether a great deal that is longingly personal, sentimental in a high sense, intensely human, desperately nostalgic, sinning and singing, freshly childlike under the prison dirt.

A more intimate look at details tells us:

In line 1—The image suggests a reminiscence of a nativity scene, pertinent to a Christian rebirth, and it is also what any sensitive child might see that is out of the way for his wayward glance alone. Little, he typically bends down to the little gleam in the hollow, below. Here, the light is coming down, like a blessing, through a chink in the stable wall, singles out an insignificant blade of straw, seen by "me," who am maybe if not a favorite son, at least a comforted one. Later, in Rimbaud, the light, with the impartiality it has in Vermeer (e.g., on a loaf of bread), touches a *pissotière* gnat with glory; and "la lumière donne sur une merde."

2—Verlaine instills in us pity for the vulnerable fearing "child," himself, together with the balm of the soothingly maternal voice, which protects from all outside the circle of her love.

3—Her on-going presence, like the river of Proust's mother's voice reading to him and following him far through life, is in "toujours" as it is in Baudelaire's "Longtemps! toujours" (*La Chevelure*) and in Claudel's "là pour toujours." Her affection is mingled with the sun's, a tender "Father's."

4—The injunction to sleep extends the soothing note out from a hypothetical bed into the surroundings; the whole peasant scene is safe, at peace with the world, having said grace perhaps at table or just at home in the simple rural setting. One easily sees Verlaine in that posture, perhaps because of *Le Coin de Table* where he appears with Rimbaud leaning on his elbow. It is crisp, concrete, alive as a Van Gogh portrait, that touch.

5—The modesty of the glass of water "au moins" adds to our affectionate concern; perhaps the child is sick, can take no more than that. He is pale and poor, a near-ghostly "âme."

---

[2]For example, one can see the floating between odd and even as in "Midi sonne," thanks to the uncertainty of the mute *e* (Verlaine's *Art Poétique* itself plumps for the *flottement*: "l'indécis au précis se joint"); but one can find these aesthetic generalities at work in any good poem. That is not the gravamen of the sonnet at all.

6-8—*dors-dorloter* is incantatory, right for cradling a "child." And the summery humming of *chantonner* is apt for this near-nothing simplicity, almost as natural as the wasp's.

9—*Midi* is well coupled with *grâce*, suggestively, at this calming point at mid-day, a good time to fall asleep, at middling home in the cosmos. Catholic bells then take us to the core, lull, promise. The incantatory appeasement is partly in *sonne-étonnant-résonnent-sonne* (as it was in *automne-monotone* of another langorous poem).

10—In *dort*, the light of summer (*or*) filters into sleep; the *pas de femme* were discussed in our earlier pages. It *is* astonishing what they do to penetrate to an early core and reassure. Baudelaire's *Le Beau Navire* lingers over the effect on our instincts of a woman's walking.

11—*cerveau*: just as the "tête sonore" of *Green* resonates with kisses, this modern and understatedly concrete "brain" communicates very directly with the abdomen of plunging sensation. Indeed, like the "tête sonore (qui roule)," it is a loose-hanging, in this sense, as the soft head of a young elephant in *Le Beau Navire*. And it is sonorous as the image in *Le Bateau Ivre*: "plus sourd que les cerveaux d'enfants."

12—*arroser* continues the tone of solicitude, summer refreshment, and chimes with *roses*; *sonne* seems "sunny" and "filial" appropriately, to us English or German readers and perhaps to this bummer-around-England and visitor to Germany.

13—The *caillou* has the comforting gleam and something of the round sufficiency of the "golden ball" of childhood myth (*The Frog Prince*), which anthropologists like Robert Bly connect with the radiant integrity of our quondam innocence. The *creux* may suggest a place of rebirth and at-homeness, the womb, whence the reintegrated self may emerge clean and fresh. Such was the "trou chaud qui souffle la vie" in Rimbaud's poem about desperate children, *Les Effarés*.

14—Baudelaire's two masterpieces chanting the maternal calm in Jeanne Duval's hair or "blotti dans tes genoux"—*La Chevelure* and *Le Balcon*—both end with a question mark. So does Verlaine's sonnet. The greater the bliss, the more anguishing the thought of losing it, and it is partly faced in this way, offering a more open and vibrant ending, consonant with the undecidables of modern art (Rimbaud's defeated closes are a more radical expression of this mood). Moreover, the *septembre* and the absence of the roses further the elegiac, wistfully hopeful note, very typical of Verlaine.

And yet, the plenitude of what is hoped-for is in the *rondeur* of the *roses*, as it is in Dante and, as in him, *la boucle est bouclée*, at least suggestively: the hope of the beginning ("L'espoir") is restated. What progress is there then? We are obviously in an ultimately circular poetic universe, where Eden is lost and can be regained only at severe cost: winter, it is hinted, lies not far off ahead. We are not sure at all. Yet the promise is there, or far-out there, at least. Death seems less threatening in childlike faiths of this sort:

> Qui cherche, parcourant le solitaire bond
> Tantôt extérieur de notre vagabond
> Verlaine? Il est caché parmi l'herbe, Verlaine
>
> A ne surprendre que naïvement d'accord
> La lèvre sans y boire ou tarir son haleine
> Un peu profond ruisseau calomnié la mort.
>
> (Mallarmé)

Sartre versus Proust

In his latest important work, *Critique de la raison dialectique*, Jean-Paul Sartre writes from a frankly neo-Marxist position, a highly theoretical Marxism laced with modern French existentialism and a renewed phenomenological approach. In some broadly-sketched early pages of the book, he describes the sort of compromise position—midway between the old "escapist" bourgeois idealism and the new "totalizing" commitment to the struggle for liberty—which characterized Parisian university thought in his student days, around 1925, when he was twenty years old.

> We set out blindly along the dangerous path of a pluralistic realism which sought men and things in their "concrete" existence. Nevertheless we remained within the framework of the "dominant ideas"...

We are reminded of the earthy Nietzschean individualism and *déculture* of Gide's influential *Nourritures terrestres*, and we understand better the word "dangerous" here if we think of Céline and Montherlant and their affinities with fascism. The scandal of the underprivileged had begun to haunt the consciences of the upper classes (including the academic world) with a fresh insistence, bringing inner conflict and "disaggregation"—familiar Marxist terms—but still, in Sartre's view, the youth managed, through the ever-available *mauvaise foi*, to skirt the deep issues. This hidden conflict was evidenced by the ambivalent attitude of the writers of the time, who not only turned against the tradition of the ruling society—while remaining in its framework, depending on it for their livelihood—but also revolted against the very language which expressed and justified it: hence phenomena like dada, futurism, literary "terrorism," and the myriad voices of Cretans calling all Cretans liars.

Though we may feel that the Marxist glasses are hardly the most favorable for a clear view of such matters, Sartre's refurbished lenses will do for a rough estimate; and we may go on from there to add that the Sartre of *La Nausée* (1938, aetat 33) was still very much a child of this

119

climate: the epigraph from Céline: "He's a fellow without collective importance, he's just a plain individual," the parodies of modern figures like Proust and Gide, the atmosphere of thorough revulsion against the rentier self (Roquentin is financially independent and mortally bored), frenzied discontent with all manner of patness or smugness... And, true to the doubleness of the mood, the half-way nature of the revolt, even as he tries to purge himself of the past via symbolic vomitives, he is held by its magnetism and owes his best pages to its delicate, highly-evolved means of expression. The very nature of pastiche implies this doubleness, as it had with Proust's own parodies of Balzac, Flaubert, the Goncourts; and, whatever the relative dosage of irony and subjugation, Proust is surprisingly often present in this little masterpiece: in the uneasy and cerebral love-affair of Anny and Roquentin, with its "privileged moments" and their awareness of the "irreversibility of time"; in the themes of solitude, of perversion, of the visions induced by place names, of the sudden crystallization of emotion triggered by insignificant objects (like the muddy shingle, the oak-tree roots), and above all the haunting little melody (here modified to a saxophone air) which brings on the revelation of a possible artistic vocation. Ironic, certainly; and also a study in fascination amounting to something like obsession.

There are some other aspects of the *entre-deux-guerres* era which Sartre does not mention. For example, it seems likely that the impact of World War I, in many ways more horrible than II, and coming as it did after a long interval of peace amidst the pleasure-whirl of *la belle époque*, had much to do with the "breakdown" aspects of art; a sort of symbolic purging of the shell-shocked nightmare. More importantly, I believe, the eccentric, fitful, compulsively provocative manifestations have to do with the formidable challenge of the Symbolist masters—Mallarmé, Valéry, Proust, Joyce, etc.—and in this the sensitive youth were undoubtedly behaving like some well-known examples of individual sons of mercilessly eminent men. Proust, accordingly, along with some other Symbolists,[1] will continue to show up in Sartre's pages like a revenant father-ghost, a bit reminiscent of the one in *Hamlet*, or *Wilhelm Meister*. His attempts to exorcise it are, like much of his writing, fairly peremptory, but nonetheless worthy of attention, considering the stature of the opponents.

---

[1] Sartre has long been preparing a book on Mallarmé which, it is said, will try to make up for the unfair "job" he performed on Baudelaire. The title of *Un Coup de dés* haunts the memory of a character in *Le Sursis*, and there are many allusions to Mallarmé in his study of Genet. Rimbaud is often present in *Les Chemins de la liberté* (particularly *Le Sursis*) and *L'Enfance d'un chef.* Joyce's influence is obvious in various episodes of *Le Mur* and *La Nausée.*

In *L'Etre et le Néant* (1943), Sartre deals Proust a glancing blow:

> Proust seeks continually to discover, by intellectualistic decomposition, in the temporal succession of psychic states, bonds of causality between these states. But at the end of these analyses, he can offer us nothing but results like the following: "As soon as Swann could think of [Odette] without horror, as he saw once more kindness in her smile, and as *the desire to keep her away from everyone else was no longer added by jealousy to his love*, this love *became* again a taste for the sensations that Odette's person gave him, the pleasure he derived from admiring as a spectacle or from interrogating as a phenomenon the lifting of one of her looks, the formation of one of her smiles, the emission of an intonation of her voice. And this pleasure, different from all others *had ended by creating in him a need of her*, which she alone could appease by her presence or her letters... *Thus by the very chemistry of his suffering*, after having *made jealousy with his love*, he began again to *manufacture affection*, or pity, for Odette." (Sartre's italics; *L'Etre et le Néant*)

Now, it is abundantly clear from the nature of his novel that Proust is speaking metaphorically and not "causally," i.e., pseudo-scientifically. Such metaphors as "chemistry" and "manufacture" are quite rare in him and it is really unjust—if typical of point-scorers like Sartre—to single out and doctor a passage like this one. Even so, though ungraceful, it is not certain that they are altogether inept. For, granting that causality had long since gone out with Hume—and Proust along with his cousin Bergson and his entire era, in full revolt against positivism, was certainly aware of it—still, *faute de mieux*, his metaphors manage to point to a recognizable course of psychic events. Proust's terms may remind us of certain mysterious symbols of his coeval, Odilon Redon, the generation of emotions from their opposites through spiraling coils reminiscent, in turn, of the whirlpool of the Tao. Can the vertiginous *en soi—pour soi* merry-go-round of Sartre do any better? Let us consult his familiar pages on love in *L'Etre et le Néant*:

> To transcend the transcendence of the Other or, on the contrary, bury in myself that transcendence, without removing the character of transcendence, there are the two basic attitudes that I take toward the Other... Each of these two attitudes is the death of the other one, that is to say that the failure of one *motivates* the adoption of the other. (401; my italics)

The notion of *motivation*, it is apparent, is even more "causal" than Proust's *chemistry* which (like Baudelaire's *alchemy* of art) is, though barely so, more suggestive. And conceding that Sartre's terms are more complex than Proust's on their discursive philosophic plane, underneath them there is the same primordial oscillation of emotion from negative to positive and back, since it is the sense of "failure" which "motivates" the changes. On a more fully realized, artistic plane, Proust, in other pages of his novel, depicts psychic phenomena with the intricacy of Sartre: for example, Swann's desire to win the esteem of Odette, and hence of himself, by overbidding ("transcend the transcendence of the Other") and, conversely, to see himself as she sees him and become an *object* of affection, or pity, for himself. Hence his generosity on the one hand and on the other the odd "pleasure of the intelligence" he takes in being victimized by her infidelity, *knowing* the awful truth. The convolutions of this affair embrace rather more of the involved inter-human reality than Sartre's abstractions. Moreover, it has been noted by critics that Sartre seems to be describing a pair of incredibly cold and gamy lovers who never really touch each other, and this is true of his "novels" as well; the emphasis is obsessively on one-upmanship and no wonder, then, that Sartre shows so little elevated interest in the opposite sex, reserving all his warmth for proletarians and the dream of fraternity.

Proust can easily defend himself against the charge of "intellectualism," and on occasion has been goaded into taking the trouble to do so explicitly: "The book is in no way a work of reason... its most trifling details have been supplied to me through feeling; because I first of all noticed them deep within myself, without understanding them, having as much trouble to change them into something intelligible as if they were foreign to the realms of the intellect..." (quoted in Hindus, *The Proustian Vision*). And *A la Recherche* almost throughout testifies to the man's concern with "synthesis" and a "total" view: the eternal Return of the privileged moments, the kaleidoscopic modulations of the persons and the places, the roundaboutness of the little promenades and the eventual meeting of the two main Ways, the bending on itself of the macrocosmic whole which, like the Kabbalistic serpent, through spiraling coils "bites over and over its dazzling tail" (Valéry), creating, as much as possible in the strung-out condition of writing, a feeling of the variegated harmony and simultaneity of life.

And what is synthesis without the primary building force of existence: love? Tolstoyan love of life—not just some sector or faction of it à la Sartre—is what gives us so often, particularly in the early volumes, Proust's good candid voice, the bell-tone of his poetic prose. Sartre's tone—allowing the authenticity of his writing in certain pages of *La Nausée*, e.g., the Sunday promenade and, more rarely, in *Les Chemins*—is too frequently mechanical, forced, *voulu*, demonstrative, hurried, polemical. Proust is more patient, sweeter, more *there*. He is an artist.

To dub Proust "analytic" is double unworthy of Sartre, not only because he is far less of an artist than Proust but also because he knows that analysis is a necessary moment of the knowing process, that it is even built into (though integrated out of sight) the subtlest instinct or vision. Proust knew, as well as Pascal, Hegel, Bergson, Sartre himself, that if the last word is for synthesis ("instinct" in the following passage, "imagination" elsewhere in his novel), *up to* that last, analysis plays a decisive role in any creativity. And so Proust writes: "each day I attach less value to intelligence [but] if intelligence does not merit the supreme crown, it alone can bestow it. And if in the hierarchy of virtues it has only the second place it alone can proclaim that instinct must occupy the first place" (preface to *Contre Sainte-Beuve*).

By 1945, when he wrote his introduction to *Les Temps Modernes*, Sartre had worked up considerable momentum, and chose this terrain for a frontal assault on Proust:

> This legend of the poet's irresponsibility that we denounced a moment ago, springs from the analytical mind. Since the bourgeois authors consider themselves as peas in a can, the solidarity which unites them with other people seems strictly mechanical to them, i.e., a mere juxtaposition. Even if they feel strongly about their literary mission, they think they have done enough when they have described their own nature or that of their friends. Since all men are alike, they will have helped all of them by enlightening everyone about himself. And as they start from the same postulate as analysis, it seems very simple to them to use the analytical method to know themselves. Such is the origin of intellectualist psychology, the perfect example of which we find in Proust's works. A paederast, Proust thought he could use his homosexual experience to describe Swann's love for Odette; a bourgeois, he presents this sentiment of a rich, idle bourgeois for a kept woman as the prototype of love. Obviously, then, he believes in the existence of universal passions, the mechanism of which does not vary much when one modifies the sexual characters, the social condition, the nation or the time of the individuals who feel them. After thus "isolating" these unalterable affections, he will be able to start converting them, in their turn, into elementary particles. Abiding by the postulates of the analytical mind, he does not even think that there may be a dialectic in sentiments, but only a mechanism. Thus social atomism, the position of retreat for the contemporary bourgeoisie, brings about psychological atomism. Proust has *chosen to be a bourgeois*, he has made himself the accomplice of the bourgeois propaganda, since his work contributes to spreading the myth of human nature.

> We are convinced that the analytical approach is dead and that its unique role today is to trouble the revolutionary conscience and isolate

men in favor of the privileged classes. We do not believe any more in the intellectualist psychology of Proust and we consider it harmful. Since we chose his analysis of passionate love as an example, we will probably enlighten the reader by mentioning the essential points on which we disagree with him entirely.

First, we do not accept *a priori* the idea that passionate love is an affection constitutive of the human mind. It could very well have, as Denis de Rougemont suggested, a historical origin related to Christian ideology. More generally, we think that a sentiment is always the expression of a certain way of life and a certain conception of the world, common to a whole class or time, and that its evolution is not caused by I know not what inner mechanism but by these historical and social factors.

Secondly, we cannot admit that a human affection is composed of molecular elements that are juxtaposed without modifying one another. We consider it to be not a well adjusted machine but an organized form. We do not conceive the possibility of *analyzing* love because the evolution of this sentiment, as of all others, is *dialectic*.

Thirdly, we refuse to believe that a homosexual's love has the same character as a heterosexual's. The secret, forbidden character of the former, its aspect of black magic, the existence of a homosexual freemasonry, and this damnation to which the invert is aware of dragging his partner with him: it seems to us that all these facts influence the whole sentiment to the very details of its evolution. We maintain that a person's various sentiments are not juxtaposed but that there is a synthetic unity of emotional functions and that each individual moves within an emotional world which is his own.

Fourthly, we deny the individual's origin, class, milieu, nation, to be mere concurrents in his sentimental life. On the contrary, we think that every affection, as any other form of his psychic life, *manifests* his social situation. This worker, who gets a salary, who does not own his working tools, who is isolated by his work from the substance of his material, and who protects himself from being oppressed by becoming conscious of his class, could not feel, under any circumstances, like this analytical-minded bourgeois, who, because of his profession, entertains polite relations with other bourgeois.

So, against the analytical mind, we turn to a synthetic conception of reality, the principle of which is that a whole, whatever it is, is different, by nature, from the sum of its parts.

We have already dealt with Proust's supposed intellectualism, so let us address ourselves now to the other issues in some detail. firstly, Sartre reveals here considerable and willful ignorance about the nature of the "poet's responsibility"—willful because in his *Qu'est-ce que la littérature* he made a sharp (and arbitrary) distinction between poets and prose writers in the matter of *engagement*, leaving the former a free independent status to create the "ornaments" of culture; and Proust is nothing if not a poet. But actually the fuller truth is more elusive than Sartre would have it in *either* of these two texts. Perhaps the best answer to Sartre's simplifications is to quote his rejoinder to a journalist who had questioned Gide's manhood on the grounds that he was "chilly" and preferred to stay indoors, wrapped in a shawl; Sartre righteously replied "mais il y a *des* courages"—there is more than one kind of courage. Might we not say with equal justice "Il y a *des* engagements"?

The lesson of labor, patience, self-discipline, devotion, unsentimental idealism involved in a work like *A la Recherche* would seem to some of us to be a sufficient commitment to society. After all, it is the civilizing force which ultimately counts, not the particular direction of it. Though Proust showed considerable interest in social questions—especially the Dreyfus case—obviously, given his temperament and build, he could no more have cut the kind of figure Sartre does than the latter could effectively imitate Maurice Thorez. And *do* the Calas pamphlet of Voltaire, Zola's *J'accuse*, Gide's *Voyage au Congo* bulk as large in our estimation of these men as Sartre claims? Only for the trivial, and essentially philistine, view which would run down Shakespeare because of a few unthoughtful pages on women or Jews, slight Yeats because of his inconsequential and naïve reactionary politics.

Secondly, Sartre calls Proust flatly and unsportingly a "pederast" (a technique he could have learned from Senator McCarthy), all the while knowing better, *vide* the following passage from *L'Etre et le Néant*:

> He does not wish to allow himself to be considered as a thing He would be right in fact if he understood that phrase "I am not a pederast" in the sense of "I am not what I am." That is to say if he declared "To the degree that... I performed these acts I am a pederast. To the degree that human reality defies all definition by acts, I am not one."

Proust precisely reveals this human complexity by (a) admitting fairly openly that he had performed homosexual acts and (b) in his novel, condemning homosexuality from a socially responsible viewpoint (not quite Sartre's) either directly, in some outright attacks, or indirectly by the grotesque quality of most of the portrayed inverts or again, tacitly, by refusing to have his protagonist, or Swann, be one. This attitude, as opposed to Gide's, to whom he confided it—"You can say anything provided you do not say 'I'"—is part of the subtle moral force which gives his art, unlike Gide's, vital direction. Proust *is* a pederast, in sum, but not *simply* one: he is a struggling and very much concerned human being.

Equally unproductive is the charge that "Proust thought he could use his homosexual experience to describe Swann's love for Odette." In the first place, it is idle to assume that a pederast—if he is not *simply* one, and is there such?—cannot have a sincere experience of love, either active or imagined, for the opposite sex. In the case of Proust, there is a wealth of evidence that he had heterosexual experience as well as feelings. And in any case, an awareness of the nature of love's genesis (after an initial vague polymorphous phase), from love of the mother, and father, to all sorts of other people, including the female who "replaces" the mother—as various mistresses of *A la Recherche* do, in Proust's own honest and knowing words—should have rendered Sartre's views more just and flexible here. Proust, whose work is a study in the evolution of emotion through quite specific historical conditions is easily more "dialectical" than his assailant: certainly than Sartre in these pages where, with a boorish heaviness, he implies that there are *only* differences between any two experiences of love, or sex. In other pages of *L'Etre et le Néant*, which he has apparently forgotten, Sartre discusses the reversible nature of sexual possession, involving both active and passive aspects in both sexes (see "the hole," 706). And though we will gladly, gratefully, grant "la petite différence," still, from Plato's androgyne to modern biological teaching about the evolution of sexual differentiation and the "suppressed potentialities," we have learned to approach the subject with some tolerance of ambiguity. Hence, for example, the male novelist has a right to describe the inner world of his feminine characters (Madame Bovary, Anna Karenina, Molly Bloom) providing he is conscious of his margin of deficiency and is shrewd enough to avoid it. And by the same token, even more clearly, Proust can understand the feelings of a man for the opposite sex, particularly if his man is a civilized, sensitive, and cerebral one like Swann or Marcel.[2] Sartre, who was raised by his widowed mother, and informs us most convincingly about the inner life of Daniel, his pederast, ought to tread more lightly in these realms.

The invective implied in the word "bourgeois" hurled at poor Proust similarly loses much of its power when we remember that Sartre terms himself a bourgeois—as well as a "slimy rat" (he seems to have gone to school to David Zaslavsky)—elsewhere; the reputations of both men will probably survive despite this sad condition. Though no Proust, Sartre is obviously a powerful somebody.[3] Hence—and because he has had an

---

[2]Proust was not so successful in avoiding his margin of deficient insight or experience in the Albertine episodes mainly because he died before he could revise them.

[3]Occasionally he returns to more honest views on art, even in regard to Proust: "I know... in the greatest artists there is much beyond [mere escapism]... in Proust one

unfortunate influence on artistic evaluations, and we can ill afford such losses at a time when the sense of value is generally so shaky—he is to be taken seriously, even when he is being as careless as he obviously is in the quoted passages.

We may thoroughly understand Sartre's response to the needs of mid-twentieth-century France, which seem objectively to call for a renewed emphasis on action, choice, will, *praxis*, commitment to urgent issues. We are also aware that French literature does not stop with Proust, that much has been added, even in the despaired-of genre of the novel, by a dozen lively figures and some fresh perspectives; conversely, that the cult of masterpieces can be deadening, academic, or, as Sartre puts it, that a return to the eternal debate of Montaigne and Pascal may be an excuse for ignoring Malraux or Camus. But, though we may welcome this youthful revolt for its own sake, as a sign of continuing life or, secondarily, as a "breather" after a rich symbolist harvest which threatened to overwhelm us, the time always comes again when we feel that youth and revolt are not the whole story and we need the challenge of past glories. And we begin to wonder: must we really bury Proust in order to pitch in with the period of Beckett and Sarraute? Camus—as indeed Beckett and Sarraute themselves—managed to reconcile something like awe for Proust (*L'Homme révolté*) with contemporaneity; and though Sartre is conceivably the more impressive figure of the two, there can be no doubt as to which has the greater commitment to art.

In conclusion, we may say that the whole force of Sartre's wrong-headed intent in regard to art is summed up in his attitude toward post-humous fame. He is dead against any attempt to achieve it, and sees this as another kind of escapism, a failure to pitch in like a man and take the consequences of struggle and mortality. Yet a belief in transcendence, to which Sartre subscribes in other forms, seems indispensable to human striving, however reservedly, hesitantly, and belatedly expressed. If, as he repeatedly says, man is not what he is, and this is the condition of his freedom, his humanity, then the desire to be something beyond the whole of our limited given condition of self is a very human one. That is why most men continue to desire progeny and, some, the spiritual equiv-alent implied in creativity. Or would Sartre really, as he unconvincingly proclaims in his dazzling slap-dash rampage through literature, have his exemplary image of man die out with his last *ad hoc* gesture? Has he really forgotten the Socratic lesson? According to the enlightened views

finds a human experience, a thousand paths" (*Qu'est-ce que la littérature*, 208). Elsewhere, however, he calls him a "fat lady stuffing herself with candy bars" and in the midst of an article on Husserl he exclaims: "At last we are rid of Proust!"

of the Greek, it is Sartre who is the escape-artist, eluding the fuller responsibilities of the hour; and it is only a naïve materialism which denies that a Mallarmé, whose personality produced a vivid impact on an extraordinary group of individuals, a Proust, with the magnificent look of a "Persian prince," Joyce with his air of utter confidence, Kafka, whose eyes were memorable for their pure expression, were exceedingly *present* in their own times, but present with the glow that says: "I have wonderful news. But it will take years for even the most sympathetic friend to fully understand, because, under my guidance, he *and eventually all men* must learn to see in new ways." What more—or as Tolstoy put it, how much land—does a man need? To be recurrently cited in the newspapers and literary gossip sheets? To be played on Broadway? *Libre à lui.*

The ABC's of Richard Wilbur

As a graduate student at Yale, fresh out of uniform, I happened upon a little magazine called *Foreground*, edited in Cambridge, Massachusetts. Its second number (Spring-Summer 1946) featured poetry and prose by Richard Wilbur, the first I had ever heard of him. If my memory of a conversation I had with him at Harvard is correct—he was also a graduate student of literature, in the Society of Fellows, and I had gone to be interviewed by them—he had previously done very little serious publishing. He told me he had not developed his gifts until, exiled from his loved ones as a soldier in Europe, he had taken to communicating with them through poems.

Everything about him interested me extraordinarily because, upon reading the *Foreground* group of pieces, I had immediately seen in him *the* poet of his time, at least for me. I told him so in a fervent letter, the only such I have ever written to anyone, and he wrote back a wonderful letter full of ideas and friendliness.

I saw him only once again after the Fellows episode: rejected, I stayed on at Yale where I got my Ph.D. in French literature working under Henri Peyre. But we had a spate of correspondence, some of it having to do with his contributing translations of Villiers de l'Isle-Adam to a review I launched in 1948, *Yale French Studies*. In later years, the exchange slacked off—only a few letters from time to time—but I never lost my conviction that he was our finest voice, and I often said so in public, in various of my books. He graciously allowed me to quote lines of his.

Though I used Wilbur on occasion to make aesthetic points, he remained for me largely what painting was for Baudelaire or, indeed, for Wilbur himself: "What wholly blameless fun" (*A Dutch Courtyard*, B[1]).

[1]Symbols of collections: A: *Advice to a Prophet*; B: *The Beautiful Changes*; C: *Ceremony*; M: *The Mind Reader*; N: *New Poems*; T: *Things of this World*; W: *Walking to Sleep*.

He dwelt outside the professional realm, *au-dessus de la M.L.A.*, gratuitous, entire. On the other hand, I feel much the same way about Baudelaire, Mallarmé, Rimbaud, yet I brought myself to write on them, occasionally at great length. The point is to do so in a way that would likely win their approval.

Once Wilbur passed on for my appreciation a translation of Mallarmé's *l'Après-midi d'un faune* that a young woman had sent to him—we referred to her as the "Mallarmé lady"—but, aside from the fact that he spoke of my own work on Mallarmé which he had perused, I really do not know, to this day, what his relation with the figure that Sartre anointed "out greatest poet" might be. He has never translated him, to my knowledge. On the other hand, my predilection for Mallarmé's poetry, and likewise Wilbur's, suggests a possible affinity. And, why be coy, I *know* there is one, and it has to do with the rare combination of extreme sophistication and childish naïveté in their choice of words, particularly in terms of the specific poetic charge the letters of the alphabet carry, in shape and/or sound.

Wilbur has not spoken of this aspect of his art, so far as I know. Mallarmé, all to the contrary, wrote a book called *Les Mots anglais* in which he demonstrated the impact of most of the letters of the English alphabet (he singled out the *initial* letters of words, but that doesn't matter for our purposes).

Before reading that work, I had been spontaneously smitten by the effects of certain letters in his poems, just as my sister and I had been tickled as school-children when we discovered that we both saw bubbles in the *b*'s of Keats's "beady bubbles winking at the brim" (*Ode to a Nightingale*), or a related swelling in the *p*'s of "plump and hazel gourd" (*Ode: To Autumn*). This too was gratuitous, pure fun, having nothing to do with official studies and *le sérieux de la vie* (or Sartre's *esprit de sérieux*). Later, I learned that Paul Valéry, in an essay, and Paul Claudel, in a radio talk—both were close to the Master, among his favorites—saw *Les Mots anglais* as the primary key to understanding his poetics. Even before knowing that, I had worked out the effects of all the letters in a book on Mallarmé's *Un Coup de dés*, being careful to insist on the gingerliness of the enterprise, which can be fruitful at all only if it remains tentative, intuitive, elfin.

When a heavy-handed disciple named René Ghil tried to systematize what he called "l'instrumentation verbale," Mallarmé gently chided him and spoke of truths which one keeps to oneself (preface to the *Traité du verbe* 857). But, after all, Mallarmé had subtly committed himself (in *Les Mots anglais* and "Crise de vers") and so, it turned out, had Victor Hugo,

Proust, Plato, and many other superb writers over the centuries. Given that my attempt was welcomed by leading poets and critics abroad, it is not inconceivable that it may find favor with some Americans who are unfamiliar with Mallarmé studies.

At first I restricted my comments to Mallarmé, merely noting in passing that *grosso modo* his effects were applicable to French poets generally, roughly in proportion to their excellence and that they emerged from objective qualities of the language as well as the pertinent reality, however delicate the process might be (different contexts bring out different aspects; the danger of subjectivism is considerable). Later, I extended my remarks to poets close to him: Baudelaire, Verlaine, Valéry, in an essay called "The ABC's of Poetry."

Given the proximity, parallel evolution and huge overlap between French and English, especially in terms of alphabet, it was elementary to assume that Mallarmé's demonstrations on English letters were, with certain adjustments, applicable to his own French art. Clearly, an *o*, for example, leaps off the page to our grateful eye in the "O miroir" of *Hérodiade* or the "ronds de fumée / Abolis en autres ronds" of *Toute l'âme résumée* (referring to smoke rings) just as it does in "the ping-pong's optative bop" of Wilbur (*My Father Paints the Summer*, B) or else in his piece entitled simply *O*: "filling by one and one / Circles with hickory spokes" (B). Similarly W. R. Rodgers evokes "the loops and blooms of cherries." I hope to get around to him more fully another time: he is certainly ripe for the approach. Meanwhile there are ample pickings of blooming words in Wilbur, so much so that I found myself in a book devoted mainly to French writers (*Modes of Art*) bringing in Wilbur as an exemplar of letter-symbolism (or what Gérard Genette has dubbed "cratylisme," nodding to Plato's pioneering efforts in this area). In a lyric poem Frank Jones hailed as one of the very best in our language, the title piece of the collection *The Beautiful Changes*, there is this memorable passage:

> Your hands hold roses always in a way that says
> They are not only yours;

My comment was:

> The seven y's... are an extremely feminine gesture of a hand [or a pair of hands] opening up around a proffered gift, corollary to the v-shape (q.v.) opening up and out like a cornucopia or, inversely, a calyx, a siren-whirlpool inviting promisingly down and in. (*Modes of Art* 62)

For now, to give an idea of the v-shape, I might mention the *Vertige!* of Baudelaire's *Le flacon*, where the whole image has to do with a dizzying descent into a maelstrom of love, death, dangerously deep memory associated with rummaging after a perfume vial in a maternal drawer...

Is there a better explanation of "always in a way that says" and the rest—i.e., of why our finest poet in one of his miraculous achievements would allow himself to use seven *y*'s in swift succession? Similarly, in *Le Démon de l'analogie* Mallarmé has a passage:

> Je fis des pas dans la rue et reconnus en le son *nul*
> la corde tendue de l'instrument de musique.

Later in the same prose poem:

> la boutique d'un luthier vendeur de vieux instruments
> pendus aux murs.

I won't go into the reason here, having largely to do with the womb-shape of a lute—it is developed at length in my book on his prose poetry (*Mallarmé's Prose Poems*)—but Valéry and Claudel were right: these intimate microcosms take one to the heart of the *oeuvre*.

There is no point that I can see in going systematically over Mallarmé's practice as defined in the mentioned studies. It will be sufficient to note, at the outset, that every effect distinguished in Wilbur is close to the equivalent effect in Mallarmé. Anyone interested in checking this can look them up in *Toward the Poems of Mallarmé* or *Modes of Art*.

Before going further with our alphabet, I'd like to make a global comment or two about Wilbur. Earlier, I mentioned the unusual joining of complexity and simplicity (which Mallarmé saw as an ideal in *Divagations*). A comparable union of opposites was Pascal's aim as well (*finesse* and *géométrie*); Leonardo clearly had mastered it. In Wilbur and his French "uncle" there is the quality, at one extreme, which Mallarmé admired in Banville:

> rajeuni dans le sens admirable par quoi l'enfant
> est plus près de rien et limpide. ("Solennité" *OC* 333)

Everything Wilbur writes has that limpidity, even in prose (comparable in this regard to Lionel Trilling's), underneath whatever complications. His whole personality exudes, in whatever I know from him or of him, that American boyish, wholesome, transparent quality. He taught us afresh—unlike so many lesser, defensive writers—not to be afraid of using simple words like "love." The dust-jacket of his first collection aptly calls it "romantic in mood." There was a little wave of neo-Romanticism at Harvard in his time—his fellow student and companion, André du Bouchet, himself an excellent poet, was part of that (he published an article on Géricault in *Foreground*)—and Wilbur never broke with those late-Western tides of basic psychic power, even though he tended to become wittier and less overtly musical as he went along.

Wilbur's handwriting loops rather roundedly, like Mallarmé's, and I can just see him mouthing it as he goes, for he is naturally "oral"; impressed by the banana-yellow of the cover of *Yale French Studies*, he pronounced it "succulent." Like Proust, to whom the walls of the Church at Combray were "edible," Wilbur *eats* the delectable things of this world:

> Imminent towns whose weatherbeaten walls
> Looked like the finest cheese
> Bowled us enormous melons from their
> Tolling towers. (*The Terrace*, C)

One can hardly miss the good round *B* and *o*'s.

Someone should do a study of the image of milk in our tradition of art and literature, going back to Christian items like Saint Bernard's epistolary "sucking the teats of Christ" or the stream of milk spurting across the canvas of a Spanish Baroque painter from the breast of the virgin in a neat arc into the mouth of a lucky sinner. Keats is prominent in the line-up, Chateaubriand (*Atala*), Nietzsche (*Nachtgesang*), Rimbaud (see Cohn, *Poetry* 14), Mallarmé (see Cohn, *Toward the Poems* 261). Wilbur weighs in with *Two Voices in a Meadow* (A):

> *A Milkweed*
>
> Anonymous as cherubs
> Over the crib of God,
> White seeds are floating
> Out of my burst pod.

That crib and subtle early whiteness bring him close to Hölderlin, to whom he is very partial, as well as to Blake.

The child in Wilbur speaks sometimes very directly to other—American—children, viz. *Juggler* (C): "whee," "Damn," "boom." It seemed to me, upon reflection, that there were only so many epiphanous opportunities in an American childhood—such as his fire-engine or his bucket of perfectly lucid water—and that Wilbur had scooped practically all of them up.

The other extreme is his complexity, his density of texture, his Shakespearean range of vocabulary, his precise vision and wisdom, his wittiness, his brilliantly informed and curious mind, his cultural rootedness and erudition, his cosmopolitanism and remarkable command of many languages. And the crowning wonder is that he knows the dead right dosage of those two directions of the spirit and exhibits, poem in poem out, the sort of nimble balance that McEnroe used to have at the net.

Back to his *abc*'s. And what better place to start than with his *a*?

In English, as in French, the *a* in some of its tones—as in "cat" or "father"—is right in the center of the vowel-pitch scale: French *i, é, u* are very high, the nasals and *ou* are low, their *a* like ours is smack dab in the middle, hence ideal for expressing flatness, matness, calm, vapidity... We easily say "aah," "blah," "banana oil" for utter banality or dreary non-sense. Carson McCullers got a deserted atmosphere like *Bagdad Café*'s out of *Ballade of the Sad Café*. Gautier used nine *a*'s in his "La caravane humaine au Saharah du monde" (*La Caravane*). Anyone who doubts this process might try "peenoreemee" or "poonoroomoo" in the place of "panorama" to see just how appropriate the sound of the last-named is for its broad-screen serenity: whence Wilbur's "a final panorama" (*In Limbo*, M). Accordingly, our laureate, to bring home the generous stretch of the relaxed season, says "Summer, luxurious Saharah" (*My Father Paints the Summer*, B). As a soldier on furlough in Paris during World War II, like the rest of us he had been drearily fascinated by the *peuple*, corny, and flat ambiance of the *Place Pigalle* (B) and so entitled a poem, reminding one of Mallarmé's "banale et vaste place" ("Catholi-cisme"). When I objected to its overblown ending, he explained in a letter that he was seeking an effect of "bombast"; again, obviously, the *a* is part of that purposeful *broadness* which we have learned to appreciate in camp, kitsch, and pop art (rows of Campbell soup cans, Marilyn Monroes, Coney Island Queens...). To be sure, these matters are elusive and contextual: snobs tend to affect a broad *a* for class.

Further examples: "the plate / Lies flat on the table top" (*Juggler*, C). There the *a* in "flat" is effective and the other *a*'s tend to reinforce it visually (although the chief reinforcement comes from the direct images of "table" and "plate," naturally). Valéry set a whole major poem in that tone, *Palme*, with repeated "Calme, calme, patience, patience, palme," and so on, and it begins:

> Un ange met sur ma table
> Le pain tendre le lait plat;

which is close to Wilbur's image. André Gide demurred (*Journal*, Jan. 16, 1933) at the "lait plat" until, with the awakening of a keener sen-sitivity, he realized that nothing was flatter, or more mat, than milk in a bowl. We have to *learn* to like pop art: to an astonishing extent, the critical story of our time is the enhancement or appreciation of the horizontal. (Where all this *fuite en avant* leads is another story, and critical).

Another common tone of *a*, as in "mate" is acute—the "Lace," "lake," "shade," of *The Beautiful Changes*—and that is apt for the meanings. The association with the broader *a* brings about, even in the above cases, a very subtle nuance of spread or serenity.

On to *b*:

> A ball will bounce but less and less. (*Juggler*, C)

Or in the same: "ball by ball." Or: "a burst balloon" (*Giacometti*, C).

This is like taking candy from a (bouncing) baby. A lot of infantile Rimbaud, comparably, depends on that *b*: "L'aube et l'enfant tombèrent au bas du bois" (*Aube*). Mallarmé used eighteen *b*'s in his sonnet on Baudelaire: "bouche... d'égout bavant boue et rubis..." As usual, he took a cue from his name, since, according to *Les Mots anglaise* the *b* expresses "bouffissure... fécondité," not least, no doubt, because of its buttock shape (particularly in the capital form) as well as its belly shape. Joyce played with the capital *B* in *Finnegans Wake* and favored the little *b* too: "bend of bay," "baubletop" on the first page. Wilbur likewise: "a bauble at the tip" (*A Courtyard Thaw*, C); "your buttocks, the convex curve of your belly" (*A Shallot*, M); the visual curve of the *c* helps here too.

A plausible cosmogonic view recently aired in the press is that the world is made of bubbles, formed by chains of exploding supernovas. So what else is new? Shakespeare knew that instinctively, along with his era: "the bubble reputation," "all melt into thin air," "bubble bubble toil and trouble." Combine bubbles with milk and you get a milkshake, a fair emblem for Wilbur's airily sublimated simplicity, at times unpretentiously cosmic in its reach (e.g., *A Dubious Night*, B).

The impact of *c* is more staid, usually: it is crisp, articulatory, defining, strict, dry, classic, as in Verlaine's *Nuit de Walpurgis classique* where the garden à la Lenôtre is "correct, ridicule et charmant." Thus Wilbur: "There's classic and there's quaint" (*Objects*, B); "She teaches leaves to curtsey and quadrille" (*Ceremony*, C). Wilbur magnifies the paradoxical play between form and nature, which is what the poem *Ceremony* is about (Ovid, Shakespeare, Pascal, Donne preceded him in that bemusement). A curtsey is one of those ideal points of balance, a meeting between the pair: the bottomless charm of the natural girl and what she makes of it as nature's Queen. The *c* and the *q* have that touching classic strictness he wants here. In *C Minor* (M) "bran-flakes crackle" as a poet breakfasts; "crickets quicken," abruptly, in a languorous summer evening (*Cicadas*, B); ping-pong "scatters... knocks / Like crazy clocks" (*My Father Paints the Summer*, B).

His *d*, like his *t*, akin to *c*, is decisive, hard, penetrating: "Dig deep" (*Digging for China*, B). "Dive, dodo" (*The Walgh-Vogel*, B). In a moving prayer for his daughter, he sees a desperate bird beat against a pane, "drop like a glove / To the hard floor" (*The Writer*, M). He ends by wishing, "my darling... What I wished before, but harder." The *d* is subtly determining of this tender stoicism. It is the toughness of:

> The hardest headlands
> Gravel down,
> The seas abrade. (*La Rose des vents*, C)

e, in its eh tone, is a self-effacing letter. Sartre, in *What Is Literature?*, saw its very quietness as functioning in his vision of florence. Classical writers, like Mme. de Lafayette, favor it, along with John Updike and *The New Yorker* altogether. It's cool: "a freshness ever the same" (*Then*, C; note the understated title). It contributes to the courtly decorum and decency in the title of a whole collection: *Ceremony*. The dryness of an insect is partly expressed by the dryness of the sound, as in Valéry's "l'insect net gratte la sècheresse" (*Le Cimetière marin*). For Wilbur, "crickets quicken" the evening air; their plain song is "thin uncomprehended" (*Cicadas*, B).

But *e* as in "these" is bright, intense, like French *i*: "the Eden trees" (*My Father Paints the Summer*, B); "fearfully free" (*Objects*, B); "Any greenness is deeper than anyone knows" (*The Beautiful Changes*, B).

Plato in his *Cratylus* identified *f* (Greek *fi*) as "the windy letter." It surely is. Hugo got carried away:

> Un frais parfum sortait des touffes d'asphodèle.
> Les souffles de la nuit flottaient sur Galgala. (*Booz endormi*)

In *Poplar, Sycamore* (B) we see a tree

> faithless to wind, troweling air
> Tinily everywhere faster than air can fill.

In *Lightness* (B), a "brute gust lifted-and-left in the midst of the air..." In *The Peace of Cities* (B), "the Luftwaffe waft" (rushes of air through broken windowpanes).

> Aloft
> On the ocean shelf he saw the soft
> Signals of trees
> And gulls, and the sift
> Of the sea's long landward airs offering trails to him.
> ....(*Sunlight Is Imagination*, B)

> Tasting the frothy mist, and the freshest
> Fathoms of air. (*The Terrace*, C)

In French, *g*, as in "gourmet" is the glottal, appetitive letter par excellence: glotte, gourmand, gargarisme, glouton, goulet, glouglou... Mallarmé saw it that way in English too and noted that the addition of l, as it were, *satisfied* the desire in an exultation: "gloire du long désir" (*Prose*), "torp grand glaïeul" (stunning flower, ibid.; its calyx seems to mirror our convulsing throat). I give these French examples to show how his own art was affected.

First, the unaccompanied *g*: "Twisted trunk, by rooted hunger wrung" (*Grasse: The Olive Trees*, C); these trees have a "great thirst." Old Andrew Mellon is "consumer with greedy ire" (*A Dutch Courtyard*, B):

> The cocks... with vulgar joy
> Acclaim the sun. (*A Black November Turkey*, T)

In *Playboy* (W), "What so engrosses him... grips his fancy."

The exultant *gl*: "glory lay wherever he might turn" (*Parable*, C); "Let us have music... in glory" (*C Minor*, M); "with strangled rale" (*A Black November Turkey*, T) is a gobbling sound, corollary.

h hardly exists in French as a sound. It seems to function mostly as an expression of emotional exhalation, in art, e.g., "ha!" or "ha! ha!" or vehemently pronounced "haine." Wilbur sometimes uses it that way:

> with a holler punch the life
> Out of a swallow in the air (*Tywater*, B)

> be bleak
> And howling-hollow. (*Two Songs...*, B)

In *Marché aux oiseaux* (C) there is a vehement "by Hell." None of this is very impressive for our purposes: *h* is pretty inert.

i, as in "pin," helps to convey a light, slender impression:

> Troweling air
> Tinily. (*Poplar, Sycamore*, B)

The song of "crickets" is "thin uncomprehended" in *Cicadas* (B), bringing a "slim false-freshness, by this trick of the ear."

i as in "lie" is a diphthong in sound with a twisting or squirming pain-release as in French *aïe* (and other Mediterranean equivalents) and is so used by Wilbur: "Damn, we cry" (*Juggler*, C); "the summer people sigh, 'Is this July?'" (*My Father Paints the Summer*, B); "the cry of the buried child" (*The Waters*, B); "cries and cries" (*Two Songs...*, B).

Some of that poignancy gets into frequent allusions to "sky," "high," "fly." Here we have rather the associative phenomenon of "clustering" (Kenneth Burke): certain groups of words forming an overtone-series, as in "fly-sky-high." Actually, the shape of the *y* tends to be more active, a sort of opening up to the beyond, as we have witnessed in the seven *y*'s of *The Beautiful Changes*. We will return to that.

j gives a violent thrust, jab, dig, but maybe for that reason does not occur frequently in Wilbur: "Jabbing among the chips" (*A Black November Turkey*, T); "Jewsotted Jews" (*Water Walker*, B); "I caused his work to jar" (*The Proof*, W).

k is like *c*, as in "the crackle of bran-flakes," above.

l is ubiquitous. A liquid, it lolls languidly, caresses like water or a curved tongue:

> The Queen Anne's Lace lying like lilies
> On water (*The Beautiful Changes*, B)
>
> Valleys my mind in fabulous blue Lucernes (ibid.)
>
> Lucent as shallows slowed by wading sun (*Ceremony*, C)
>
> the slip
> Slip of the silken river. (*A Simile for Her Smile*, C)

m is the initial sound in the word for mother in just about every language. Sir Richard Paget attributes this phenomenon, rightly I think, to the position of the lips in sucking. It is soft on the ears and soothing, as in *mmm*, especially in "hum," "yumyum," "summer." It looks pillowy, breast-like or motherly, receptive. Cf. *w*, an inverted *m*.

A Simile for Her Smile is addressed to Wilbur's wife, the mother of his children; the two *m*'s seem appropriate, as in:

> with your mother's milk the mother tongue,
> In which pure matrix... (*The Etruscan Poets*, M)

"Summer" is one of Wilbur's favorite words. "Maternal murmurs" (*The Waters*, B) are a part of its lullaby, as in "sometimes summer" (*Praise in Summer*, B). Wilbur, in sum, is a summery Sunday child, one of Dylan Thomas' "boys of summer."

n is apt to be negative, unsurprisingly: occasionally it is appetitive, as in "banana," "ninny." Sometimes it is used for its little mound:

> The walrus: head hunched from the oxen shoulder.
> (*Castles and Distances*, C)

This "hunch" and the negation are both in "the spine of the rock. No" (*Sunlight Is Imagination*, B).

In a word like "tender," the hardness of negation is utterly swamped by the softness of the *r* and the meaning. Benjamin Whorf was right: these elusive phenomena emerge by a cooperation of various aspects of language, incrementally, through "overdetermination." The *n* seldom emerges in Wilbur's poetry; negation is not his forte.

o is for his plenitude, all over him:

> The ping-pong balls
> Scatter their hollow knocks   (*My Father Paints the Summer*, B)

> the ping-pong's optative bop.   (ibid.)

We earlier invoked his *O* (B) with its one and one "circles." We can securely pass on.

p is cooperative. It is plump, like the *b* of "belly" (which is it, up-side down):

> veins pump, pump and burst their seams.   (*Folk Tune*, B)

We recall the wonderful "pod" of *Two Voices in a Meadow* (A). The fat little shape of the ampersand causes this:

> Porter, poor pander ampersand.   (*&*, B)

Pears and plums bear us out:

> that picked pear you tossed me, and your face
> As legible as pearskin's fleck and trace,
> Which promise always wine.   (*June Light*, B)

The plum is in *Two Songs...* (B). And the *u*, we shall see, has to do with its pendulous shape.

q is like *c*, we noted, but it has a twist, as in "queer" or "queasy." Wilbur uses that aspect in "There's classic and there's quaint" (*Objects*, B). But there isn't much to go on.

r is a lovely, liquid effect in both languages (in the right context). In French it gives much of the melodious flow of tendresse: "L'ombre des arbres dans la rivière embrumée (Verlaine, *L'Ombre des arbres*). In this case the combination with *b* brings a vibrancy which is close to Debussy's "drowned" appogiatura. What would we do without that *r* in their names: Renoir, Mallarmé, Verlaine, Valéry? "Verlaine? Il est caché parmi l'herbe Verlaine" (Mallarmé, *Tombeau de Verlaine*). Like them, Wilbur wields it often in combination with *a*, and then it becomes part of a fair overtone series, a "cluster": air, clair, art, clarté, transparence, Paris, parfum, paradis... In English, clear, art, stare, pear, air, darling, fair hair, grace, transparency...

Clearness (C) begins:

> There is a poignancy in all things clear,
> In the stare of the deer.

Castles and Distances (C) has a closely related effect in the gaze of a stag, "the eyes clear with grace." The rhymes of the first stanza of *June Light* are "there-stare-air." To his wife he says, "You are clarion hair" (*Sunlight Is Imagination*, B).

The *r* alone is watery, flowing. "Long landward airs offering trails" (ibid.). In his gorgeous *Hamlen Brook* (N):

> At the alder-darkened brink
> Where the stream slows.

In *The Waters* (B):

> From powdery Palmyre, the tireless wind,
> Braided by waves but cradling to this shore,
> Where folding water...

s is silkily caressing often in Wilbur:

> The sea so sings us back to histories (*The Waters*, B)
>
> such soft air
> That real caresses (ibid.)
>
> A phosphorous girl is singing,
> Up whispering galleries trellised notes (*A Song*, B)
>
> the slip
> Slip of the silken river. (*A Simile for Her Smile*)

t is strict, neat, erect, staccato:

> Scattering stutter of windmills (*A Song*, B)
>
> Electric towers. (*Attention Makes Infinity*, B)

The title of the last-mentioned is noteworthy for its *t*'s. Also:

> the stuff of stones (*Epistemology*, C)
>
> the nets and cages of my thought. (*An Event*, T)

u presents marvellous opportunities of skulk, slump, urn, glum, sump, in its sagging shape, and sometimes Wilbur exploits this pendulous aspect.

> guttural sucks (*The Beacon*, T)
>
> The forests strummed as one loud lute (*Folk Tune*, B)
>
> summer's easy / Wheel ruts (*Wyeth's Milk Cans*, N)
>
> let's not turn down our thumbs (*In a Bird Sanctuary*, B)
>
> the shucked tunic of an onion. (*Lying*, N)

In "fabulous blue Lucernes" (*The Beautiful Changes*, B) the valleyed calyxes are almost like buttercups.

The French *u* is more acute, penetrating, complex: whence Mallarmé's obsessive streaks of them, as we noted.

According to an eminent Belgian psychoanalyst, Charles Baudoin (234), *v* is a routine symbol for the feminine organ in the unconscious mind of patients. It is an ancient archetype: Venus, Eve, the lower half of Solomon's seal (Joyce's "maids-apron") for the Kabbalah, virgin, vulva, vagina, vase, and so on. Mallarmé used it subterraneanly in connection with the naked virgin Hérodiade:

> Vers lui la femme nativement se dévoile
> ...J'aime l'horreur d'être vierge et je veux
> Vivre...

So its shape is apposite for valleys and the like. Wilbur knows that:

> Now all this proud royaume
> Is Venice. (*Winter Spring*, B)

> the slightest shade of you
> Valleys my mind (*The Beautiful Changes*, B)

> Failure, the longed-for valley, takes him in. (*In the Smoking Car*, A)

w is perhaps Wilbur's favorite letter (it's importantly in his name). It is double: in French *double-v*, in English *double-u*, with parallel impact. Mallarmé saw its duality as an essence of the feminine—wife, woman, womb, wench—the fertile fluctuation of existence—wave, waver—the twin shape of the female organ (labia), the two sides of his metaphysical boat, in the *Coup de dés*, and so cosmogonically on. Wilbur construes it much the same way:

> mermaid you in the grass waving away. (*Sunlight Is Imagination*, B)

w has little twin wings: so *Walgh-Vogel* (B) is a good name for a bird which has "two token wings," "wings wavy wide as heaven."

> A rowdy wind... swoops the lake. (*Sunlight Is Imagination*, B)

This is clearly multiple, fluctuant, like a sweeping broom.

> Everywhere
> Walls wince, and there's the steal of waters. (*Winter Spring*, B)

Winter spring is an unsure season, wavering.

> Winter spring is winnowing the air of chill. (*Winter Spring*, B)

The "wa-wa" of wind (and waves) influences the "wind's white shudders" (*The Ride*, N).

One of the most resonant clusters in our language is winter-wind-window-winnow. The rattling of casements is in it, the flurry of snow, the stir of excited childhood indoors looking out. Wilbur cherishes all this and shows it:

who from a window watch the blizzard blow (*Orchard Trees, January*, N)

See, every yard, alive with laundry white,
Billowing wives and leaves, gives way to air (*Attention Makes Infinity*, B)

One wading a fall meadow... water. (*The Beautiful Changes*, B)

The intimate growth gently parts or *gives* in this yielding nature, a beloved Woman, his wife. The parting is further in the *v* of "Valleys" and the sustained series of *y*'s, sheer generosity: "such kind ways."

x is hard to find in our poet. Mallarmé built a whole sonnet on it ("Ses purs ongles") where it functioned like "the X of an unknown" and the Baroque mystery of paradox-phoenix-quincunx, fall crossing rise in an absurd cancellation, presented as a geometric crispness laid on nature in thought. But Wilbur scants it. I don't know why.

y: we saw its power from the first, in the seven *y*'s of *The Beautiful Changes* (B) passage:

Your hands hold roses always in a way that says
They are not only yours.

That is a major image of Wilbur, that feminine "cornucopia" offering generously or opening up to the beyond on high, like a calyx reaching up its invitation to the bee or the sunlight and rain, or two arms held up embracing the All:

Shall I say you are fair
In the sun,
Or mermaid you in the grass waving away? (*Sunlight Is Imagination*, B)

I toss circles skyward (*O*, B)

a branchy shape. (*Under a Tree*, N)

z is another puzzle, a zigzag, much more available in French where Mallarmé used it for a tacking boat's path and the maze of existence. The maze (often Baroque or Rococo) is closely related to the quincunx and the other *X*-shapes. The word "amaze" adds to its feeling of puzzlement one of dazzlement:

We're amazed as windows stricken bright (*Winter Spring*, B)

Its [summer's] perfect blaze. (*My Father Paints the Summer*, B)

Dazzling as summer's leaf-stir
Chinked with light (*A Storm in April*, M)

blizzard. *Orchard Trees, January*, M)

As a reward for our joint analytic efforts, in a move to put this world back together again, here now is one whole poem: *The Beautiful Changes* (B). I recommend reading it twice: first, noting in a lingering way the riffs of *w, l, y*, and the meaningful play of other letters too (*o, u, a*) in this masterpiece. Second, forgetting the ill-mannered pointing, submit to it for its own incomparable sake.

THE BEAUTIFUL CHANGES

One wading a Fall meadow finds on all sides
The Queen Anne's Lace lying like lilies
On water; it glides
So from the walker, it turns
Dry grass to a lake, as the slightest shade of you
Valleys my mind in fabulous blue Lucernes.

The beautiful changes as a forest is changed
By a chameleon's tuning his skin to it;
As a mantis, arranged
On a green leaf, grows
Into it, makes the leaf leafier, and proves
Any greenness is deeper than anyone knows.

Your hands hold roses always in a way that says
They are not only yours; the beautiful changes
In such kind ways,
Wishing ever to sunder
Things and things' selves for a second finding, to lose
For a moment all that it touches back to wonder.

Works Cited

Baudoin, Charles. *De l'instinct à l'esprit*. Belgium: Bruges, 1950.

Cohn, Robert Greer. *Mallarmé's "Un Coup de dés."* A Yale French Studies Publication. New Haven: Yale University Press, 1949.

_____. *L'Oeuvre de Mallarmé: Un Coup de dés*. Paris: Librairie Les Lettres, 1951.

_____. *The Poetry of Rimbaud*. Princeton: Princeton University Press, 1973.

_____. "The ABC's of Poetry." Rpt. in *Modes of Art*. Stanford French and Italian Studies 1 (Saratoga: Anma Libri, 1975).

_____. *Toward the Poems of Mallarmé*. Berkeley: University of California Press, 1980.

_____. *Mallarmé's Prose Poems*. New York: Cambridge University Press, 1988.

Mallarmé, Stéphane. *Traité du verbe*. Preface. In *Oeuvres complètes*. Paris: Gallimard, 1945.

Valéry, Paul. "Sorte de préface." *Ecrits divers sur Stéphane Mallarmé*. Paris: Gallimard, 1950.

Desire: Direct and Imitative

Envy or, in a more civilized way, desire which imitates another desire—little John wants what little George grabs for—is familiar in our experience and our lore. Dante presented a poignant example in his Paolo and Francesca episode: reading about Lancelot's desire gave the ill-fated pair "ideas." La Bruyère wryly commented that if the word *love* hadn't existed, people wouldn't think of making it, again illustrating thereby the dialectical relations between form and matter, word and deed. Stendhal's Count Mosca knew that and worried that if the word *amour* arose between his nephew and his girlfriend, he was *perdu*. In sum, words and other forms—models we imitate—limit or mold a chaotic reality, make a specific reality possible. So fads are an important part of life.

The animal and human propensity to imitate, which is an integral part of learning and survival, was widely discussed in the eighteenth century, for example by David Hume, in his *Treatise of Human Nature* and Adam Smith in *The Theory of Moral Sentiments*. Smith wisely tempered this view with his insistence that although imitation and "custom" are powerful forces, humans nevertheless have spontaneous and original tastes. In sum, for Adam Smith, the two inclinations constitute two dimensions of psychic drive which cut across each other in all areas of desire or "sentiment."[1]

The fuller dialectic is widely recognized in our time by critics, philosophers, psychologists, e.g., Jacques Lacan, who in a long essay, "Some Reflections on the Ego"[2] makes a distinction between "the object of the animal's needs which is emprisoned in the field of force of its desire" and "the object of man's desire, and we are not the first to say this, which is essentially an object desired by someone else." We note the *two* kinds of

---

[1] (Oxford: Clarendon Press, 1976) 199-200.
[2] Translated by Mary Elizabeth Beaufils; in *International Journal of Psycho-analysis* 34 (1953) 11-17.

desire, the direct animal kind connected with needs, and the indirect and mimetic sort connected with "higher things," in humans. What Lacan does not say clearly, but implies, is that these two desires are dialectically related—as is upper (civilized) and lower (animal) in the rounded human generally—and this is dramatically manifest in problematic phenomena such as religious eroticism. More recently, René Girard, the well-known scholarly critic, radically alters this perspective and sees "mimetic desire" everywhere, practically to the exclusion of the other kind of desire, the equally familiar direct kind easily observable in the self or others. His stubborn research on this has produced some illuminating and influential results but, as often happens, a good thing tends to go too far and indeed, in this instance, to become wildly runaway.

The fundamental error of his system can be summed up as unidimensionality: In terms of desire, he has a strong tendency to eliminate, or "put on a back burner," its deep, "vertical" dimension, the "metaphorical" one, where highest aspiration, as in religion or art, and lowly hungers and needs, as in lust or aggression, meet, ultimately, in a union of extreme opposites. This is the dimension of tragedy and glory, of ironic reversals, of God's benefits and monstrosities—Mother Teresa and Auschwitz—and altogether the "problem of evil" vis-à-vis our eternal dream of sheer beauty and goodness, of Paradise.

In this direction, he fails to see that lowly *need* and sublime *aspiration* can be construed in a continuum, as well as different. And that both together form a dimension at right angles to the tempered, more ordinarily "human" one of civilized appetites, and desires, including prominently those based on envy, or, more complexly, imitating the desires of others.

A vivid illustration of this one-sidedness is provided in his well-known scenario of the "double" as a harbinger of a crisis of violence. It *can* be: if two leads to one, as in rivalry for an object. But two can lead *away* from one, as in "divide and rule" or simple proliferation. In that case it can appear as benign: "two is better than one," and does so in many myths.[3]

---

[3]In Frazer's *Golden Bough* (*The New Golden Bough*, ed. Theodore h. Gaster [New York: Doubleday & Co., 1959]) almost all the doubles are positive in their magic. Likewise in Joseph Campbell's *The Masks of God*. There are also examples of a two-one tension, as in Lévi-Strauss's ambiguous myths of vegetable-animal generation. It also is the core of George Sand's *La Petite Fadette*: an adaptive two-one tension in the female protagonist who reflects the author (a tomboy girl who grows up to marry a rich peasant) is carried out also in the relation of the twins, who learn how to get along. It is all very mild, no threat of violence at all—just one of insipidity.

This arbitrariness reflects the mobility of all such basic concepts as we know since Zeno, Plato, Aristotle, as well as the modern paradoxalists and "absurdists." Unity, seen on a deep "metaphorical" dimension, is both an ideal harmony and a frightening concentration which can explode in destruction.[4] Multiplicity (beginning with two) is an appeasing temperateness, or reassuring repetition (e.g., of children: one child is too vulnerable against fate) as well as its opposite, an eventual boredom, dull repetitiousness, passivity, shallow "quantitative" spirit, and ultimately the death of spirit...

In other words, there is a *dilemma of dimensions* which is more profound than a mere crisis of violence. We often do not know which way to turn; ;throughout our lives we bounce from one dimension to another, oscillating, as Schopenhauer noted, between boredom and pain. We go one way for a while, as in a prudent working career and settled home life, and then we get intolerably bored, restless, kick up our heels, take terrible risks on weekends, and so on. If we get badly hurt or psychically wounded, guilt-ridden, in this new direction, we pivot back to "normal" life for a forgetful while...

Such is humankind, even in the context of frightfully destructive war. Thoughtful people realize that even if we decide to make permanent peace with the Russians, for fear of nuclear holocaust, the old human propensity to *risk* will at some point arise, out of the immemorial fear of inertia, passivity, mediocrity, utter flatness of spirit, lifelessness...

This view of human becoming may easily appear as hopeless; yet somehow we have survived and muddled through, with the help of faith, and probably will continue to do so. It helps too, I think, to look at the tough realities *squarely* and not just through the polarized lenses of a reductionist theory which slights the tragic depths of the *fully human* dilemma.

Among Girard's favorite whipping-boys is Sigmund Freud. Freud's view of desire—libido in its fuller sense—over his entire evolving career can be summed up on a Cartesian cross: the vertical axis goes from the superego down through the ego, which is fundamentally a zero-infinite node, or point of origin (the empty ego of which Sartre and Lacan also speak) all the way down to the id; the horizontal axis extends through all the tempered (partial, fragmentary) entities of the social perspective—e.g., others—and ordinary, sane existence.

---

[4] It is the *one* eye of the monster in *La Dolce Vita* that is awesome.

We can picture the Eros-Thanatos polarity[5]—life-death, positive-negative, love-hate, pleasure-pain, etc.—as a swirling wheel of the Tao, generating mysteriously interpenetrating opposite emotions welling like a vortex from the Being-Nothing core of life at the crossroads of the two axes and coloring all the poles of the Freudian chart.[6]   Or else as a macrocosmic blown-up version of that wheel in a total "divine" scheme such as the Venus-mars couple of Empedocles (there is an obvious exchange between the micro and the macro...).

Freud's later doctrine makes it clear that the relation between Eros and Thanatos is ambiguous. It is also evident from his (and Lacan's) work on the dream-life and the unconscious generally that the articulations of mind from the upper region interpenetrate with expressions even from the lowest levels of the psyche (see XXIII, 1924: "The Economic Problem in Masochism" in *Collected Papers*).[7]   Cf. Lacan's "ça parle," referring to the unconscious.[8]

Crucially, it is through *grace* that these tensions tilt on merciful occasion to something arational and beyond even a pure love, an Edenic glimpse, the goal of faith—the "peace that passeth understanding"—to which we aspire throughout our existence. Here we leave Freud behind.

Now, the superego is the extreme locus not of *imitation*, but as Freud says, "emulation" (op. cit.)—of the ideal model, a divinity, and, in general, the region *above* the ego is the area of Form in that sense, of cultural formation or structuring.

This, we are persuaded by Freud and Lacan, comes about (at least in a major phase, I would add) via the Oedipus complex, castration fear, sublimation into culture (the vibrant symbolic chain stemming from the yes-no Eros of the phallus).

The completer pattern, going beyond Freud and Lacan, is an ever-recurrent attempt to pull off a major Promethean coup, ever-rebuffed, whereupon the cringing psyche *pivots* into our on-going Adamic or existential expressions (cf. Hegel's master-slave, Mallarmé's *Coup de dés*).

---

[5]When seen as a separating, a duality, that is the beginning of a linearity (two points make a line) characterizing the horizontal (metonymic) axis. But the tilt of grace of which we speak below, toward a positive beyond Eros, is a deeper, more intimate matter, central and mysterious like all faith (our occasional assignment of it to the "metaphorical" axis is merely approximate).

[6]The paradoxical (dialectical) mobility of the polarity is what undercuts the hypostatized and optimistic view of the ego in psychologists (particularly American) of the sort Lacan attacks.

[7](New York: Basic Books, 1959).

[8]Since the relation between upper and lower is dialectical, the nature of the unconscious is profoundly problematic, vibrant—it is and is not separate from consciousness—and those who like Sartre and René Girard deny its existence are self-deceptive.

The drama with the actual father is merely one version of the drama whose prologue is "in Heaven" (Goethe, *Faust*, 1).

In the fragmentary ("metonymic") mid-realm of the psyche where the humiliated ego extends through social relations, divine Form—in the beginning was the Word—emanates, becomes tempered into social versions, especially the symbolic chain, language itself. it is in this realm of everyday ta-ta-ta, measured forms of practical—in linear, operational, irreversible time—fallen or Adamic existence that "mimetic desire" occurs along with all other imitation (as opposed to deep originality). Emulation, to use Freud's term, pertains to the holistic dimension of the vertical or metaphoric—the realm of faith, vision, tone, beauty, originality as our tradition from Plato through Augustine to Baudelaire, Mallarmé and beyond has praised and glorified it. It is as far as can be from mimetic, though Girard tries to cram it under that heading in *Deceit, Desire, and the Novel*[9] and all his writing, thus skewing the whole picture of life and its authentic texts. Adoration (the Church's and Proust's "adoration perpétuelle"—the early title of part of his masterpiece; later he settled for *intermittent* adoration, more realistically) is the stuff of the *Imitatio Christi*, for example, or even Don Quixote's relation to Amadis de Gaula. But, although Quixote is also enormously imitative, he is clearly "cracked." His freakish case serves mainly to obfuscate the crucial distinction we are making here. That perhaps, is why Girard chose him to lead off his specious argument...

Regardless of that unlikely particular instance, in true emulation—following an *inspiration*—a subject may imitate nothing specific at all but merely go on "in the spirit" of his inspirer, say a god or demigod, as we refer at times to culture heroes. To repeat, it is a radically separate *dimension* of reality which it is ruinous to scant in a serious discussion of great literature, let alone life through the western ages.

The id pole features the reverse of Form: *sparagmos*, scattering, dispersal as in death, defecation, and sex. But, as we observed in Freud's later view of Eros and Thanatos, worship *above* and the relaxation of the mediocre social ego into an oceanic dispersal—"comme un prêtre mis en pièces," as St-John Perse exclaimed ecstatically in *Anabase*—*below* are mysteriously joined "far out" or far in. Hence, again, the bemusing fact of religious eroticism...

Freud and Lacan have taught us to see desire on a metonymic axis. But desire is rooted in the central "core of existence" (Freud), and maintains a nostalgia for that purity even in its most "forgetful" (Heidegger) mediated forms, as in Dostoevsky, where the most flatly ordinary

[9](Baltimore: Johns Hopkins University Press, 1965).

"buffoon" is sooner or later struck by a dazzling reminiscence. At times, in literature like that and in life, a petty desire, which is inevitably at this level partly "mimetic" in adults, conceived in rivalry and resentment, can take off to a superior, noble, almost divine, Olympian dignity of "male" spirit, vertically. Or, horizontally, it can transcend all-too-human limitations in a flash and become a truly generous love for a woman—Dostoevsky's Sonia—or a child, for example, furthering "female" or on-going, healthy life. Likewise, the petty negative elements involved in the process can descend, on this chart, to pure murder, Thanatos. And the two impulses, alas, are related and can produce strange, tragic reversals, as we read in the daily papers (e.g., the Jonestown cult). But, with grace, man and woman transcend all that dialectical to-do and muddle through toward a faithful beckoning peace, an Edenic hope, undimmed.

There are impulses in these holistic directions and more or less of movement in them all through life, interspersed with, or oscillating with, through "intermittences" (Proust), the minor phases of desire. This oscil-lation or balance, tending to equality like all the other polar opposites of existence, is far closer to the truth than the critic's one-sided emphasis on mimetic desire either in existence itself or on the pages of a novel (in the latter case, the novelist may lend himself to this mutilated perspective by his own inadequacy of vision).

A person tends to move in *both* these directions—whole and partial—when he desires *at any time*, although one or the other may be empha-sized momentarily, along the usual dissociative "operational" path of becoming. But, to repeat, over a longer period the two will tend to even out:

Thus, for example, in infants purity prevails for a while, during the phase of "primary narcissism," involving the isolated self (coalesced with the mother) in a singular self-sufficiency, as Freud has demonstrated in "On Narcissism: An Introduction." Even here, as Derrida would claim, there is *some* mediation epistemologically or metapsychologically, some formal principle or "trace," but Freud is nonetheless substantially correct. Not only is the child largely self-sufficient in this sense as compared to the adult but, as Freud compellingly shows, this is true of very "femi-nine" women as well and, further, the lost Eden glowing in the infant is sought in parental adoration, vicariously, and an equivalent male ado-ration of sublimely feline and "indifferent" women (here we may think of the adolescent Gilberte in Proust).[10]

---

[10]D. H. Lawrence contrasts women's self-sufficiency and high-low fusion of the psyche, integrity, and grace, with the weak, split psyche of males, dependent "anaclitically" on women's wholeness (*Psychoanalysis and the Unconscious* [London: M. Secker, 1923]).

Girard sees all that as sentimental myth masking the only real game in town, the male-male rivalry. The women naturally feel left out and occasionally—in an ironic turn for the feminists—give him whatfor, notably Sarah Kofman, in *Diacritics*.[11]

The alternations of infantile narcissism and adult realism are a prime example of the bent toward homeostasis which goes on altogether in existence, but this tendency to equilibrium occurs intermittently all along, as ubiquitously as essence (or "totalization") is interspersed with existence, synthesis with analysis, female Being or immanence with male Doing and transcendence... And the fullness is reflected in the great novels Girard discusses, and misuses, particular *A la Recherche du temps perdu* which he leans on heavily for his demonstration, in *Deceit, Desire and the Novel*.

Girard, like all critics, not only uses selected passages for his argument, he also, to repeat, indulges a semantic sleight-of-hand. Instead of seeing two kinds of desire at work, he sees only one, mimetic, and divides it into the two aspects of "external and internal" mimesis or "mediation." The first is exemplified by Don Quixote since he is not a rival of his model (Amadis de Gaula) who is dead, fictive, a sort of deity, *hors jeu*; but, as we noted, this worship (and emulation) is, basically, no longer "mimetic desire" at all; it is on the radically different dimension of metaphor, verticality. Girard is converting a cross of two dimensions and four poles into a triangle.[12]

The other kind of "mimetic desire," "internal," is illustrated by typical Dostoevsky characters—e.g., the Adolescent, the Man from Underground, and the Eternal Husband who resent the people they admire because they are too close for comfort; they are thus engaged in smallchange rivalry for an object with them. Sure, but the pure desire so powerful in Dostoevsky is ignored in all this. To repeat, one needn't have a model or rival in order to desire: the infant needs none in order to seek his mother's breast—at most she steers his blundering little mouth in the

---

[11]Sarah Kofman, "The Narcissistic Woman: Freud and Girard," *Diacritics* 10.3 (Fall 1980) 36-45.

[12]This is a common tactic of incomplete thought: Hegel's triad has been rightly attacked on similar grounds of smugness, premature conclusion. Also Lévi-Strauss's triads. Adding a fourth pole (which I call "antisynthesis") is what opened up post-Hegelian thought, in Kierkegaard and Mallarmé. Girard's thinking is a throwback... See Julia Kristeva's *The Revolution of Poetic Language* (New York: Columbia University Press, 1984) for a discussion of the "4th term." Also Derrida's *Dissemination*, introduction (Chicago: University of Chicago Press, 1981). And my own previous discussions, e.g., in *L'Oeuvre de Mallarmé: Un Coup de dés* (Paris: Librairie Les Lettres, 1951).

right direction—and that kind of spontaneous greed or love along with higher forms of it—worship (and Jesus' *sitio*, Mallarmé's equivalent in *Les Fenêtres*)—recurs very frequently in later phases of life till we die. There are thousands of little cults in daily life and some very deep ones, such as the adulation of artists, musicians, sports heroes.

Dostoevsky is useful to Girard because he is obsessive in *revealing* hitherto sentimentally slighted aspects of human personality, nasty, and complex, but he overdoes it and the effect is one of imbalance, often exaggeration to the point of caricature. The total absence of *nature* in his novels furthers this disequilibrium. People (even Russians) neither appear in the way he describes nor do we recognize a fully adequate description of the inner life in his portrayals, for all of his genius and for all of the dramatically revelatory quality of his work. Tolstoy strikes us as more complete or human in this sense: Thomas Mann, Albert Camus, and George Steiner, among others, have helped us to see this.

Cervantes, too, is unbalanced in the presentation of a naïvely credulous hero, purer than life, childlike to the point of extreme improbability. Again we settle for these contrivances because of his genius which carries us along with wit and brio and causes us to "suspend disbelief."

Don Quixote and Sancho Panza and the Man from Underground together in one character (i.e., one who "touches all the bases" as Marcel does in his affair with elusive Gilberte), would begin to tell us something about the true rounded nature of human desire.

Girard's triangle of rival-subject-object (as in the Oedipus complex), represents only a fragmented (mediated) kind of love or desire, as we noted. The integral emotion occurs for Girard only as a finality based on Catholic theology; in Proust, for example, in the last volume of *A la Recherche: Le Temps retrouvé*, where there is an ascension to artistic, Olympian joy, freedom, salvation of the spirit. But great novels, particularly Proust's, aren't written in this naïvely linear way (let alone life): the final, total joy *spirally*, as it were—in reflection of the well-identified spiral nature of the plot—bathes the entire narration to some large extent, and this is surely the case with those numerous "privileged" or beacon moments along the way. Such clearly is Marcel's Edenic adoration ("perpetual") for his mother or Combray, both unreplaceable, unshakable, authentic, as Proust states at the end of the "Combray Section," and little Gilberte Swann is a part of that adoration: in addition to the mimetic element (influenced by Bergotte) he obviously wants us to feel the wild totality of that wonderful puppy love—the "vert paradis" of Baudelaire—which yearns to "carry off" the child "body and soul" recalling the narcissistic greed of the infant: thus Swann opens his mouth wide as if to swallow Odette; he bites her cheeks. Proust puts the whole emphasis on this:

> cette joie... il n'y avait pascollaboré... elle lui restaitextérieure... C'est d'elle-mêmequ'émanait... cette vérité.[13]

Of course, the other side of Swann's love is presented, for example, in the passages where he *collaborates* with his infatuation, imitates art. But finally—following his usual spiral from naïve faith through adolescent skepticism up to a return of faith (as in the beauty of the Duchesse de Guermantes), sublimated, *aufgehoben*—the truest Proust is on the side of faith; the parts on pure love, spontaneous, original, are powerful and sustained:

> Ainsi un voyageur arrivé par un beau temps au bord de la Méditer-ranée, incertain de l'existence du pays qu'il vient de quitter, laisse éblouir sa vue, plutôt qu'il ne leur jette des regards, par les rayons qu'émet vers lui l'azur lumineux et résistant des eaux. (ibid.)

The moving pages on the "petite phrase" are all in that register of authentic love. This is indispensable Proust: Girard tries to make us forget it. So, in sum, the "final" joy is really pantheistically ubiquitous, as Eden is in our later tradition, all around us; original, final, above, below (in certain writers) and even, "quintessentially," at the core of "here and now" as in Kierkegaardian Instants and the various equivalents discussed by Poulet, that eternal present which is rather often felt in Proust, enough to make certain commentators speak of his "eudae-monia." These are moments of his *vraie vie*, which is constant in a sense, or intermittent, at least latent or implied in his narrative as a whole.

One must grant that Proust's narrator becomes skeptical of love as he grows up, but this is fully compensated by his faith in original creation—that of Vinteuil, Elstir, Bergotte, Berma—and in Creation, nature. And there is a great deal of human warmth not only in those early pages satu-rated with childish belief but in many a subsequent page concerning Jupien, his niece, Charlus himself, Saint-Loup, the Prince de Guer-mantes, not to speak of his enduring attachment to his family and Swann. Girard's insistence is depressing, a sort of debunking, a demo-lition of the art. The one-sided idea that sentimental subjectivity gives way to novelistic maturation denies the view of Proust himself who apologized for a mounting dryness in his work (due, in part, to his pre-mature aging, an aggravation of his weakness). The last pages of *Le Temps retrouvé* return to this notion, try to excuse the less inspired

---

[13]*A la Recherche du temps perdu* I (Paris: Gallimard, 1957).

passages. Well, these assaults on poetry are periodic: "*Phèdre*, qu'est-ce que cela prouve?" The "vraie vie" goes on. It was the "admirable poète" that Mauriac, in a short documentary on Proust, cherished most of all. The pilgrimages go to Combray...

Proust comments somewhere that adolescence, peopled with "gods and monsters" is the only period when we ever really learned anything. Assuredly for an artist there are losses as well as gains in growing up— if not for scientists or businessmen. Is prose always better than poetry, generically? Is a disenchanted truth always superior to the "glorieux mensonge" (Mallarmé) of our youthful illusion? For a sophisticated mind— "jeune et pourtant très vieux"—there are grounds for fertile hesitation here. "Do not speak to me of the wisdom of old men" (T. S. Eliot). Eden is located in *both* directions according to Plato and Christianity. It is childhood and Reminiscence of what precedes it that fascinates figures like Wordsworth, Hölderlin, Rimbaud. Even according to the doctrine of original sin, which occurs with the fall of Adam, the primordial innocence is rediscovered at the *beginning* of life, in baptism. Hence existence itself is in a sense redeemed, for a sane and balanced view which the Church has espoused for centuries. Girard's scheme is excessively teleological, final, a sort of horizontal angelism which empties existence, as Camus noted of Marxism. Marriage is a sacrament, for Catholicism, and the events of this world are often good. Jesus wanted us to become like those little children, as did Dostoevsky.

The generous élan of love toward the woman as object—we spoke of this in our opening paragraphs—refutes Girard's persistent, almost Manichean, deflation of usual existence which he punctures with little mimetic tacks strewn everywhere. He attempts to knock down Freud's Oedipal triangle in *Violence and the Sacred*, for similar reasons, denying that the son's yearning for his mother is anything more than a subterfuge and construct masking mimetic desire. But in truth, the child's love for his mother in this authentic phase becomes the generous transcendence toward woman as mate in his later years. This movement of transcendence is the relatively horizontal equivalent of the self-sacrificial rise to purity of spirit which can solve the problem of life's constant contests when they threaten to become orgiastic murder, as Girard shows. In this sense, the "horizontal" transcendence provides an escape from the excessively fascinating male-male mimetic (and non-mimetic) whirl, just as Becoming, metaphysically, allows an escape from inert Being, providentially. We see this in animal behavior, across the spectrum of species: the male abandoning his hypnotic concern for the rival and *turning* toward the female...

Here one is aware again of the interchangeability of dimensions: totality can be achieved (or approached) "far out" along the horizontal which tends to meet the vertical ultimately in an Einsteinian space-time globality (or far in, at the microcosmic core, as in contemplation). And even well short of that ultimate, there are *approaches* to the purity or directness of unmediated love in that on-going healthy direction all along life's Adamic way, intimations of the power of the feminine: Goethe's *Ewigweibliche* (*Faust*), Mallarmé's "magnifique et aveugle instinct de vie" (J.-P. Richard's reference to the mother in *Pour un Tombeau d'Anatole*), as there are approaches to "Olympian" joy in the vertical "male" direction. Here Girard falls short of the lucidity of Lacan, for example, who shows the interpenetration of metaphoric and metonymic in a tetrapolar pattern, followed by Guy Rosolato (*La Relation d'inconnu*) and others.

Girard's excessive admiration for Sartre as critic points to certain affinities: Sartre is a pretty heavy-handed and insistently tendentious deflater of the romantic and late romantic tradition of great bourgeois writers. Girard's religious belief is very different from Sartre's atheistic pro-proletarian one (*engagement*), but both use devastating techniques of knocking down everything in the way of their goal. Girard has fallen in with the Byzantine deconstructivism of his time at least *methodically*, the same bent that produced Sartre's one-sided emphasis on existence and the almost McCarthyist quality of his criticism of Baudelaire, Mallarmé, Flaubert, and Proust. In this respect Girard has come close to structuralism with its arid insistence on differentiae alone and cold "structures," an "emptier than thou" dandy posture, a myopic addiction to narration, slighting the holistic and visionary aspect of life and art.

My main emphasis has been so far on Girard's approach to literature: although he prefers art to science, theoretically, as being suppler, embodying imperfection, in practice by leaning so heavily toward prose (the debunking novel) and depreciating the romantic (poetry, the metaphoric and visionary) he abets the encroachment of science into the humanities. His extensive use of anthropology furthers this unhelpful trend.

In the broader realm of culture-criticism—biblical exegisis and social foundations—he is less damaging, and I have a personal sympathy for his religiosity, specifically Catholicism, though again I find his dosage less wholesome than Saint Thomas' faith-reason balance, and, even though Pope John-Paul II has shown interest in his ideas, I sense a heretical bent in his concrete anti-transcendentalism.

Girard invokes, notably, the old procedure of the scapegoat: men resort, from time to time, to an orgy of murder in a sort of psychic entropy or totalization. This social crisis—which he thinks to be exclusively "mimetic" (Lévi-Strauss, whom he attacks, is more correct in seeing a drive to disorder)—incites people to seek a common adversary who attracts and diverts their bad energy. The victim is lynched and then divinized. We know all this from Frazer and Mauss, particularly.

The Girardian approach to the problematic of sacrifice is defective. Kierkegaard had understood, in his treatment of the Abraham-Isaac drama, that the deepest faith is based on the absurd (*credo quia absurdum est*); it is absurd for a loving God to ask us to sacrifice that which we love most, our son. It is the same essentially with Christ on the cross. But that dilemma had to be lived to the life-death core before a graceful, merciful turn, or pivoting, could occur, a way out for Abraham, an eternal glory for Jesus. Mallarmé and Camus, each in his way, wrestled with the same problem, and so do we all, to whatever extent. That is the meaning of authenticity, that not-cheating or not-haggling with your Maker or life as a whole. We lived that terrible dilemma on the battlefield as soldiers, thanking God if he saved us *in extremis* while others less graced went down under the gunfire. Our honor was at stake; some of us owed no less to the martyr-children of Auschwitz, for example.

Does the revelation of Judeo-Christianity and the internalization or symbolization of sacrifice through "le savoir biblique" and the innocence of Christ as Girard claims (*Des choses cachées...*)[14] do away with the crucial question? Well, we no longer believe in ritual murder of the scapegoat victim, true enough. But did not God *in some sense* murder Jesus for us? and murder man? That bitter query of writers like Hugo, Joyce, Vigny, Dostoevsky, Mann is still the challenge of our Christian tradition, and no clever verbalism can obviate the tragic fact, anymore than in the case of Abraham's intense suffering, perhaps worse than death. And if any person imitate Jesus in this and take upon himself a martyr's death —say in rescuing a child from fire and in thou-sands of other actual ways —how has the inmost dilemma really ever disappeared? Only by a leap of faith such as typically occurs at this juncture. As at the aporia of man-God. As man, can he be entirely "innocent"? This presents grave problems to Girard's thesis, another "absurd" he fails to deal with in depth. In *Le Sacrifice*, Guy Rosolato solidly confirms this view.[15]

The bipolar dilemma of the absurd in sacrifice may at this point, alternatively, be crossed by another dimension of itself (the absurd, squared) which makes the solution to the problem problematic: Jesus'

---

[14]*Des choses cachées depuis la fondation du monde* (Paris: Editions Grasset et Fasquelle, 1987).
[15](Paris: Presses Universitaires de France, 1987).

eternal glory—and our salvation through his death (murder)—both *is and is not* a way out: the question remains as all life's deepest questions do but is deepened epistemologically in these terms. We go on only through a graceful leap amidst this now tetrapolar (and conceivably poly-polar) situation, a leap of faith as in Kierkegaard's "The Absolute Paradox" (from *Philosophic Fragments*) at the node of the tetrapolar cross of inner crucifixion, which position might be called "quintessential."

This was the way of the late Camus, in *The Rebel*: his early formula of the absurd was crossed by itself, made problematic, and then he, torn at the crossroads, followed the impulse of a good heart (like his humble hero, Grand) and refused to follow the nihilistic Nazis through what was an after-all arbitrary logic of the absurd. Most of us, after a long-enough life, know that turning away from harm to self or others *in extremis*, as we offer up thanks for being allowed to live and let live. But who among us of any sensitivity does not also know the anguish of realizing life is not always that kind? "There but for the grace of God go I." Girard's rationalistic approach to these realms is shallow com-pared to a Kierkegaard's. (Girard's exaggerated praise of Sartre as critic is understandable in these terms).

The polydimensional cross in Kierkegaard and the other visionaries cited above is a common denominator of philosophic depth. Sometimes, as essentially in Saint Thomas and the healthy Catholic view since him, it takes the form of a balance of faith and reason conceived as epistemological dimensions (parallel to a metaphoric-metonymic cross and the basic Christian axes of divine and human). Fanatics of all sorts, contrariwise, get "hung up" on one or the other dimension: religious or rational excesses of the sort Camus decries in *The Rebel*. His doctrine of "limits" uses one to check the other, just as Leonardo's masterpieces reveal an ideal science-art equilibrium, or Einstein in the face of terrible threats to the world proposed that "Science without religion is lame." In other words, we recognize the intrinsic innocence, infinite value, of any dimension but also, like Pascal, recognize that we live in a middle ground of existence—Plato's and Voegelin's "metaxy"—where one must offset the other, as in Leonardo's paintings, Montesquieu's republic or anything else that is fully human.

The two dimensions limit and marry each other, in a sort of dance, rhythmic, warmly persistent, in our best artists, of all eras and, *mutatis mutandis*, in our great thinkers. Girard displays almost nothing of that incarnate beauty (Shekhina), that swelling, present, and thickset existence. Instead, an almost Manichean insistence, obsessed, monistic, uni-dimensional. The same terms keep coming back, all events are the same.

This recalls painfully the aging Tolstoy, the one who betrayed his human beauty, Anna Karenina, substituting for her a monolithic and boring belief. All right, religious and philosophic thought have always had that tendency, agreed; but to that extent? After Bergson, after Heidegger? At least Girard should respect that median warmth in the writers he comments on. But no: for him Proust writes well only when he is debunking, denying the young Romantic and his "lies," while we, the "Romantic and Symbolist critics" Girard rails at, believe that it is youth and maturity *together* which create, spirally, the intensely human union, the vibrancy of "la vraie vie."

Dosage, in this sense, is all-important: a bit too much of this or that ingredient spoils the dish; a bit more of scientific meticulousness in Leonardo would have marred his masterpieces. A minimal flaw in judgment exploded Challenger and Chernobyl. An excessive Faustian spirit has seriously damaged our universities. A wave of social engineering has devastated families in America. The West is in crisis, and Girard's heavy insistence on science in a science-literature "fusion" he extols seems to me to be not what we need now in humanistic study.

Girard uses all sorts of ruses: if Plato favors originality, "we must restudy Plato," thus putting him on a back burner. If a certain myth doesn't reflect his scheme, it is because the mechanism must remain hidden in order to be effective... Accept that formula and nothing can be disproven...

Girard betrays a similar dexterity concerning vendetta. There is an imitative side to it, of course, but at bottom there is a *symmetric* raising of social barriers, liberating relatively *spontaneous* or pure emotions (which may interpenetrate in love-hate).

Finally, there is not a single "mimetic crisis" which does not imply also a dialectic of pure love-hate, in *Midsummer Night's Dream, Macbeth*, anywhere. Shakespeare lives... but we can't detail everything here.

Girard is, after all, a remarkable writer and thinker, in spite of our foregoing strictures. Profound flaws will never stop a thinker—Mortimer Adler reminded us not long ago—from being deemed stimulating and even important. He got us to rethinking various grave matters, and for that we are grateful.

APPENDIX

Derrida at Yale

In the new biography of Sartre by Annie Cohen-Solal, I came upon the following line, which gave me an almost Proustian shock of pleasure and total recall: "[in 1948] the excellent review, *Yale French Studies*, devoted a whole issue to Sartre and existentialism." Those were the years... What a haven Yale was for a young literary person then! Fresh out of World War II, we were eager to make up for lost time. Henri Peyre— who loves to reminisce about that generation—gave us his southern French warmth, his brilliance, his immense erudition. Out of a desire to give something back, I proposed that we graduate students start a magazine, on a shoestring, and since existentialism was in the transatlantic air, that was our first issue. It soon had to be reprinted.

I ran the founding number and the next one, "Modern Poets." On the banana-yellow cover (Richard Wilbur pronounced it "succulent") appeared names like Sartre (he sent us his then unpublished play, *Les Mains sales*), Henri Peyre, and Wallace Fowlie. Roger Shattuck, home from flying the "hump," gave us Apollinaire translations; Richard Wilbur sent down Englishings of Villiers from Harvard; Richard Ellmann offered us Michaux; Pierre Schneider did an article (his first) on Valéry and automatic writing.

I could go on, but enough. It is enough to make a man weep, especially when he thinks of what came after—after roughly 1968, that is.

Despite the gathering fog, the growing chill of dehumanization in literature and art, those cited names go on proudly, of course. Comforted by my awareness that they were out there somewhere, I went on to pursue my lifelong affair with Mallarmé, lesser flings with Rimbaud, Baudelaire, Proust, others...

In 1971 Paul de Man published *Blindness and Insight*, where I came upon the following:

159

Recent interpreters of Mallarmé, such as Jacques Derrida and Philippe Sollers, anticipated in some respects by the American critic Robert Greer Cohn, find in Mallarmé a movement that takes place within a textual aspect of language as mere signifier, regardless of a natural or subjective referent.

I was not altogether surprised, because by then I knew, from published statements, etc., that I had influenced the *Tel Quel* group generally, which at that time loosely included Derrida as well as Sollers, his wife Kristeva, et al. But, although I was naturally pleased in a way, I was also bothered. How had I, in pursuit of that warmly—and as Sartre claims, "passionately"—wonderful poet Mallarmé (whom all those other charming Yale-days writers admired and often wrote about), come to this chic emptiness?

I made my independent position known in my writings and teaching and watched my classrooms empty out as the youth flocked to the showy new banners of ideology and skepticism about values. I hung onto my belief that one day all this would fade away like a bad dream. Alas, the nightmare from which we are struggling to awaken goes on and on. We were forcefully reminded of this by a lengthy article on Derrida and the Yale "Gang of Four"—which includes Geoffrey Hartman, J. Hillis Miller, and the late Paul de Man—by Colin Campbell in *The New York Times Magazine* a few Sundays back (February 9, 1986). Before I too become a fading dream, I decided to try to put the record straight, so far as I know it.

Derrida has indeed been influential in our time, and singularly at Yale, but it is helpful to know what *his* sources were. He leans heavily on Nietzsche, Heidegger, Blanchot and, not least, Mallarmé, who, as Roland Barthes remarked, was at the fountainhead of modern linguistics and all the critical, semiotic, and general intellectual to-do that came out of that. ("All we do is repeat Mallarmé. And we do very well when it is Mallarmé that we repeat.") In what is widely regarded as his best book, *Dissemination*, Derrida devotes the bulk of his energies to a deconstructive reading of Mallarmé's *Mime* and some related texts.

Now, deconstruction is very ancient, going back at least to the Sophists Socrates took on in various dialogues of Plato. Those debunkers had understood what we later sophomores got excited about, that all truth is problematic by the very nature of the knowing process (which interferes with it, as in current physical notions of "indeterminacy"). Zeno of Elea made an early formulation of the dilemma, and Plato and Aristotle dealt with it variously.

Mallarmé, after Hegel and Kierkegaard—he knew the former's work glancingly, the latter's not at all—gave the definitive modern formulation with his "fiction [is] the very process of thought," "A throw of the dice will never abolish chance," and so on. Accordingly, Sartre placed him "at the threshold of our era" in respect to the doctrine of the absurd, the meditation on suicide, and the rest.

But Mallarmé also formulated the antidote to this youthfully alluring half-truth. In a remarkable passage from *Igitur*, he showed that paradox turns against itself, making the absurd problematic, both true and not true. This complex dialectic, in the lineage of Kierkegaard's "absolute paradox," became the syntactical skeleton of his sketch for a Great Work, which was to become *Un coup de dés*. In his 1894 speech at Oxford, he identified the formula for this paradox as "the symphonic equation proper to the seasons"—that is to say, a four-polar dialectic, as in paradox crossed by itself. Camus repeated the maneuver in his elusion of suicide in the *Myth of Sisyphus*, and of murder in the preface to *The Rebel*.

At the heart of these evasions of evil lies an arational "leap," like Kierkegaard's leap of faith from between the "crucifying" poles of dilemma. Camus ended up with a simple, good-hearted impulse not to follow the Nazis through what was, after all, an arbitrary logic of the absurd.

Now, Mallarmé had already come to a solution in his own way when he told a tinkering poetaster, René Ghil, "You can't do without Eden." That is a modest form of belief, like Camus's "sacred," and certainly undogmatic, but it makes all the difference. His poetry was accordingly rooted in a distant, lost totality, or Eden, as he put it, and made its way, however tentatively, toward it again.

This movement constitutes what he called elsewhere (in the Oxford speech, "Music and Letters") the "omnipresent Line" of existence, which gives existence meaning—in French, *sens* (both "direction" and "sense"). That omnipresent Line (which is traditional, normative, classic, metonymic), together with the "vast Circle" (of vision, cosmos, poetry, metaphor), affords some approximation to a plenary truth, as opposed to the one-sided, chic views of the deconstructionists. The fuller dialectic is found in all the major artists and thinkers: Proust's fusions of space and time, Joyce's Shem and Shaun, Lacan's interchange of metaphor and metonymy.

And yet it is a strange fact that Derrida himself, as I know explicitly from conversation with him on just that point, does not attempt a fuller dialectic. In fact, he distanced himself from it specifically. He comes closest to it in his notion of *la clôture* and *la différance*. Why he stops short is a source of some puzzlement to me, especially since in his *Dissemination* he announces his intention to explore these ideas in a future work.

But at any rate there it is: the imbalance remains, in Derrida and his disciples. The most essential dialectic—the one that produces the "higher balance" (as Camus called it in "Helen's Exile")—is between faith (corresponding to metaphor) and reason (corresponding to metonymy). This has been the healthy Catholic view since Saint Thomas and *should* have been the healthy modern view since Mallarmé. The Yale bunch illustrates the heretical pathology of runaway pride and critique: tone, beauty, and vision are lost, as is the faith-oriented line of meaning which leads to them. All that is left is a *dotted* line of debunking and point-scoring, plus the gloating face of the clever critic himself.

Not long ago, I attended a talk by a young professor who was illustrating how Godard, in his *Prénom Carmen*, had "trashed" Beethoven, as well as Mérimée, Bizet, and the whole bourgeois-elitist past which believed in individual personality as opposed to the systems-view which, she ritually restated, has replaced that in our day. A few weeks before, in the same spot, a former student of mine who had gone on to teach at Harvard reduced to rubble everything that her former professor (myself) had taught her about the—however elusive—meanings of Mallarmé's superb texts, including *Un Coup de dés*, a page of which she exhibited on a projector screen, pronouncing it "irrecoverable." Stunned by this betrayal, I began, in the question period, to point out the perfectly obvious (even to the uninitiated) meaning in the beautiful text up there. I wondered aloud, to the audience, why, if the words meant whatever any reader wanted to put into them, my particular readings had elicited the enthusiastic response of Hermann Broch, Ungaretti, and Derrida himself, who in spirited pages of his *Dissemination* defended my interpretation against that of Jean-Pierre Richard! Taken aback by the audience's clear sympathy for making some sort of sense in Mallarmé, my former student limply admitted that she had gone that route because it was the "in" thing to do now, and she needed to swim with the tide in order to get a better post.

Well, those Yale professors, most of whom I have known, can afford to give a little ground here and there about sense: they don't need jobs. Some of them, as quoted in the *Times*, seem to have suspicions that they may have gone too far. One hopes, for example, that J. Hillis Miller, now that he is president of the Modern Language Association—an organization from which many of us resigned long ago because of the orgy of modish mediocrity—may come to regret the incredible obtuseness of putting Wallace Stevens in the same artistic sack with Robbe-Grillet or John Cage, as he did in his *Poets of Reality*. Perhaps Geoffrey Hartman, the owl, will eat a little crow for declaring the critic the generic equal of the artist. Who? Proust, Baudelaire? How Yale has changed since the days of Henri Peyre and René Wellek! At their feet we used to "crave to adore." Faith like theirs may have gone underground for a dreary while in academia, but if the millions of folk who flock to worship Mozart in *Amadeus* give any inkling—or the pilgrimages to Proust's Illiers-Combray—Cage, Godard, and the Yale pedagogues have a certain distance to go to prove their points.

This is a modern appraisal, even if it denies modern luminaries
and as Derrida or
Camus (& Baudelaire) is read in the light of modern science —
Baudelaire of modern linguistics

If it denies Derrida
his influence is perceptible

eminently readable
Lively, stimulating, often provocative
the essays collected in this volume have
in the main been published before

He examines B's famous 'frisson nouveau' chiefly from the
angle of sound patterning (this bi, fr, rr, cr & other r)

Elements of pure dogmatism creep in.
He is dogmatic 'his finest pure poem, Les Veuves'. There
are other candidates.